create, update, remake

TRANSCONTINENTAL BOOKS

1100 René-Lévesque Boulevard West
24th floor
Montreal, Que. H3B 4X9
Tel: (514) 340-3587
Toll-free: 1-866-800-2500
www.canadianliving.com

Bibliothèque et Archives nationales du Québec
and Library and Archives Canada cataloguing
in publication

Main entry under title :
Create, update, remake : DIY projects for you, your
family and your home
"Canadian living".
ISBN 978-0-9813938-3-4
1. Do-it-yourself work - Handbooks, manuals, etc.
2. Handicraft - Handbooks, manuals, etc.
I. Canadian living.

TT155.C73 2011   643´.7   C2010-942528-6
Project editor: Christina Anson Mine
Senior editor: Austen Gilliland
Copy editor: Jill Buchner
Knitting technical editor: Kate Atherley
Art direction and design: Chris Bond

Printed in Canada
© Transcontinental Books, 2011
Legal deposit – 1st quarter 2011
National Library of Quebec
National Library of Canada
ISBN 978-0-9813938-3-4

We acknowledge the financial support of
our publishing activity by the Government
of Canada through the Canada Book Fund.

For information on special rates for
corporate libraries and wholesale purchases,
please call 1-866-800-2500.

Canadian Living

create, update, remake

DIY PROJECTS FOR YOU, YOUR FAMILY AND YOUR HOME

From the editors of Canadian Living

Transcontinental Books

editors'
note

We can't imagine a life without crafting.
As lifelong makers-and-doers, we can barely a
remember a time when we didn't have at least one
craft project on the go. Austen's happiest childhood
memories involve sitting cross-legged in front of
the television, cutting and pasting along with
Mr. Dressup. Tina started out in Brownies, winding
yarn around Popscicle sticks, and cross-stitching
alongside her mom. As the years passed, our
interests have grown to include knitting, quilting and
DIY projects. We believe a hand-knit sweater is
warmer than one from the mall, and that you really
can feel the love in every stitch of a quilt. Funnily
enough, neither of us will forget the satisfaction of
reupholstering a chair for the first time (Tina even
upcycled an old shirt to make the cushion – surely
the seed of an idea that has bloomed in this book).

In this era of big-box stores and e-commerce,
credit cards and ready-made everything, it certainly
is possible to live a life without handmade. (What
sock-knitter hasn't had someone look at all their hard
work and say, "You know they sell socks at stores,
right?") But we would argue that the increasing
popularity of knit cafés and sew-by-the-hour studios,
not to mention the success of websites such as
Etsy – that amazing online marketplace for handmade
items – show that people still hunger for the crafty
life. And with economic and environmental
sustainability on our minds, making (or updating or
remaking) our own clothing, accessories, home and
decor items makes a great deal of sense.

In this book, we've gathered together more
than 100 of our favourite DIY projects from the past
10 years of *Canadian Living* Magazine. Whether you
want to make something brand-new, or to bring new
life to something you already own, there are projects
for the needleworker and woodworker, the gardener
and scrapbooker, for kids and adults alike. You'll find
a range of seasonal crafts, and a whole chapter of
ways to bring DIY to the kitchen – complete with
Tested-Till-Perfect recipes from our Test Kitchen.

Shakespeare wrote, "Joy's soul lies in the doing."
With this book, we wish you much joy.
– *Christina and Austen*

Christina Anson Mine
executive editor,
food and books

Austen Gilliland
senior editor

contents

CANADIAN LIVING | CREATE. UPDATE. REMAKE

sewing

bags • linens • curtains • organizers • pillows • rugs • toys

Simple Tote Bags

Lightweight, sturdy tote bags are a must-have – and it's not hard to make your own.

YOU NEED:

Simple Tote

- Piece of sturdy canvas, denim or upholstery fabric, 101 x 50 cm (39¾ x 19¾ inches) or, if using oilcloth, 96 x 50 cm (37⅞ x 19¾ inches), for bag

- Strip of contrasting or coordinating sturdy fabric, 50 x 44 cm (19¾ x 17⅜ inches) or, if using oilcloth, 50 x 42 cm (19¾ x 16½ inches), for reinforcing (optional)

- 1.1 m (43⅜-inch) long flat, firm 2.5 cm (1-inch) braid, for handles

- Matching thread

- Dressmaker's chalk pencil and ruler

Large Lined Tote

- Piece of sturdy canvas, denim or upholstery fabric, 105 x 58 cm (41⅜ x 22⅞ inches) or, if using oilcloth, 100 x 58 cm (39⅜ x 22⅞ inches), for bag

- Piece of contrasting or coordinating sturdy fabric or oilcloth, 95 x 58 cm (37⅜ x 22⅞ inches), for lining

- 1.1 m (43⅜-inch) long flat, firm 2.5 cm (1-inch) braid, for handles

- Matching thread

- Dressmaker's chalk pencil and ruler

Notes:
- If using oilcloth, read Sewing with Oilcloth, right, first.
- Use 1 cm (⅜-inch) seam allowance unless otherwise indicated.
- If desired, bind seam allowance with machine zigzag.

Simple Tote

TO MAKE:

1| If using reinforcing fabric strip, press under 1 cm (⅜ inch) along each long edge.

2| Centre strip, right side up, across right side of bag piece; pin, then edgestitch in place.

3| Fold bag piece so right sides are together and short (top) edges are even; stitch along each side edge to form bag.

4| Cut braid into 2 equal lengths. Turn bag right side out. Press under 2.5 cm (1 inch) twice around top edge of bag (if using oilcloth, fold under 2.5 cm/1 inch once). At bottom fold, mark centre front and centre back. Measure 4 cm (1⅝ inches) from front mark at either side, push 1 cut end of braid 2.5 cm (1 inch) under fold at either side, to form handle, and pin. Repeat with remaining braid and back. With handle loops down inside bag, edgestitch bottom fold in place, catching handle ends in stitching.

5| Fold each handle back against wrong side of top edge so loop is up; pin, then topstitch in X-shape to secure [A].

6| Turn wrong side out.

7| Flatten bag, then slide palm along bottom fold to crease. Working on 1 corner at a time, open out, then refold flat against work surface so side seam aligns with crease. Measure along each new fold and mark 12 cm (4¾ inches) from corner; stitch straight across from mark to mark. Trim off corner, leaving 6 mm (¼-inch) seam allowance.

8| Turn right side out.

9| If desired, form boxy bag sides as follows: Measure along top edge of front and mark 9 cm (3½ inches) from each side seam; fold front from each mark down to corresponding corner of base and edgestitch along fold. Repeat for back to complete tote [B].

Large Lined Tote

TO MAKE:

1| Follow Step 3 for Simple Tote. Increasing seam allowance by 1 mm (⅟₁₆ inch), repeat with lining piece. Follow Step 7 for Simple Tote. Repeat with lining.

2| Turn bag right side out. Aligning all corresponding seams, slide lining right down into bag (top edge is below top edge of bag). Follow Step 4 for Simple Tote, folding top edge of bag over lining, pushing 1 cut end of braid 5 cm (2 inches) from each centre mark at either side, and catching handle ends and lining in stitching. Follow Step 5 for Simple Tote.

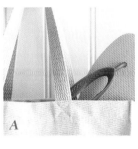

A

B

Dressed-Up Bedding

Breathe life into plain-Jane sheets, pillowcases and pillows. Dig through your stash for pretty leftovers from other projects, or pick up a special ribbon or fabric to tie the room together.

YOU NEED:

Satin-Edged Bedding
- Set of white or neutral bed linens
- Satin ribbon
- Matching thread

Organza-Overlay Throw Pillow
- Organza fabric, in a print to cover a plain pillow or in a shiny solid colour to cover a patterned pillow
- Throw pillow
- Matching thread

Satin-Edged Bedding
TO MAKE:

1| Prewash and dry bed linens.

2| Topstitch ribbon with matching thread for a pretty, detailed effect, if desired.

3| Place ribbon 10 cm (4 inches) down from top edge of sheet or in from opening edge of pillowcase, starting end of ribbon at side seam. Pin in place and edgestitch.

Organza-Overlay Throw Pillow
TO MAKE:

1| To determine the amount of fabric needed, multiply pillow width by 2½, then add 12.5 cm (5 inches), for total width; add 15 cm (6 inches) to pillow height for total height.

2| Cut organza to total width x total height. Finish side seams with 1.3 cm (½-inch) hem.

3| With fabric right side up, fold 1 of the sides in to centre, then fold other side toward centre, overlapping the other flap. Pin flaps in place, ensuring that width measures that of pillow plus 12.5 cm (5 inches).

4| Sew 1.3 cm (½-inch) seams along top and bottom of folded rectangle. Trim seams and corners; turn right side out.

5| To form border, measure 6.5 cm (2½ inches) in from edge of fabric and mark with pins. Topstitch along this outline. Press organza; insert pillow.

Vintage Tea Towel Treasures

Repurpose an old-fashioned tea towel to bring vintage panache to a modern kitchen.

sewing

CANADIAN LIVING | CREATE. UPDATE. REMAKE

YOU NEED:

Café Curtain
- Decorative curtain rod

- Vintage embroidered or lacy tea towel, tray cloth or tablecloth, for curtain

- Matching 1.3 cm (½-inch) wide twill tape or ribbon, cut in 35 cm (13⅞-inch) lengths

- Matching thread

Tea Tray Liner
- Vintage embroidered or lacy tea towel, table napkin, doily or tray cloth

- Wooden tray*

- ¼-inch thick glass** cut 6 mm (¼ inch) shorter than inside-tray length and width

Available at craft supply and home decor stores

**Available at glass and mirror stores*

Café Curtain

TO MAKE:

1| Install curtain rod, aligning with horizontal window sash on sliding window or positioning partway up picture window.

2| Fold each cut length of twill tape in half to form loop. With folded edge about 6 mm (¼ inch) down from top edge of curtain fabric and cut ends up, machine-stitch 1 loop to wrong side of curtain at each top corner and at approx every 10 cm (4 inches) in between.

3| Loosely knot each pair of twill ends beneath and above rod.

Tip:
If you prefer a no-sew version, omit loops and use squeeze clips to fasten curtain to rod (look for clips and rod at drapery stores).

Tea Tray Liner

TO MAKE:

1| If necessary, trim fabric to fit inner dimensions of wooden tray, cutting carefully to highlight decorative embroidery or lace, and finishing with 6 mm (¼-inch) hem.

2| Starch and press fabric.

3| Lay, right side up, inside tray; cover with glass.

Tip:
When you're having the glass custom-cut for this project, ask that the corners be slightly rounded and the edges polished. If you're planning to serve hot beverages on the tray, specify tempered glass.

Using Vintage Linens

Beautiful vintage linens are inexpensive at flea markets (and sometimes free from your great-aunt). Made to last, most still have lots of life left in them.

Look for pure linen or cotton (or a blend). Don't shy away from dinginess, or the odd hole or stain. With a little TLC, these treasures can be restored to their former glory.

Repairing:

• Use pure cotton or linen floss or thread, such as the kinds designed for fine sewing, embroidery or crochet. You'll also need sharp, pointed embroidery scissors, No. 7 and 8 embroidery needles, and a magnifying lamp with a daylight bulb.

• Mend fabric, then wash.

• Turn a hole into a lacy feature. Trim hole edges to desired shape. If desired, press under a scant 3 mm (⅛-inch) edge; stitch to an inset of lace or fabric (cut with a pinked edge to prevent fraying).

• Turn a scattering of small holes into eyelets by buttonhole-stitching around each. Or stitch a small flower around each – add stems and leaves for an embroidered bouquet. Cover small spots with lazy daisies or bullion-stitched roses.

• Mending sheets with torn sides or bottoms is easy. Trim off the edge along the grain, then rehem.

Removing Stains:

• For rust marks, try Rit Rust Remover or Whink Rust and Iron Stain Remover. (Caution: These are powerful chemicals, so read and heed warnings.)

• To spot-clean before laundering, centre stain over a bucket. Squirt clear liquid dish detergent onto stain. Leave for 15 minutes, then, if necessary, rub gently with an ultrasoft toothbrush. Pour rinse water through fabric into the bucket.

• Or soak stain in a bucket half-filled with water and liquid dish detergent, pretreater, laundry booster or stain remover (such as Biz Stain Fighter, OxiClean or borax; or try Restoration, a stain remover designed for delicate fabrics).

• Use hydrogen peroxide or chlorine bleach as a last resort. Mix one part bleach with five parts water, dampen the stained area with water and carefully dab solution onto the back of the fabric with a cotton swab. Leave for 15 minutes, then rinse. Repeat if needed.

• Add white vinegar to the final rinse to remove any soap residue.

• Avoid prolonged soaking. Some of the fabric will float, making it patchy.

• To remove undyed candle wax, gently scrape off what you can, then freeze the cloth so the remainder will flake off easily.

Drying:

• Lay damp linens flat outside on the grass and hang wet fine linens to dry outside on a calm, sunny day.

• Check periodically for dryness. When the fabric is almost dry (it will feel cool), press it.

Pressing:

• Use an iron without steam vents in the soleplate. Look for these at flea markets.

• Always press cotton or linen when it's still slightly damp; if using spray starch, apply only to damp fabric.

• Use a dry iron. To avoid creating shiny spots, press from the wrong side and use a clean cotton pressing cloth.

• Always press the edging or border of a flat cloth to help restore its shape.

Canvas Pocket Organizer

Maximize your closet space with a panel of generous pockets.
They're ideal for stashing socks, undies and small accessories.

YOU NEED:

- 1.2 m (47¼ inches) tightly woven medium-weight canvas, 1.5 m (59⅛ inches) wide

- Matching thread

- Three ½-inch grommets with assembly tools and instructions*

- Dressmaker's chalk pencil, ruler and set square

Available in kits at fabric stores

TO MAKE:

1| From canvas, cut out panel, 92 x 55 cm (36¼ x 21⅝ inches), aligning edges with fabric grain, then draw line 3 cm (1⅛ inches) inside each edge. Fold panel in half so long edges (sides) are even, then press fold to mark vertical centre. Open out and refold each side, one at a time, parallel to and 16 cm (6¼ inches) from each side edge, then press folds to mark positions of pocket centres. Open out, fold bottom edge, parallel to and 29 cm (11½ inches) from top edge, then press fold to mark position of bottom edge of first pocket strip. Set aside.

2| From remaining canvas, cut out 4 pocket strips, each 60 x 22 cm (23⅝ x 8⅝ inches). Along 1 long edge (top) of each, press 2 cm (¾ inch) toward right side (on printed fabric, press toward wrong side); with closely spaced machine zigzag, stitch in place so bottom edge of stitching aligns with raw edge. Draw vertical centre line on each strip, then, 14 cm (5½ inches) along bottom from each side edge, place pin to mark pocket centre.

3| Sew on strips, 1 at a time, as follows: Place first strip on panel, aligning bottom edge with pressed line on panel and aligning vertical centres; pin down centre line. Aligning each side edge with drawn line at side edge of panel, pin side edges in place. Matching pins on strip to panel's corresponding pressed pocket-centre lines, pin bottom edge to panel, forming inverted box pleat at each pocket centre. With closely spaced machine zigzag, stitch pleated bottom edge in place so bottom edge of stitching aligns with raw edge. Reinforce with line of topstitching along top edge of zigzag, and another, 6 mm (¼ inch) above. Aligning folded top edge of each strip with bottom edge of previous strip, pin and stitch next 2 in same manner, then pin last strip in place at bottom, but do not stitch. With wide, closely spaced machine zigzag, stitch vertical centre line from folded top edge of first strip to bottom edge of last.

4| Trim 1 cm (⅜ inch) from panel edges to remove any fraying. Press 2 cm (¾ inch) along top, bottom, then side edges of panel, toward right side, and pin, enclosing unsewn pocket edges. With closely spaced machine zigzag, stitch in place so inside edge of stitching aligns with raw edge. Reinforce with line of topstitching along inside edge of zigzag.

5| Following manufacturer's instructions, set grommets in double layered top edge, 1 about 3 cm (1⅛ inches) in from each side and the third at centre.

Easy Apron

Rescue a favourite old fabric and give it a new life. Here, a set of 1940s-style floral drapes (destined for the dump) was recycled into a great accessory for the discerning cook or crafter: a handy apron.

YOU NEED:

- 1.3 m (51¼ inches) medium-weight fabric, 1.15 m (45⅜ inches) wide, such as chintz, denim or twill

- Matching thread

- Brown paper

- Pencil, ruler and set square

- Dressmaker's chalk pencil

Note:

**Pin pressed edges
before stitching.**

TO MAKE:

1| Enlarge pattern
(page 260) by squaring
method as follows: On
brown paper, draw grid
of horizontal and vertical
lines 2.5 cm (1 inch)
apart. Each square on
diagram equals a square
on brown paper. Enlarge
pattern by redrawing
each line of pattern onto
corresponding square.
Transfer any markings.
Seam allowance
is included.

2| Fold fabric in half so
selvages are even; using
pattern, cut out apron
and (if desired) pocket,
then cut 2 ties, each
110 x 7 cm (43⅜ x
2¾ inches) and 1 strip
70 x 7 cm (27⅝ x
2¾ inches). Set pocket
and ties aside.

3| Press top edge of
apron under 1 cm
(⅜ inch), then 7 cm
(2¾ inches); edgestitch
along inside fold. Around
each armhole edge,
press under 1 cm
(⅜ inch), clipping seam
allowance if necessary,
then press under
1 cm (⅜ inch) again;
edgestitch along inside
fold. Press bottom edge
under 1 cm (⅜ inch)
twice; repeat with each
side edge. Edgestitch
along inside folds.

4| Press under 1 cm
(⅜ inch) along all raw
edges of ties and strip;
fold each, so wrong
sides are together and
long pressed edges are
even, then edgestitch.
On wrong side of apron
at each dot, overlap 1 tie
end 2 cm (¾ inch) so
each tie is perpendicular
to side edge; topstitch in
place. On wrong side of
apron at each X, overlap
1 strip end 2 cm (¾ inch)
so each strip end is
perpendicular to top
edge and strip forms
loop; topstitch in place.

5| If making pocket,
press top edge under
1 cm (⅜ inch) then
2.5 cm (1 inch);
edgestitch along inside
fold. Press bottom edge
under 1 cm (⅜ inch);
repeat with each side
edge. On right- or
left-hand side of apron
front as desired, pin
pocket, right side up,
where indicated by
broken lines; edgestitch,
then topstitch 1 cm
(⅜ inch) from side and
bottom edges.

Easy-Make Dopp Kits

These pouches are perfect for packing cosmetics or shaving supplies for travel. A great way to use up fabric scraps, the bag takes less than two hours to make.

YOU NEED:

- 2 pieces lightweight or medium-weight fabric, each 50 x 30.5 cm (19¾ x 12 inches), for bag and lining

- 1 piece lightweight or medium-weight fabric, 25.5 x 20.5 cm (10 x 8 inches), for handle (optional)

- 1 piece medium-weight interfacing, 50 x 30.5 cm (19¾ x 12 inches), optional

- 35 cm (13⅞-inch) zipper

- 2 pieces 1.3 cm to 1.5 cm (½- to ⅝-inch) wide matching or contrasting ribbon, 5 cm (2 inches) long

- Matching thread

- Dressmaker's chalk pencil, ruler and set square

A

Note:

Use 6 mm (¼-inch) seam allowance throughout, unless otherwise indicated. Backstitch at each end of stitching and, once or twice, over ribbon, zipper and handle ends in seams.

TO MAKE:

1| Interfacing: Place bag fabric, right side up, on interfacing so edges are even; using 3 mm (⅛-inch) seam allowance, stitch together around edges.

2| Handle: With wrong sides together, fold in half so long edges are even; press. Open out. With wrong sides together, fold over each long edge to pressed line at centre; press. Fold in half again so pressed edges are even; press. Pin, then topstitch 6 mm (¼ inch) in around edges.

3| Bag: Press each short edge under 1 cm (⅜ inch). With right sides up, centre 1 pressed edge over 1 edge of zipper; pin. Using zipper foot, edgestitch in place. In same manner, pin and stitch remaining pressed edge and zipper edge, forming tube.

4| Holding zipper along 1 folded edge, flatten tube and press fold along opposite edge to mark centre line of bottom. Open zipper halfway.

5| Fold 1 ribbon length so wrong sides are together and raw edges are even. Centre over 1 end of zipper so raw edges are even; using 3 mm (⅛-inch) seam allowance, stitch in place. Repeat with remaining ribbon length at other end of zipper.

6| Turn tube wrong side out. With raw edges even and zipper centred over pressed centre line, pin across each end of tube; stitch. Trim excess from zipper ends. With zipper centred over pressed centre line, flatten tube and press fold along each long edge to mark centre line of side.

7| Referring to diagram [A]: Working with 1 hand inside, open out 1 corner. Refold so end seam aligns with pressed centre line of side; pin layers together. Measure and mark point 5 cm (2 inches) down seam from corner; with set square, draw line straight across corner, from edge to edge, through mark. Stitch along line; trim seam allowance to 6 mm (¼ inch), discarding corner. Machine-zigzag raw edges together to reinforce.

8| Repeat with other corner on same end. In same manner, open and refold each remaining corner, marking line, then tucking 1 handle end 1.3 cm (½ inch) beyond line, inside corner and centred over pressed centre line of side (handle should lie, untwisted, between right sides of bag); pin and stitch. Trim seam allowance to 6 mm (¼ inch), discarding corner; turn right side out.

9| Lining: Press each short edge under 1.5 cm (⅝ inch). With right sides together, fold so pressed edges are even along (top) edge; flatten and press to mark centre line of bottom. Open out. With right sides together, fold over each

Tips:

• If using lightweight fabric, such as quilting calico, interface bag fabric, following Step 1. If using medium-weight upholstery fabric, or sturdy twill, linen or canvas, omit Step 1.

• If no handle is desired, omit Steps 2 and 8, and follow Step 7 for all corners.

pressed edge to 3 mm (⅛ inch) from centre line of bottom. With raw edges even, pin across each end; stitch.

10| Follow Step 7 to mark, sew and trim all corners.

11| With wrong sides together, fit bag over lining, aligning seams and matching corners. Aligning pressed edge of lining with stitching line on corresponding zipper edge, pin each lining edge in place, placing pins perpendicular to edge; using zipper foot and working from right side, topstitch 3 mm (⅛ inch) in from stitching line.

Upcycled Necktie Tea Cosy

Spend a few dollars at the thrift store and a few hours at the sewing machine – that's all it takes to create these lovely little teapot toppers.

YOU NEED:

- Silk neckties (3 or 4 for small tea cosy; 4 or 5 for large)

- 2 pieces each coordinating broadcloth, for lining, and flat cotton quilt batting, each 30 cm (11⅞ inches) square for small tea cosy or 40 cm (15¾ inches) square for large tea cosy

- 2 pieces standard-loft polyester quilt batting, each 30 cm (11⅞ inches) square, for small tea cosy, or 2 pieces high-loft polyester quilt batting, each 40 cm (15¾ inches) square, for large tea cosy

- Tassel or large ball button

- Matching thread

- Brown paper, pencil, ruler and set square

Note:

Unless otherwise indicated, use 1.3 cm (½-inch) seam allowance.

TO MAKE:

1| Carefully clip open centre-back seam of each tie, then remove and discard lining. Wash by hand using gentle detergent; hang until dry, then press.

2| Enlarge pattern (page 261) by squaring method as follows: On brown paper, draw grid of horizontal and vertical lines 2.5 cm (1 inch) apart. Each square on diagram equals a square on brown paper. Enlarge pattern by redrawing each line of pattern onto corresponding square. Seam allowance is included. Cut out (for small tea cosy, follow wide and broken lines; for large tea cosy, follow wide and narrow solid lines).

3| Fold each square of broadcloth, and cotton and polyester batting in half; lay pattern on each and cut 1 front/back from each. Set aside polyester batting front/backs.

4| Lay cotton batting front/backs flat on work surface; on top, lay tie strips in desired pattern of vertical stripes. Set aside, maintaining each arrangement. Along left-hand edge of 1 front/back, lay first tie strip, right side up and overlapping edges slightly; on top, lay second strip, right side down, so right-hand edges of strips are even. Machine-stitch through all layers, 6 mm (¼ inch) from right-hand edges of strips. Open out second strip, right side up, and press seam line. Continue across front/back, sewing, opening and pressing in same manner. Turn right side down.

5| With batting edges even, lay 1 polyester batting front/back on top; baste together through all layers, 6 mm (¼ inch) from outside edge, then trim tie strips even with batting. Assemble second front/back in same manner. With right sides together and edges even, stitch assembled front/backs together along side and top edges to make cover; do not turn right side out.

6| With right sides together and edges even, stitch broadcloth front/backs together along side and top edges; do not turn right side out. Lay assembled cover flat on work surface; with edges even, lay assembled lining on top and pin. Using 1 cm (⅜-inch) seam allowance, and starting and ending 6.5 cm (2½ inches) up from bottom edge, stitch lining to cover along side and top edges [A]. Trim seam allowance across tip; turn cover right side out. Pull lining open inside.

7| Around bottom edge of cover, press 2.5 cm (1 inch) up between layers. Around bottom edge of lining, press 2.5 cm (1 inch) up between layers; pin pressed edges together. Topstitch 6 mm (¼ inch) from bottom edge.

8| Handstitch tassel at tip of tea cosy.

A

Embroidered Pillows

Embroider a tiny picture – inspired by a favourite wallpaper, fabric motif or child's drawing – then frame it with linen and appliqué it onto a simple pillow – or anything you like.

YOU NEED:

• Chosen motif

• Scrap of medium-weight, plain, smooth cotton for stitchery (choose opaque fabric that floss won't show through)

• Embroidery floss in desired colour(s)

• Scrap of medium-weight, plain, coarse linen for appliqué patch

• Pillow form of desired size

• Medium-weight, plain or printed upholstery fabric for pillow cover (see Step 4 to determine required amount)

• Matching thread

• Tracing paper, carbon paper and pencil (optional)

• Dressmaker's chalk pencil

• Ruler and set square

• Pins and sewing needles

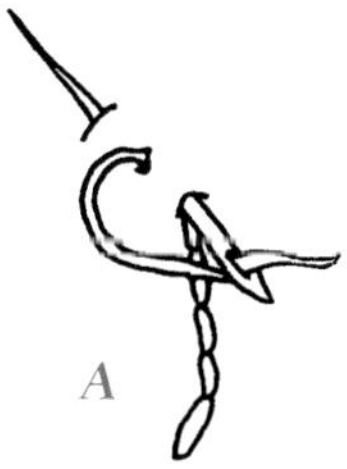

Notes:

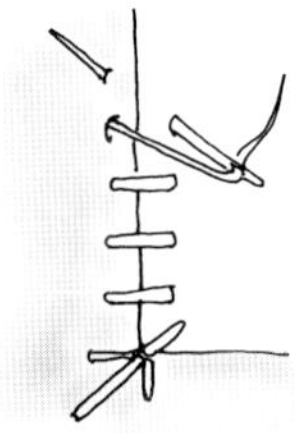

• Preshrink all fabrics before use.

• When retracing or drawing motif, align vertical centre of motif with straight grain of fabric.

• When positioning each consecutive patch, align pressed edges with straight grain of fabric below before pinning.

• Remove pins as you stitch.

• In Step 2 through Step 4, each time stitching is complete, lightly press, wrong side up.

A

B

C

D

TO MAKE:

1| Lay tracing paper on motif and trace, then position traced motif on right side of cotton; slide carbon paper between layers and retrace. Or, using chalk pencil, draw motif directly onto cotton.

2| With 3 strands of floss in desired colour(s), backstitch [A] motif lines and satin-stitch [B] to fill in any spots and shapes. Using chalk pencil, ruler and set square, draw rectangle or square around motif, allowing 3 mm (⅛-inch) turning allowance on each edge; cut out along lines. Press under 3 mm (⅛ inch) along side edges, then top and bottom edges.

3| Pin embroidered patch, right side up, to right side of linen. With 3 strands of floss to match cotton, overcast-stitch [C] in place, adding decorative backstitches at each corner if desired. Using chalk pencil and ruler, draw linen frame of desired width around embroidered patch, allowing 3 mm (⅛-inch) turning allowance on each edge; cut out along lines. Press under 3 mm (⅛ inch) along side edges, then top and bottom edges.

4| To pillow form width, add 2 cm (¾ inch) for total width; to length, add 2 cm (¾ inch) for total length. From upholstery fabric, cut cover front and back, each total width x total length. Pin linen patch, right side up, where desired on right side of cover front. With thread to match linen, handstitch [D] in place.

5| With right sides together and using 1 cm (⅜-inch) seam allowance, stitch cover front to back, leaving opening for pillow form centred along bottom edge. Trim seam allowance across corners and turn right side out. Press edges; press under 1 cm (⅜ inch) around opening, insert pillow form and slipstitch opening closed.

Tip:

To make zippered cover, cut front as given in Step 4, then, adding 4 cm (1⅝ inches) to total length, cut back. Approx three-quarters of the way down back, cut straight across from side edge to side edge for zipper opening. Machine-zigzag each just-cut edge to bind. With right sides together and using 2 cm (¾-inch) seam allowance, sew bound edges together, starting at each side edge and stitching 7 cm (2¾ inches) along, then backstitching to end seam. Press under 2 cm (¾ inch) along each edge of opening, then sew zipper in place. With right sides together and using 1 cm (⅜-inch) seam allowance, stitch cover front to back (remember to leave zipper open so you can turn cover right side out). Trim seam allowance across corners and machine-zigzag seam allowance to bind. Turn right side out, press edges, then insert form and zip.

Maple Leaf Quilt Squares

The classic maple leaf quilt square is perfect for all kinds of projects: quilts (of course), bags, pot holders, pillows and so on.

sewing

YOU NEED:

- 1 fat quarter (approx 46 x 56 cm/18 x 22 inches) white or neutral fabric, for background

- 1 fat quarter (approx 46 x 56 cm/18 x 22 inches) red or red print fabric, for maple leaf

- Rotary cutter, acrylic ruler and self-healing cutting mat

- Pencil or disappearing-ink fabric marker

- Matching thread

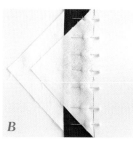

Note:
Because quilting convention works in imperial measurements, these instructions use only imperial units throughout.

TO MAKE:

1| Using rotary cutter, ruler and cutting mat, square up white fabric edges and cut 2 white strips [A], one 4½ x 9 inches and the other 4⅞ x 9¾ inches. Cut 4½- x 9-inch strip into two 4½-inch squares.

2| Square up red fabric edges and cut 3 red strips, one 4½ x 13½ inches, another 4⅞ x 9¾ inches and another 1¾ x 7 inches. Cut 4½- x 13½-inch strip into three 4½-inch squares.

3| To make stem: Cut 1 white square diagonally in half. Fold each triangle in half along long edge to find midpoint and finger press; fold red 1¾- x 7-inch strip in half so short ends meet and finger press at midpoint. With right sides together and matching creases at midpoints, sew 1 edge of red strip to 1 of the white triangles. Repeat with second triangle and other edge of red strip [B]. Press seams open; trim to 4½-inch square.

4| To make half-square triangles: Stack 4⅞- x 9¾-inch rectangles, right sides together and with white on top. Using pencil and ruler, mark down centre to create two 4⅞-inch squares. On left-hand square, mark diagonal from top left to bottom centre; on right-hand square, mark diagonal from top right to bottom centre. Mark seam lines scant ¼ inch on both sides of both diagonals; pin. Starting at top right of right-hand square, stitch along top seam line to centre line; pivot and stitch to top left [C]. Repeat with second set of seam lines. With rotary cutter and ruler, cut pieces on marked lines. Press seams open; trim blocks to 4½-inch squares.

5| To assemble rows: Arrange pieces as shown (see photo, opposite). With right sides together and using ¼-inch seam allowance, sew squares together into 3 rows; press seams open. Square up edges if necessary.

6| To assemble block: With right sides facing, align row seams; using ¼-inch seam allowance, sew 3 rows together. Press seams open. Trim edges to make 12-inch square block.

Tips:

• It's essential to prewash fabric at least once (or more) when working with red to ensure the colour won't bleed. Imagine making a red-and-white quilt only to have it turn pink upon its first washing!

• "Fat quarter" is a common quilting term. It refers to a piece of fabric formed by cutting a yard of fabric in half lengthwise, then crosswise. A typical fat quarter measures approx 46 x 56 cm (18 x 22 inches) – more generous than a traditional quarter-yard cut (hence the label "fat").

• Each fat quarter will give you enough fabric for at least two maple leaf blocks. Save leftover fabric to use for quilt binding, or for other scrappy projects.

Knitting Basket

Line a deep basket with a roomy drawstring bag that you stitch yourself, then stash all your knitting or needlework paraphernalia neatly inside.

YOU NEED:
- Basket
- Fabric (see Step 1 to determine necessary amount)
- Medium-weight cord
- Matching thread and heavy-duty thread, such as buttonhole twist
- Measuring tape, ruler, set square, dressmaker's chalk pencil and scissors
- Large safety pin or bodkin
- Soft sculpture dollmaker's needle

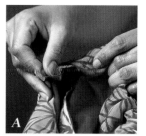

TO MAKE:

1| Measure basket circumference and add 4 cm (1⅝ inches) for total width. Measure basket diameter, then height; add together plus 12 cm (4¾ inches) for total height. With ruler, set square and chalk pencil, draw rectangle, total width x total height, on fabric; cut out. Cut cord 76 cm (30 inches) longer than total width; set aside.

2| Fold fabric in half so right sides are together and short edges (height) are even; pin together down short edges and along bottom to fold. Using 1 cm (⅜-inch) seam allowance, machine-stitch along pinned edges; machine-zigzag seam allowance to bind. Press under 1 cm (⅜ inch), then 5 cm (2 inches) around top edge; pin. Leaving 1 cm (⅜ inch) unstitched and backstitching at beginning and end of seam, edgestitch along pressed edge; topstitch 1 cm (⅜ inch) above seam to make casing for cord. With safety pin, thread cord through casing [A]; tie overhand knot in each end of cord. Turn bag right side out.

3| Place bag partway into basket, leaving enough above rim to gather closed at centre top. Sewing back and forth with dollmaker's needle and heavy-duty thread, handstitch bag to basket just below rim [B].

sewing

Penny Rug

Turn a stack of old wool blankets into a fabulously retro rug.
This craft is so old it's new again.

YOU NEED:

- At least 1 clean wool blanket, plus additional blankets or scraps of boiled or felted wool fabric

- Matching or contrasting heavy-duty thread (if using as floor mat)

- Crochet cotton, fine yarn or embroidery floss (if using as decorative mat)

- Soft lead pencil or dressmaker's chalk pencil

- Yard stick, set square and pins

- Basting thread

- Coins or jar lids of desired circle sizes (to trace)

TO MAKE:

1| Determine desired size of rug; add 8 cm (3⅛ inches) to each dimension for total width and length. With pencil, yard stick and set square, mark rectangle, total width x total length, on 1 blanket; cut out, approx 1 cm (⅜ inch) outside rectangle. With basting thread, sew vertical- and horizontal-centre lines, then sew lines between diagonally opposite corners to use as guidelines when placing appliqués.

2| With pencil, trace around coins or lids to mark circles of desired number, colours and sizes onto contrasting blankets; cut out.

3| With heavy-duty thread or crochet cotton, blanket-stitch [A] 1 small centred circle to each circle of next size up, beginning and ending stitching with secure knot on wrong side of work. If using 3 circles for each appliqué, blanket-stitch each pair of sewn circles to 1 circle of next size up.

4| Placing at least 4 cm (1⅝ inches) inside marked line, arrange appliquéd circles as desired on rug; pin or baste in place, then blanket-stitch to rug. Remove all basting.

5| Trim rug along marked line. Turn up 2 cm (¾ inch) around each edge, mitring at corners, and pin; blanket-stitch in place to bind edges (or, if desired, bind only long edges, then cut scalloped or zigzagged fringe along each short edge).

Tips:

• Old wool blankets – especially those with the odd moth hole or mark that won't wash out – are bargain buys at flea markets. Cushy but durable, and available in a rainbow of solids and plaids, these blankets make the perfect materials for penny rugs. Simply cut around the bad bits.

• As well as the blanket stitch, other embroidery stitches – such as the feather or the herringbone stitch – can be used for both appliqué and decorative stitching.

• If you prefer to machine-stitch, use a wide machine zigzag, beginning and ending stitching by pulling thread ends through to wrong side of work and securing with overhand knot.

• Before determining your final design, experiment with contrasting and matching thread, or try incorporating simple shapes, such as squares or triangles, into your appliqués.

• Place a nonslip underlay below when using as a floor mat.

• Reminiscent of retro '70s designs, the concentric circles of contrasting colours – in eye-popping arrangements of straight rows, alternating rows, diamond shapes or even flowers – belie this craft's true age. The appliquéd rugs made their appearance about two centuries ago. Backed with burlap or linen, they became bed coverings, chair pads, scatter mats and table runners – and they're just as versatile and hardworking today.

• Coins – used as pattern pieces for the circles – have earned these rugs their "penny" nickname.

A

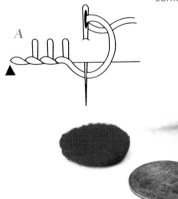

Lynx Sock Toys

Turn an ordinary pair of work socks into a couple of goofy, long-legged lynx.

YOU NEED (FOR EACH):

- 1 piece black knit fabric*, 25.5 x 6 cm (10 x 2⅜ inches)

- 1 piece grey knit fabric*, 25.5 x 12.5 cm (10 x 5 inches)

- Scraps of black and white felt

- 2 snap-on cat's eyes, 1.5 cm (⅝ inch) in diameter, or scrap of yellow knit fabric*

- Men's grey work sock with white toe and heel, and black stripe around cuff

- Stuffing

- Black, grey and white buttonhole twist thread

- Tiny scrap of black fun fur

- Needle and matching thread

- Burgundy and black embroidery floss

- Brown paper

- Compass, set square, ruler, scissors and dressmaker's chalk pencil

- Dollmaker's needle

*Such as sweatshirt fleece

Notes:

- In Step 2, using compass, set square, ruler and dressmaker's chalk pencil, measure and mark circles and squares on wrong sides of fabric, then cut out.

- Unless otherwise noted, pin and sew pieces with right sides together, using 6 mm (¼-inch) seam allowance and matching thread, and backstitching at beginning and end of each seam.

- Bind seam allowance with machine zigzag stitching.

- When handstitching and shaping, knot thread ends securely.

TO MAKE:

1| Enlarge pattern pieces (page 263) by squaring method as follows: On brown paper, draw grid of horizontal and vertical lines, 2.5 cm (1 inch) apart. Each square on diagram equals a square on brown paper. Enlarge by drawing each line of pattern onto corresponding square. Transfer markings. Seam allowance is included.

2| From black fabric, cut 4 circular paws, each 5.5 cm (2⅛ inches) in diameter. From grey fabric, cut 6 cm (2⅜-inch) square tail, then 4 ears and 4 cheeks. From black felt, cut nose, 6 cheek triangles, 2 tail spots, and 2 eye pieces (to use with snap-on eyes) or 2 eye triangles. From white felt, cut 2 inner ears and 2 inner cheeks. If making fabric eyes, cut 2 circular eyes from yellow knit fabric, each 4.5 cm (1¾ inches) in diameter.

3| Along bottom edge, trim black stripe off sock. Perpendicular to trimmed edge, cut stripe into 3 equal lengths; set aside.

4| Refer to cutting diagram (page 262). Lay sock flat. On leg, measure 2 cm (¾ inch) from each folded edge, then mark with pin at trimmed edge. Beginning at each pin and ending 3 cm (1⅛ inches) from heel, cut top layer parallel to folded edge to create centre strip (standard sock has 21 ribs, so strip is approx 5 ribs wide). Turn sock over; measure and cut in same manner, then cut straight across bottom of each centre strip. Remove centre strips for front legs. Set sock aside.

5| Fold each front-leg strip in half so long edges are even; stitch from bottom of white cuff down long edge. Pin each cuff edge around edge of 1 paw, stretching white cuff to fit; stitch. Turn right side out. Stuff paws until firm and round, then loosely stuff front legs. Machine-zigzag each top edge closed. Set aside.

6| Turn sock inside out. Fold each attached strip in half so long edges are even; stitch from bottom of white cuff down long edge. Stitch paws onto white cuffs; turn right side out, then stuff paws and legs, as in Step 5.

7| Form firm, lemon-size ball of stuffing; push into toe of sock. With white buttonhole twist, sew running stitches around edge of white toe. Pull up thread to shape snout and knot.

8| If using snap-on eyes, push each through eye piece at dot, then through sole (sole is face and back of lynx), approx 1.5 cm (⅝ inch) above snout stitching and 1 cm (⅜ inch) from centre front; affix.

9| Form firm orange-size ball of stuffing; push into sock against snout. With grey buttonhole twist, sew running stitches around sock, approx 7 cm (2¾ inches) above snout stitching. Pull up thread to shape head and knot.

10| Form 1 cm (⅜-inch) deep fold along sole, approx 2.5 cm (1 inch) behind head on each side; into each fold, push top edge of 1 front leg, then topstitch in place through all layers. Stuff body. Turn under 6 mm (¼ inch) around opening; slipstitch closed.

11| Sew 1 stripe length (cut in Step 3) to 1 end (tip) of tail, then fold tail in half so long edges are even; stitch across tip end and down long edge. Turn right side out and stuff. Turn under 6 mm (¼ inch) around opening; slipstitch to centre of heel. Handstitch 2 tail spots to top of tail.

12| Centre 1 inner ear on right side of 1 ear; edgestitch in place for ear front. Repeat. Fold 1 stripe length in half so wrong sides are together and long edges are even; with cut edges even, baste to 1 ear front, along right-hand edge from bottom corner to tip. Repeat with remaining stripe length and left-hand edge of other ear front. Stitch 1 ear front to each remaining ear, leaving bottom edge open. Remove basting, then turn right side out. Turn under 6 mm (¼ inch) around opening; slipstitch closed. From fur, cut 2 small tufts; stitch 1 to tip of each ear. At centre of bottom edge of each ear front, pinch fold to shape ear; pin, then slipstitch bottom edge to head.

13| Centre 1 inner cheek on right side of 1 cheek; edgestitch in place for cheek front. Repeat. Stitch 1 cheek front to each remaining cheek, leaving straight edge open. Clip seam allowance at corners, then turn right side out. Handstitch 1 cheek triangle to each point on cheek front. Turn under 6 mm (¼ inch) around opening; slipstitch 1 cheek at each side of face, along snout stitching.

14| With 6 strands of burgundy floss, satin-stitch nose all inside broken line; handstitch nose to centre of snout. With black buttonhole twist, make 6 mm (¼-inch) stitch just beyond nose edge at each top corner, knotting ends close to snout; trim to make two 6 cm (2⅜-inch) whiskers on either side of nose.

15| If making fabric eyes: With buttonhole twist, sew running stitches around edge of each yellow eye circle; centre small ball of stuffing on wrong side. Pull up thread tightly to shape eyeball and knot. With 4 strands of black floss, satin-stitch long pupil on each, then outline with backstitch; with white buttonhole twist, satin-stitch highlight at top. Slipstitch each eyeball to head, 6 mm (¼ inch) from centre front; handstitch eye triangle alongside.

16| With grey buttonhole twist, make series of 6 mm (¼-inch) wide vertical stitches, back and forth, above each eye. Pull tightly to shape brow and knot. Make similar series of horizontal stitches, 1 cm (⅜ inch) wide, between eyes. Pull gently to shape bridge of nose and knot. With dollmaker's needle, make several stitches, back and forth, from inner bottom corner of each eye to centre bottom of chin at snout stitching. Pull gently to embed eye and knot. With 6 strands of black floss, satin-stitch 3 claws on each paw.

Hassle-Free Hassock

Informal but stylish, a hassock can serve as a soft perch or a comfy footstool. And anywhere space is at a premium, several can be stacked away until they're needed.

YOU NEED:

- 2 pieces vinyl, leather, synthetic suede or sturdy upholstery fabric, each 75.5 cm (29¾ inches) square, for rectangular hassock; or each 64 cm (25¼ inches) square, for cube

- Matching sturdy thread, such as buttonhole twist

- Heavy-duty metal or plastic zipper, 20 cm (7⅞ inches) long, for rectangular hassock; or 18 cm (7 inches) long, for cube

- Beanbag pellets

- Dressmaker's chalk pencil, ruler and set square

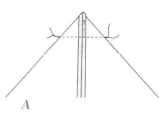

A

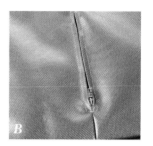

B

Notes:

- Backstitch at beginning and end of each seam and use 1.5 cm (⅝-inch) seam allowance throughout.

- Finished rectangular hassock is approx 51 cm square x 21.5 cm high (20⅛ inches square x 8½ inches high); cube is approx 30.5 cm (12 inches) square and high.

TO MAKE:

1| With right sides together and edges even, pin squares together, leaving opening long enough for zipper centred on 1 edge; using medium-length straight machine stitch, sew. Stitch again, 3 mm (⅛ inch) outside first stitch line, to reinforce seam.

2| Finish each corner as follows [A]: Working with 1 hand inside, open out corner; refold, pushing corner point flat and in line with side seam so seams align. About 10 cm (4 inches) from corner, pin layers together at seam. Lay refolded corner flat on work surface. Using chalk pencil and ruler, measure and mark each folded edge 15 cm (6 inches) from corner for rectangular hassock or 21 cm (8¼ inches) for cube. Draw line from mark to mark: 21.5 cm (8½ inches) long for rectangular hassock or 30.5 cm (12 inches) long for cube, and perpendicular to seam (check with set square and redraw if necessary). Stitch along line, reducing bulk at seam by turning seam allowance on top and bottom in opposite directions, if desired. Stitch 3 mm (⅛ inch) outside first stitch line. Trim seam allowance to 6 mm (¼ inch), then machine-zigzag raw edges together to bind.

3| Turn right side out. Turning under seam allowance along each side of opening, pin zipper in place. Using zipper foot, stitch, then pull top threads through to inside and tie all 4 threads in overhand knot. If desired, reinforce seam at each end of zipper with (hand or machine) stitches sewn across and perpendicular to seam [B].

4| Open zipper and fill hassock with beanbag pellets, then zip closed.

Jean-Pocket Wall Organizer

Faded to a fabulous range of indigos, well-worn blue jeans provide the perfect patches to sew into this over-the-desk organizer.

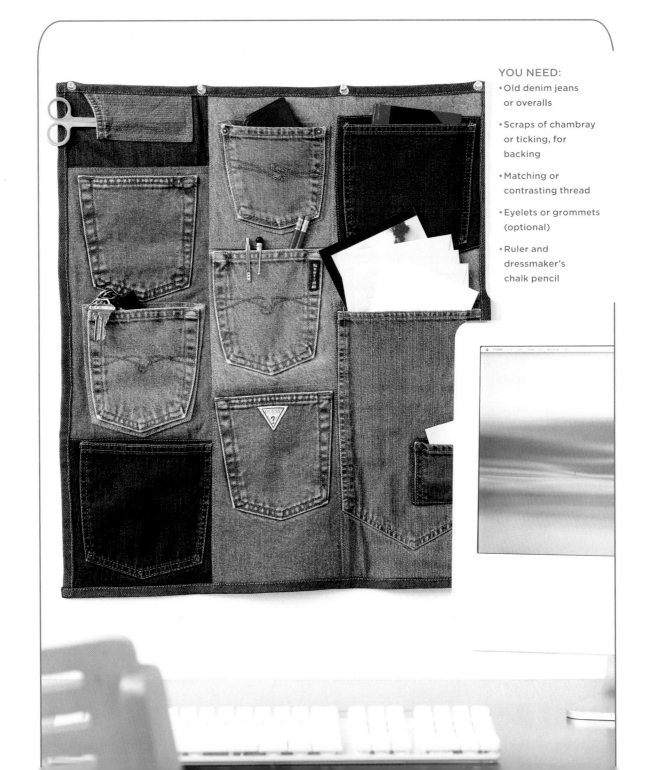

YOU NEED:

• Old denim jeans or overalls

• Scraps of chambray or ticking, for backing

• Matching or contrasting thread

• Eyelets or grommets (optional)

• Ruler and dressmaker's chalk pencil

TO MAKE:

1| Cut out plain denim pieces in desired sizes and pocket patches, then topstitch pockets onto larger pieces as desired.

2| Arranging in vertical rows of same-width pieces on work surface, lay out patched organizer front as desired.

3| Working from top to bottom, sew pieces together along top and bottom edges to patch left-hand row. Repeat to complete remaining row(s).

4| Sew right-hand row to adjoining row. Repeat to complete front. If necessary, trim outside edge even; with ruler and chalk pencil, mark line on right side, 1 cm (⅜ inch) in from each edge.

5| Lay front, right side up, on wrong side of backing fabric; trim backing 2 cm (¾ inch) out from edge. Press 1 cm (⅜ inch) to wrong side of backing around edge; fold pressed edge over front to match chalk line and pin. Edgestitch along pressed edge, pivoting and topstitching small square over each corner. Topstitching along seam lines where desired, sew front to backing.

6| Follow manufacturer's directions to affix eyelets for hanging, if desired, about 1 cm (⅜ inch) in from side edge at each top corner, then at desired intervals along top edge.

Tips:

• Add to your blues with inexpensive pairs from thrift stores, then customize this project to suit your selection and sizes.

• Look for thread specially created for blue jeans (shown above). It comes in variegated denim blue (use for seams you want to hide) or the classic gold (use for topstitching).

sewing

knitting
and
crochet

mitts • totes • afghans • slippers • scarves • socks

Mulled Wine Mitts

A pair of fingerless mitts is the perfect accessory to take you from fall to winter.

YOU NEED:

• 1 skein (50 g/137 m) Malabrigo Silky Merino, 50% silk, 50% baby merino (shown here in Velvet Grapes)

• Set of four 3.5 mm double-pointed needles (DPN) or whichever needles you require to produce the tension given

• Stitch markers

• Stitch holder

Note:

Standard abbreviations are used (see page 284).

SIZE:

Each mitt is approx 16.5 cm (6½ inches) in circumference, and will fit hands up to 21.5 cm (8½ inches) around.

TENSION:

24 sts and 30 rows = 10 cm (4 inches) in st st using recommended yarn and DPN. Work to exact tension with specified yarn to obtain satisfactory results.

To save time, take time to check tension.

STITCH PATTERNS:

Twisted Rib: *K1tbl, p1. Repeat from * to end of rnd.

Twisted Moss Stitch:
(Note: As worked in the rnd, all rows are right side rows.)
Row 1: *K1tbl, p1. Repeat from * as required.
Row 2: As Row 1.
Row 3: *P1, k1tbl. Repeat from * as required.
Row 4: As Row 3.

TO MAKE:

Cast on 44 sts, dividing among 3 DPN as follows:
Needle 1: 22 sts.
Needle 2: 11 sts.
Needle 3: 11 sts.
Taking care not to twist sts, join in rnd.

Rnds 1 to 8: Work twisted rib.
Rnd 9:
Needle 1: P4, k1tbl, work Row 1 of twisted moss stitch over next 13 sts, k1tbl, p3.
Needles 2 and 3: P1, m1 purlwise, p1, k1tbl, work Row 1 of twisted moss stitch over next 13 sts, k1tbl, p3, p2tog.
Rnd 10:
Needle 1: P4, k1tbl, work Row 2 of twisted moss stitch over next 13 sts, k1tbl, p3.
Needles 2 and 3: P3, k1tbl, work Row 2 of twisted moss stitch over next 13 sts, k1tbl, p4.
Rnd 11:
Needle 1: P4, k1tbl, work Row 3 of twisted moss stitch over next 13 sts, k1tbl, p3.
Needles 2 and 3: P3, k1tbl, work Row 3 of twisted moss stitch over next 13 sts, k1tbl, p4.
Rnd 12:
Needle 1: P4, k1tbl, work Row 4 of twisted moss stitch over next 13 sts, k1tbl, p3.

Needles 2 and 3: P3, k1tbl, work Row 4 of twisted moss stitch over next 13 sts, k1tbl, p4.
Rnd 13 and following:
Continue to work even in pat until piece measures 10 cm (4 inches) in length (or desired length) before beg thumb gusset inc.

Thumb gusset:
Rnd 1: P1, m1 purlwise, place marker, p3. Work rest of rnd as established, until 1 st before end of rnd. Place marker, m1 purlwise, p1. 46 sts now on needles.
Rnd 2: Work even as established.
Rnd 3: P to first marker, m1 purlwise, slip marker. Work rest of rnd as established to second marker, slip marker, m1 purlwise, p to end of rnd. 48 sts now on needles.
*Rnd 4: Work even.
Rnd 5: Work even.
Rnd 6: P to first marker, m1 purlwise, slip marker. Work rest of rnd as established to second marker, slip marker, m1 purlwise, p to end of rnd. 50 sts now on needles.
Next: Repeat from * 5 times more. 60 sts now on needles.
Next: Work 1 rnd even.

To separate thumb sts:
Rnd 1: P8 sts, then slip these 8 sts and the last 8 sts on Needle 3 onto stitch holder for thumb. Work rest of rnd in pat as established. Cast on 2 sts; join to work in rnd once again. 46 sts now on needles.
Rnd 2: Work even in pat for 9 more rnds or until mitt measures 2.5 cm (1 inch) shorter than desired length, purling the 2 cast-on stitches.

Top ribbing:
Rnd 1:
Needle 1: K1tbl, p1, repeat to end of needle.
Needles 2 and 3: K1tbl, p2tog, *k1tbl, p1, repeat from * until 3 sts from end of round. K1tbl, p2tog. 44 sts now on needles.
Rnds 2 through 7:
*K1tbl, p1, repeat from * to end of rnd.
Next: CO in ribbing.

To form thumb:
Rnd 1: Pick up and k16 sts from holder; pick up and k4 sts along inside edge of thumb. 20 sts now on needles. Divide evenly over 3 DPN and join to work in rnd, beg rnd in middle of top of thumb.
Next rnd: Knit.
Next: Loosely CO knitwise.

Plastic-Bag Bags

Cut plastic shopping bags into strips and use them as yarn to crochet these eco-friendly carryalls.

YOU NEED:

Round Bag
- Plastic shopping bags, cut in strips (see Tips, opposite)
- 10 mm crochet hook

Square Bag
- Plastic shopping bags, cut in strips (see Tips, opposite)
- 6 mm crochet hook

Notes:

- Rounds of single crochet are worked in spiral.
- Standard abbreviations are used (see page 284).

Round Bag

TO MAKE:
Ch 2, join with sl st to form ring.

Rnd 1: Work 10 sc in ring; place st marker (move up in successive rnds).
Rnd 2: [2 sc in next sc] to end of rnd.
Rnd 3: [1 sc in next sc, 2 sc in next sc] to end of rnd.
Rnd 4: [1 sc in next 2 sc, 2 sc in next sc] to end of rnd.
Rnd 5: [1 sc in next 3 sc, 2 sc in next sc] to end of rnd.
Rnd 6: [1 sc in next 4 sc, 2 sc in next sc] to end of rnd.
Rnd 7: [1 sc in next 5 sc, 2 sc in next sc] to end of rnd. 70 sc now in rnd.
Rnd 8: [1 sc in next sc] to end of rnd.

Continue in same manner as for Rnd 8 until bag measures 24 cm (9½ inches) from bottom or reaches desired depth.

Next: [1 sc in next 6 sc, skip next sc] to end of rnd. 60 sts now in rnd.
Next: [1 sc in next sc] to end of rnd.

Handles:

Rnd 1: 1 sc each in next 19 sc, ch 20, skip next 10 sc, 1 sc each in next 20 sc, ch 20, skip next 10 sc, 1 sc each in next sc.
Rnd 2: 1 sc each in next 19 sc, 1 sc each in next 20 ch, 1 sc each in next 20 sc, 1 sc each in next 20 ch, 1 sc in next sc.
Next: 1 sc each in next 2 sc, fasten off.

Square Bag

TO MAKE:
Ch 40, *turn.*

Row 1: Skip 2 ch (counts as first dc), [1 dc in next ch] to end of row, ch 1, *turn.*
Row 2: Working across bottom of first row, [1 dc in next ch] to end of row, ch 1, sl st to top of first dc in Row 1 to join in rnd. Do not turn; continue to work in rnd.
Rnd 1: Ch 2 (counts as first dc), [1 dc in next dc] to end of rnd, sl st to top of first dc in rnd. 76 sts now in rnd.

Continue in same manner as for Rnd 1 until bag measures 30 cm (11¾ inches) from bottom or reaches desired depth.

Handles [A]:

Rnd 1: Ch 2, 1 dc each in next 13 dc, ch 10, skip next 10 dc, 1 dc each in next 28 dc, ch 10, skip next 10 dc, [1 dc in next dc] to end of rnd, sl st to top of first dc in rnd.
Rnd 2: Ch 2, 1 dc each in next 13 dc, 1 dc each in next 10 ch, 1 dc each in next 28 dc, 1 dc each in next 10 ch, [1 dc in next dc] to end of rnd, sl st to top of first dc in rnd.
Rnd 3: Ch 2, [1 dc in next dc] to end of rnd, sl st to top of first dc in rnd, fasten off.

Tips:

- Sort plastic grocery and shopping bags into two lots: thin and thick.
- For round bag and larger hook, cut thin bags into 5 to 6.5 cm (2- to 2½-inch) wide strips and thick bags into 2.5 to 4 cm (1- to 1½-inch) strips.
- For square bag and smaller hook, cut thin bags into 4 to 5 cm (1½- to 2-inch) wide strips.
- You can cut strips in two ways: Trim off top and bottom of bag, then, starting at top edge, cut strip in spiral, across and around bag, to bottom edge; or trim off top of bag and lay bag flat on work surface, then, starting at top edge, cut strips straight down to fold at bottom edge, cutting through both layers.
- Tie strips together, end to end, with overhand knots; enclose strip ends as you crochet to avoid weaving in later.

Striped Afghan

Striped crocheted afghans are a classic way to stay cosy. Use the colour combinations shown here, or substitute a mix of your favourites.

YOU NEED:

- 5 mm crochet hook or whichever hook you require to produce the tension given

- Patons Classic Wool, 100% wool (100 g/ 205 m each), in:

  3 balls Magenta (C); 2 balls each New Denim (A), Royal (B), Winter White (D) and Petal Pink (F); and 1 ball Yellow (E), for baby blanket

  3 balls Bright Red (C); 2 balls each Peacock (A), Leaf Green (B), Winter White (D) and Magenta (F); 1 ball Yellow (E), for full-size blanket

A

Notes:

- Standard abbreviations are used (see page 284).
- This afghan is worked in double crochet, then edged with a scalloped border.
- Instructions are written for the baby blanket; changes for the full-size blanket follow in brackets. If there is only one figure, it applies to both sizes.

SIZE:

Finished baby blanket is 91.5 x 84 cm (36 x 33 inches); finished full-size blanket is 137 x 122 cm (54 x 48¼ inches).

TENSION:

14 dc and 8 rows = 10 cm (4 inches). Work to exact tension with specified yarn to obtain satisfactory results.

To save time, take time to check tension.

TO MAKE:
With A, ch 110(163).

Row 1 (RS): 1 dc in fourth ch from hook, 1 dc in each ch to end of ch, *turn.* 108(161) dc now in row.

Row 2: Ch 3 (counts as 1 dc), 1 dc in each dc to end of row, *turn.*

Row 3: With B, ch 3, 1 dc in each dc to end of row, *turn.*

Repeat Row 3 as follows:

With A, work 2 rows.
With C, work 4 rows.
With D, work 2 rows.
With C, work 4 rows.
With A, work 2 rows.
With E, work 1 row.
With A, work 2 rows.
With F, work 4 rows.
With D, work 2 rows.
With C, work 1 row.
With D, work 2 rows.
With F, work 4 rows.
With C, work 2 rows.
With D, work 1 row.
With C, work 2 rows.
With A, work 4 rows.
With E, work 2 rows.
With F, work 1 row.
With E, work 2 rows.
With A, work 4 rows.
With B, work 2 rows.
With E, work 1 row.

With B, work 2 rows.
With C, work 4 rows.
With F, work 2 rows.
With E, work 1 row.
With F, work 2 rows.
With C, work 4 rows.

For baby blanket only, fasten off, then work edging [A]. For full-size blanket, continue as follows.

With D, work 2 rows.
With B, work 1 row.
With D, work 2 rows.
With F, work 4 rows.
With E, work 2 rows.
With C, work 1 row.
With E, work 2 rows.
With F, work 4 rows.
With A, work 2 rows.
With B, work 1 row.
With A, work 2 rows.
With C, work 4 rows.
With D, work 2 rows.
With E, work 1 row.
With D, work 2 rows.
With C, work 4 rows.
Fasten off.

Tip:

To change colours, work to last two loops on hook, draw loop of new colour through two loops on hook to complete stitch and proceed in new colour, enclosing end of old colour in stitches as you work.

Edging:

With right side facing, join B with sl st to top right-hand corner.

Rnd 1: Work 1 sc in each dc along top edge, 3 sc in corner st, 120(187) sc down left-hand edge, 3 sc in corner st, 1 sc in each ch of foundation ch across bottom edge, 3 sc in corner st, 120(187) sc up right-hand edge, 3 sc in corner st, sl st to first sc to join in rnd.

Rnd 2: Ch 1, 1 sc in same sp as sl st, [skip next 2 sc, 5 dc in next sc, skip next 2 sc, 1 sc in next sc] to end of rnd, working in corners as per Rnd 1; join D with sl st to first sc.

Rnd 3: With D, 1 sc in each st to end of rnd, working 3 sc in each corner; sl st to first sc to join. Fasten off.

Retro Crocheted Slippers

These comfy retro slippers – updated with pretty accents on top – are lovely to make as gifts or as a contribution to a craft-sale table.

YOU NEED:
- 1 ball (100 g/205 m) Patons Canadiana acrylic yarn (shown here in Cranberry and Medium Blue)
- 4.5 mm crochet hook
- Stitch markers
- Tapestry needle

Notes:

- Standard abbreviations are used (see page 284).

- Place marker at end of Round 1, then reposition to end of each successive round as you work.

TO MAKE:
Beg at toe end, ch 5, sl st to join in rnd.

Rnd 1 (RS): Work 3 sc in each ch. 15 sts now in rnd. Place marker.

Rnd 2: Work 1 sc in each sc to end of rnd, inc 1 st in fifth and 13th sc. 17 sts now in rnd.

Rnd 3: Work 1 sc in each sc to end of rnd, inc 1 st in first, seventh and 12th sc. 20 sts now in rnd.

Rnd 4: Work 1 sc in each sc to end of rnd, inc 1 st in fifth and 15th sc. 22 sts now in rnd.

Rnd 5: Work 1 sc in each sc to end of rnd, inc 1 st in seventh, 14th and 21st sc. 25 sts now in rnd.

Rnd 6: Work 1 sc in each sc, inc 1 st in second, seventh, 12th, 17th and 22nd sc. 30 sts now in rnd.

Work 17 rnds even in sc, *turn.*

Next: Ch 2 (counts as 1 dc), dc in next sc, inc 1 st in next sc, dc in next 3 sc, inc 1 st in next sc, dc in next 11 sc, inc 1 st in next sc, dc in next 3 sc, inc 1 st in next sc, dc in next 2 sc, *turn,* leaving 5 sc unworked. 29 dc now in row.

Working back and forth, work 7 rows even in dc (or until slipper is desired length), then fasten off, leaving 38 cm (15-inch) yarn end for sewing up.

Fold last row worked in half, butting edges to form centre-back seam of heel; with tapestry needle and yarn end, sew.

Tips:

- Leave plain or decorate by stitching on a simple flower cut from blanket cloth or fleece, or by embroidering a lazy daisy with yarn. Alternatively, you can sew on a tassel, bow or fancy button.

- To make the slippers nonskid, trace the sole outline onto real or faux suede, cut out, then handstitch in place using buttonhole twist or other sturdy yarn.

Uptown Cowl

This snug cowl is quick to knit and takes just two skeins of luxurious fair-trade yarn – a perfect last-minute gift. The cable pattern's staggered twists lend a sense of movement to an otherwise demure accessory.

YOU NEED:

- 2 skeins (50 g/75 m each) Mirasol Miski, 100% baby llama (shown here in Chamoise)

- 5 mm circular knitting needle, 40 cm (15¾ inches) long

- 6 mm circular knitting needle, 40 cm (15¾ inches) long

- Stitch markers

- Cable needle

- Tapestry needle

Note:

Standard abbreviations are used (see page 284) with one exception (see Stitches, below).

SIZE:

Laid flat, finished cowl measures 18 cm (7 inches) high and 24 cm (9½ inches) wide, after blocking and drying. One size fits most. See Tips, right, to alter the finished size.

TENSION:

15 sts and 20 rows = 10 cm (4 inches) in st st on 6 mm needles. Work to exact tension with specified yarn to obtain satisfactory results.

To save time, take time to check tension.

STITCHES:

C10L=Left-cable over 10 stitches: Place first 5 sts on cable needle and hold in front of work. Knit next 5 sts, then knit 5 sts from cable needle.

TO MAKE:

With smaller needles, Cast on 96 sts.

Taking care not to twist sts, join in rnd. Place stitch marker to mark beg of rnd.

Rnds 1 to 5: *K4, p2. Repeat from * to end of rnd.

Changing to larger needles, work cable pattern as follows:

Rnds 1 to 4: *K10, p2. Repeat from * to end of rnd.
Rnd 5: *C10L, p2, k10, p2. Repeat from * to end of rnd.
Rnds 6 to 9: *K10, p2. Repeat from * to end of rnd.
Rnd 10: *K10, p2, C10L, p2. Repeat from * to end of rnd.

Work Rnds 1 to 10 once more.

Work Rnds 1 to 9 once more.

Changing to smaller needles, work final 5 rnds in ribbing as follows.

Rnds 1 to 5: *K4, p2. Repeat from * to end of rnd.

CO all sts according to pat.

Wash cowl by hand according to yarn label instructions. Lay flat to dry and block to specified measurements.

Tips:

• To ensure a comfortable fit, cast on and cast off stitches loosely.

• For a larger cowl with more drape, increase total number of cast-on stitches by a multiple of 24; work pattern according to instructions provided. You will need at least one more skein of yarn.

Crocheted Carryall

Fun and fast to crochet, this reusable cotton bag scrunches up to fit into a pocket, then stretches wide when it's packed with groceries and produce.

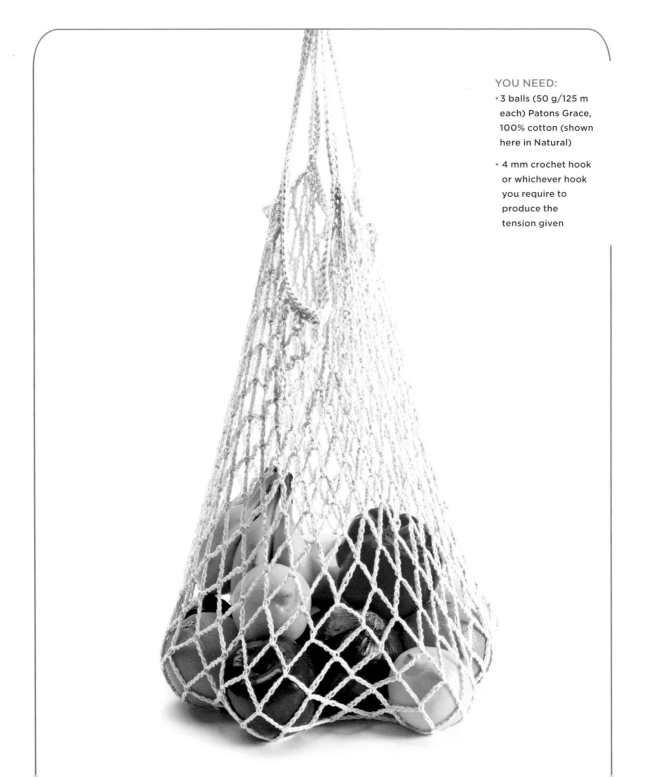

YOU NEED:

• 3 balls (50 g/125 m each) Patons Grace, 100% cotton (shown here in Natural)

• 4 mm crochet hook or whichever hook you require to produce the tension given

Note:

Standard abbreviations are used (see page 284) with one exception (see Stitches, below).

TENSION:

20 dc and 8 rows = 10 cm (4 inches). Work to exact tension with specified yarn to obtain satisfactory results.

To save time, take time to check tension.

STITCHES:

Dtr = double treble: [Yoh] 3 times, draw loop through next st, [yoh and draw through 2 loops on hook] 4 times.

TO MAKE:

Base:

Ch 3 (counts as 1 dc), sl st to first ch to join in ring.

Rnd 1: Ch 3, 15 dc in ring, sl st in top of ch 3. 16 dc now in rnd.

Rnd 2: Ch 3, 1 dc in same sp as last sl st, [2 dc in next dc] to end of rnd, sl st in top of ch 3.

Rnd 3: Ch 3, [2 dc in next dc, 1 dc in next dc] to last dc, 2 dc in last dc, sl st in top of ch 3.

Rnd 4: Ch 3, 1 dc in next dc, [2 dc in next dc, 1 dc each in next 2 dc] to last dc, 2 dc in last dc, sl st in top of ch 3.

Rnd 5: Ch 3, 1 dc each in next 2 dc, [2 dc in next dc, 1 dc each in next 3 dc] to last dc, 2 dc in last dc, sl st in top of ch 3.

Rnd 6: Ch 3, 1 dc each in next 3 dc, [2 dc in next dc, 1 dc each in next 4 dc] to last dc, 2 dc in last dc, sl st in top of ch 3.

Rnd 7: Ch 3, 1 dc each in next 4 dc, [2 dc in next dc, 1 dc each in next 5 dc] to last dc, 2 dc in last dc, sl st in top of ch 3.

Rnd 8: Ch 3, 1 dc each in next 5 dc, [2 dc in next dc, 1 dc each in next 6 dc] to last dc, 2 dc in last dc, sl st in top of ch 3.

Rnd 9: Ch 3, 1 dc each in next 6 dc, [2 dc in next dc, 1 dc each in next 7 dc] to last dc, 2 dc in last dc, sl st in top of ch 3.

Rnd 10: Ch 3, 1 dc in each dc to end of rnd, sl st to top of ch 3. 144 dc now in rnd.

Mesh:

Rnd 11: Ch 1, 1 sc in same sp as last sl st, [ch 9, skip next 3 dc, 1 sc in next dc] (arch made) to last 3 dc, ch 4, skip next 3 dc, 1 dtr in sc. 36 arches now in rnd.

Rnd 12: [Ch 9, 1 sc in centre st of next ch-9 sp] to last arch, ch 4, 1 dtr in top of dtr.

Next: Repeat last rnd 14 times more.

Next rnd: [Ch 9, 1 sc in centre st of next ch-9 sp] to last arch, ch 9, sl st in top of dtr.

Edging and handles:

Next rnd: Sl st in next ch-9 sp, ch 1, 5 sc in same ch-9 sp as last sl st, 5 sc each in next 2 ch-9 sps, [3 sc each in next 6 ch-9 sps, 5 sc each in next 3 ch-9 sps] 3 times, 3 sc each in last 6 ch-9 sps, sl st in top of first sc.

Next rnd: Ch 1, 1 sc in same sp as last sl st, 1 sc each in next 14 sc, ch 45 (handle made), skip next 18 sc, 1 sc each in next 48 sc, ch 45 (handle made), skip next 18 sc, 1 sc each in next 33 sc, sl st to first sc.

Next rnd: Ch 1, 1 sc in same sp as last sl st, 1 sc each in next 14 sc, *1 hdc in next ch, 1 dc each in next 43 ch, 1 hdc in next ch*, 1 sc each in next 48 sc, repeat from * to * once more, 1 sc each in last 33 sc, sl st to first sc. Fasten off.

Cosy Cowl

This slouchy knitted collar will keep you warm on the coldest winter day.

YOU NEED:

• 8 balls (50 g/100 m each) Sirdar Eco Wool Dk, 100% wool (shown here in Flint)

• 4 mm circular knitting needle, 60 cm (23¾ inches) long, or whichever needle you require to produce tension given

• Tapestry needle

Notes:

• The finished cowl is 45.5 cm (18 inches) high.

• Standard abbreviations are used (see page 284).

TENSION:

22 sts and 28 rows = 10 cm (4 inches) in st st. Work to exact tension with specified yarn to obtain satisfactory results.

To save time, take time to check tension.

TO MAKE:

Cast on 300 sts; join in rnd.

Rnd 1: *K2, p2. Repeat from * to end of rnd. Repeat Rnd 1 until cowl from beg measures 45.5 cm (18 inches); CO in rib.

With tapestry needle, weave in ends.

Simple Scarf

Use bamboo yarn in a bright berry colour to stitch a midwinter pick-me-up.

YOU NEED:

- **4 balls (50 g/95 m each) Sirdar Snuggly Baby Bamboo Dk yarn, 80% bamboo, 20% wool (shown here in Cherry Lips)**

- **Pair of 4 mm knitting needles or whichever needles you need to produce the tension given**

Note:
Standard abbreviations are used (see page 284).

TENSION:
22 sts and 28 rows = 10 cm (4 inches) in st st. Work to exact tension with specified yarn to obtain satisfactory results.

To save time, take time to check tension.

TO MAKE:
Cast on 35 sts.

Row 1: *K1, p1, k1, p1, k1, k5. Repeat from * 2 times. K1, p1, k1, p1, k1.

Row 2: **K1, p1, k1, p1, k1, p5. Repeat from ** 2 times. K1, p1, k1, p1, k1.

Repeat these 2 rows until scarf is 152 cm (60 inches) long or until you reach desired length. CO.

Aran Bolster Pillow

Wrapped with wonderful texture, this bolster is the perfect starter project for anyone who ever wanted to tackle an Aran knit but wasn't ready to commit to a whole sweater's worth of knitting.

YOU NEED:

- 2 balls (100 g/205 m each) worsted-weight yarn, 100% wool (such as Patons Classic Wool)

- Pair of 5 mm knitting needles

- Tapestry needle

- Bolster form, 43 cm (17 inches) long x 20 cm (8 inches) diameter

Note:

Standard abbreviations are used (see page 284) with some exceptions (see Stitches, below).

SIZE:

Finished bolster is approx 43 cm (17 inches) long x 20 cm (8 inches) diameter.

TENSION:

20 sts and 24 rows = 10 cm (4 inches) in st st. Work to exact tension with specified yarn to obtain satisfactory results.

To save time, take time to check tension.

STITCHES:

C2F: Sl1 to cn and hold at front of work; k1, k1 from cn.

C2B: Sl1 to cn and hold at back of work; k1, k1 from cn.

C3FP: Sl2 to cn and hold at front of work; p1, k2 from cn.

C3BP: Sl1 to cn and hold at back of work; k2, p1 from cn.

C4F: Sl2 to cn and hold at front of work; k2, k2 from cn.

C4B: Sl2 to cn and hold at back of work; k2, k2 from cn.

C5BP: Sl3 to cn and hold at back of work; k2, sl left-hand st from cn back to left-hand needle, p1, k2 from cn.

MB = Make bobble: [Knit, purl, knit] into next stitch, *turn* and k3, *turn* again and k3, pass the centre, then the right-hand st over last st worked (bobble made).

MW = Make wrap: With yarn at back of work sl1, yfwd, sl1 back to left-hand needle (wrap made).

TO MAKE:

Aran strip:
Cast on 91 sts.

Foundation row: K2, p1, k1, p4, k1, p1, k1, p12, k1, p1, k1, p6, k1, p1, k9, p2, k1, p2, k9, p1, k1, p6, k1, p1, k1, p12, k1, p1, k1, p4, k1, p1, k2.

Row 1 (RS): P2, k1, p1, C4F, p1, k1, p1, [C2B, C2F] 3 times, p1, k1, p1, C4F, k2, p1, k1, p9, C5BP, p9, k1, p1, k2, C4B, p1, k1, p1, [C2B, C2F] 3 times, p1, k1, p1, C4B, p1, k1, p2.

All wrong-side rows from Row 2 to Row 24: K all knit sts and p all purl sts as they appear.

Row 3: P2, k1, p1, k4, p1, k1, p1, [C2F, C2B] 3 times, p1, k1, p1, k6, p1, k1, p8, C3BP, p1, C3FP, p8, k1, p1, k6, p1, k1, p1, [C2F, C2B] 3 times, p1, k1, p1, k4, p1, k1, p2.

Row 5: P2, k1, p1, C4F, p1, k1, p1, [C2B, C2F] 3 times, p1, k1, p1, k2, C4B, p1, k1, p7, C3BP, p3, C3FP, p7, k1, p1, C4F, k2, p1, k1, p1, [C2B, C2F] 3 times, p1, k1, p1, C4B, p1, k1, p2.

Row 7: P2, k1, p1, k4, p1, k1, p1, [C2F, C2B] 3 times, p1, k1, p1, k6, p1, k1, p6, C3BP, p5, C3FP, p6, k1, p1, k6, p1, k1, p1, [C2F, C2B] 3 times, p1, k1, p1, k4, p1, k1, p2.

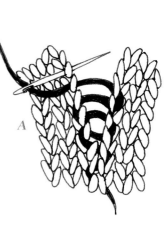

A

Row 9: P2, k1, p1, C4F, p1, k1, p1, [C2B, C2F] 3 times, p1, k1, p1, C4F, k2, p1, k1, p5, C3BP, p7, C3FP, p5, k1, p1, k2, C4B, p1, k1, p1, [C2B, C2F] 3 times, p1, k1, p1, C4B, p1, k1, p2.

Row 11: P2, k1, p1, k4, p1, k1, p1, [C2F, C2B] 3 times, p1, k1, p1, k6, p1, k1, p4, C3BP, p9, C3FP, p4, k1, p1, k6, p1, k1, p1, [C2F, C2B] 3 times, p1, k1, p1, k4, p1, k1, p2.

Row 13: P2, k1, p1, C4F, p1, k1, p1, [C2B, C2F] 3 times, p1, k1, p1, k2, C4B, p1, k1, p4, k2, p5, MB, p5, k2, p4, k1, p1, C4F, k2, p1, k1, p1, [C2B, C2F] 3 times, p1, k1, p1, C4B, p1, k1, p2.

Row 15: P2, k1, p1, k4, p1, k1, p1, [C2F, C2B] 3 times, p1, k1, p1, k6, p1, k1, p4, C3FP, p9, C3BP, p4, k1, p1, k6, p1, k1, p1, [C2F, C2B] 3 times, p1, k1, p1, k4, p1, k1, p2.

Row 17: P2, k1, p1, C4F, p1, k1, p1, [C2B, C2F] 3 times, p1, k1, p1, C4F, k2, p1, k1, p5, C3FP, p7, C3BP, p5, k1, p1, k2, C4B, p1, k1, p1, [C2B, C2F] 3 times, p1, k1, p1, C4B, p1, k1, p2.

Row 19: P2, k1, p1, k4, p1, k1, p1, [C2F, C2B] 3 times, p1, k1, p1, k6, p1, k1, p6, C3FP, p5, C3BP, p6, k1, p1, k6, p1, k1, p1, [C2F, C2B] 3 times, p1, k1, p1, k4, p1, k1, p2.

Row 21: P2, k1, p1, C4F, p1, k1, p1, [C2B, C2F] 3 times, p1, k1, p1, k2, C4B, p1, k1, p7, C3FP, p3, C3BP, p7, k1, p1, C4F, k2, p1, k1, p1, [C2B, C2F] 3 times, p1, k1, p1, C4B, p1, k1, p2.

Row 23: P2, k1, p1, k4, p1, k1, p1, [C2F, C2B] 3 times, p1, k1, p1, k6, p1, k1, p8, C3FP, p1, C3BP, p8, k1, p1, k6, p1, k1, p1, [C2F, C2B] 3 times, p1, k1, p1, k4, p1, k1, p2.

Rows 1 through 24 form cable pat.

Complete a total of 6 pat reps, working last rep to Row 23 inclusive; CO purlwise.

Circle (make 2):
Cast on 20 sts.

Row 1 (WS): Knit.
Row 2: K16, MW, *turn,* leaving rem 4 sts unworked.
Row 3: P16.
Row 4: K12, MW, *turn,* leaving rem 8 sts unworked.
Row 5: P12.
Row 6: K8, MW, *turn,* leaving rem 12 sts unworked.
Row 7: P8.
Row 8: K4, MW, *turn,* leaving rem 16 sts unworked.
Row 9: P4.
Row 10: K across all 20 sts, working each wrap and st it wraps as follows [insert needle knitwise under both at once, ktog].

Rows 1 through 10 form circle pattern.

Complete a total of 13 pat reps; CO purlwise, leaving 25 cm (9¾-inch) yarn end.

To finish:
One at a time, fold each circle so right sides are together and cast-on and cast-off edges are even; with tapestry needle and yarn end, ladder-stitch these edges together [A], then thread end through centre sts, pull to close centre and knot.

Pin to measurements: strip 63.5 x 40.5 cm (25 x 16 inches); circles, each 23 cm (9 inches) in diameter. Block, do not press. With right side out, wrap strip around form so short edges are even; pin edges tog, matching pat, then ladder-stitch. Pin 1 circle, right side out, at each end; stitch in place.

Thrummed Socks

These super snuggly socks make the perfect gift for a person with perpetually cold toes.

YOU NEED:

- 1 skein (113 g/196 m) Briggs and Little Tuffy 2-ply yarn (shown here in Red Mix)

- Approx 80 g washed, carded fleece*

- Set of four 4.5 mm double-pointed needles (DPN) or whichever needles you require to produce the tension given

- Stitch holder

- Tapestry needle

- Piece of suede 25 cm (9¾ inches) square (optional)

- Buttonhole twist or other heavy-duty thread, and darning needle or awl (all optional)

Available at yarn stores

Notes:

- Standard abbreviations are used (see page 284) with one exception (see Stitches, below).

- Instructions are written for Small (S) size. Any changes for Medium (M) or Large (L) are written in brackets. If there is only one set of figures, it applies to all sizes.

STITCHES:

K1thrum: Holding twisted thrum over forefinger, insert needle into next st. Slip thrum over inserted needle so ends are to WS of work. Wrap yarn around needle and draw thrum and wrapped yarn through st.

FINISHED FOOT LENGTH:

Small   20 cm
                    (8 inches)
Medium   23 cm
                    (9 inches)
Large   27 cm
                    (10½ inches)

All measurements are approximate.

TENSION:

18 sts and 28 rows = 10 cm (4 inches) in st st using 4.5 mm needles. Work to exact tension with specified yarn to obtain satisfactory results.

To save time, take time to check tension.

TO MAKE:

Thrums:

Pull off (don't cut) 7.5 cm (3-inch) length of fleece; split lengthwise into thin, wispy thrums. Pull fibres apart at centre of each thrum to make it thinner than ends, then fold both ends toward centre, overlapping slightly, and twist (centre of finished thrum should be almost as thick as knitting yarn). Make approx 270(300,330).

To work cuff:

Cast on 36(40,44) sts. Distribute across DPNs as follows: 16 sts on first needle and 10(12,14) sts each on second and third needles. Being careful not to twist sts, join in rnd.

Rnds 1 to 8: [K1, p1] to end of rnd.

Push work through centre of needles to turn inside out.

Rnd 9 (RS): Starting back across needle just worked, k. 10(12,14) sts each now on first and second needles, and 16 sts on third needle.

Rnds 10 to 18: [K1, p1] to end of rnd.

To begin heel:

[K1, p1] across first needle, slip all 10(12,14) sts from second needle and first 5(3,1) sts from third needle onto stitch holder. *Turn.*

Using 1 needle, p10(12,14) sts from first needle, then p11(13,15) sts from third needle. 21(25,29) sts now on single needle.

Work back and forth down heel as follows:

Row 1 (RS): K2, [k1thrum, k3] to last 3 sts, k1thrum, k2.
Row 2 (WS): Purl.
Row 3 (RS): Knit.
Row 4 (WS): Purl.

Rep these 4 rows 2(3,3) times more, then Rows 1 and 2 once more.

To shape heel:

Row 5: K17(19,21) sts. *Turn.*
Row 6: Sl1, p11, p2tog. *Turn.*
Row 7 for size M only: Sl1, k3, k1thrum, k3, k1thrum, k3, sl1, k1, psso. *Turn.*
Row 7 for sizes S and L: Sl1, k1, k1thrum, k3, k1thrum, k3, k1thrum, k1, sl1, k1, psso. *Turn.*
Row 8: Sl1, p11, p2tog. *Turn.*
Row 9: Sl1, k11, sl1, k1, psso. *Turn.*

Repeat Rows 6 through 9 one(2,3) time(s) more. 13 sts now on needle. *Turn.*

P 1 row.

With first needle, k across 13 sts. With same needle and RS of work facing, pick up and k9(11,13) sts up left edge of heel. With second needle, work 15 sts from st holder. With third needle, pick up and k9(11,13) sts down right edge of heel. With the same needle, work 6 from heel sts. 46(50,54) sts now in rnd.

To shape instep and foot:
Rnd 1: K to last 3 sts of first needle, k2tog, k1. K across second needle. On third needle, k1, sl1, k1 psso, k to end.
Rnd 2: [K1thrum, k3] to end of rnd.
Rnd 3: As given for Rnd 1.
Rnd 4: Knit.

Keeping continuity of thrum pat, repeat Rnds 1 through 4 twice more, then Rnds 1 and 2 once more. (Note: Some thrums are eliminated by dec sts. Extra sts between thrums will be taken up by following dec sts.) 36(40,44) sts now in rnd.

Work even in thrum pat as established until foot from back of heel measures 19(21.5,25.5) cm/ 7½(8½,10) inches or desired length to within 1.3 cm (½ inch) of desired toe tip, ending with Rnd 2.

To shape toe:
Rnd 1: [K2tog] to end of rnd. 18(20,22) sts now on needle.
Rnd 2: Knit.
Rnd 3: [K2tog] to end of rnd. 9(10,11) sts now on needle.

Break yarn. With tapestry needle, thread yarn end through rem sts. Draw up and fasten securely on inside.

To finish:
Turn socks WS out. Weave in yarn ends. Gently pull each thrum to tighten, then gently fluff apart fibres to cover inside surface. Turn RS out.

To add soles (optional):
Enlarge sole pattern (page 264) by squaring method as follows: On brown paper, draw grid of horizontal and vertical lines 2.5 cm (1 inch) apart. Each square on diagram equals a square on brown paper. Enlarge pattern by redrawing each line of pattern onto corresponding square. Cut out pattern; trace 2 onto suede.

Cut out soles. With darning needle, punch holes around edge of each, 6 mm (¼ inch apart) and 6 mm (¼ inch) in from edge. Centre 1 sole on sole of each slipper sock. Through holes, blanket-stitch with thread.

Weekend Socks

Knitting socks is satisfying, and this pattern is designed to help even a novice produce a pair of warm and cosy footwear.

YOU NEED:

- Worsted-weight yarn (see Quantities, opposite)

- Set of four 3.5 mm double-pointed needles (DPN) or whichever needles you require to produce the tension given

- Stitch markers

- Tapestry needle

Notes:

- Standard abbreviations are used (see page 284).

- Socks are worked in the round. Instructions are written for Small (S) size. Any changes for Medium (M) or Large (L) are written in brackets. If there is only one set of figures, it applies to all sizes.

SIZE:

Socks are 15(19,23) cm/ 6(7½,9) inches in foot/ ankle circumference, corresponding approx to women's sizes S(M,L) or women's shoe sizes 5-6(7-8,9-10).

If in doubt, knit size that corresponds to ankle circumference. If desired, knit foot of sock to different length: Trace foot on piece of paper and measure from base of heel to tip of longest toe to determine total length; subtract 5 cm (2 inches) to determine length to knit prior to starting toe shaping.

QUANTITIES:

The socks shown here were made with Louet Gems Light Worsted in Golden Rod, but we also made samples with Patons Classic Wool and Mission Falls 1824. Suggested quantities are as follows for S(M,L):

- 1(2,2) skeins (100 g/ 160 m each) Louet Gems Light Worsted, 100% merino machine-washable wool
- 1(1,2) balls (100 g/ 205 m each) Patons Classic Wool, 100% wool
- 3(3,4) balls (50 g/ 78 m each) Mission Falls 1824, 100% merino superwash wool

TENSION:

24 sts and 34 rows = 10 cm (4 inches) in st st using 3.5 mm needles. Work to exact tension with specified yarn to obtain satisfactory results.

To save time, take time to check tension.

TO MAKE:

Cuff:

Cast on 32(40,48) sts. Place marker. Being careful not to twist sts, join in rnd, dividing sts as follows: 16(20,24) sts on Needle 1, and 8(10,12) sts each on Needles 2 and 3. Rnd begins with Needle 1.

Rnd 1: *K1, p1. Repeat from * to end of rnd.

Repeat this rnd until work measures 2.5 cm (1 inch) from beg.

Leg:

Next rnd: *K3, p1. Repeat from * to end of rnd.

Repeat this rnd until work measures 13(14.5,16.5) cm/ 5(5¾,6½) inches from beg, or until desired length before start of heel.

To shape heel:

The heel flap is worked over sts on Needle 1. Sts on Needles 2 and 3 remain as they are until heel is completed.

Work heel flap over 16(20,24) sts on Needle 1 as follows:

Row 1 (RS): *Sl1, k1. Repeat from * to end of needle.
Row 2 (WS): Sl1, p to end of needle.
Next rows: Repeat Rows 1 and 2 seven(9,11) times more.

To turn heel:

Work short rows as follows:
Row 1 (RS): K10(12,14) sts, ssk, k1, *turn.*

Size S:
Row 2 (WS): Sl1, p5, p2tog, p1, *turn.*
Row 3 (RS): Sl1, k6, ssk, k1, *turn.*
Row 4 (WS): Sl1, p7, p2tog, p1, *turn.*
Row 5 (RS): Sl1, k8, ssk, *turn.*
Row 6 (WS): Sl1, p9, p2tog, *turn.* 11 sts now on needle.

Size M:
Work Rows 2 to 4 as indicated for Size S, then proceed as follows:

Row 5 (RS): Sl1, k8, ssk, k1, *turn.*
Row 6 (WS): Sl1, p9, p2tog, p1, *turn.*
Row 7 (RS): Sl1, k10, ssk, *turn.*
Row 8 (WS): Sl1, p11, p2tog, *turn.* 13 sts now on needle.

Size L:
Work Rows 2 to 4 as indicated for Size S, then Rows 5 and 6 as indicated for Size M. Proceed as follows:

Row 7 (RS): Sl1, k10, ssk, k1, *turn.*
Row 8 (WS): Sl1, p11, p2tog, p1, *turn.*
Row 9 (RS): Sl1, k12, ssk, *turn.*
Row 10 (WS): Sl1, p13, p2tog, *turn.* 15 sts now on needle.

To establish gussets:
In this step, you will pick up sts at each side of the heel flap in order to return to working the foot of the sock in the rnd. Then you will gradually dec at each side of the foot, forming gussets, which allow a smooth fit over the arch of the foot.

Slip sts from Needle 3 onto Needle 2.

Rnd 1 (RS):
Needle 1: K11(13,15) sts for heel. Pick up and k11(13,15) sts along selvage of heel flap. Move the last of these sts to the beg of Needle 2; this st will be worked as a purl st from now on. 21(25,29) sts now on Needle 1; 17(21,25) sts on Needle 2.
Needle 2: P1; work remaining sts on Needle 2 in k3, p1 ribbing as established.
Needle 3: Pick up and k10(12,14) sts along rem selvage of heel flap and k first 5(6,7) sts of heel. 48(58,68) sts now on needles: 16(19,22) sts on Needle 1, 17(21,25) sts on Needle 2 and 15(18,21) sts on Needle 3.

To shape gussets:
Work decreases
as follows:

Rnd 1: K to last 3 sts
on Needle 1, k2tog, k1.
Work sts on Needle 2
in k3, p1 ribbing as
established, beginning
and ending with purl
stitch. On Needle 3, k1,
ssk, k to end of rnd.
46(56,66) sts now
on needles.
Rnd 2: K all sts on
Needle 1. Work sts on
Needle 2 in k3, p1 ribbing
as established. K all sts
on Needle 3.

Repeat Rnds 1 and 2
seven(8,9) times more.
33(41,49) sts now
on needles.

To shape foot:
The foot of the sock is
now worked evenly with
no further dec until the
toe, maintaining ribbing
pat on top of foot
(instep) and st st on
bottom of foot (sole).
Work rnds even,
knitting or purling sts as
they appear in pat as
established, until foot
measures 13(14,15) cm/
5(5½,6) inches from
gusset or 5 cm
(2 inches) shorter than
desired length.

To shape toe:
Following an initial
set-up round, the toe is
formed with spiral dec.
The simple dec pat is
easy to remember and
eliminates the need to
graft the toe. Note that
Rnd 1 instructions differ
for each size.

Rnd 1 (Size S): *K9,
k2tog. Repeat from *
twice more.
Rnd 1 (Size M): K21,
m1, k20.
Rnd 1 (Size L): K24,
k2tog, k23.

30(42,48) sts on
needles. Rearrange sts
to have multiple of 6 sts
on each needle.

Rnds 2 and 3: Knit.
Rnd 4: *K4, k2tog.
Repeat from * to end
of rnd.
Rnds 5 to 7: Knit.
Rnd 8: *K3, k2tog.
Repeat from * to end
of rnd.
Rnds 9 to 11: Knit.
Rnd 12: *K2, k2tog.
Repeat from * to end
of rnd.
Rnds 13 and 14: Knit.
Rnd 15: *K1, k2tog.
Repeat from * to end
of rnd.
Rnds 16 and 17: Knit.
Rnd 18: *K2tog. Repeat
from * to end of rnd.

5(7,8) sts rem on
needles.

To finish:
Break yarn; use tapestry
needle to sew through
rem sts, drawing toe
together. Sew closed.
Weave in ends.

around the house

furniture • mirrors • shelves • plant pots • pet beds • lamps • curios

Wire Family Photo Tree

Simple wire from the hardware store transforms into a pretty photo tree.

YOU NEED:
- 25-foot coil of 18-gauge brass or copper wire
- Needle-nose pliers and wire cutters
- 2 small nails or tiny cup hooks
- Family photos (see Tips, opposite)
- Brown paper, pencil and ruler (optional)

TO MAKE:

1| Photocopy pattern (page 265), enlarging to desired size. Or enlarge pattern by squaring method as follows: On brown paper, draw grid of horizontal and vertical lines 2.5 cm (1 inch) apart. Each square on diagram equals a square on brown paper. Enlarge by drawing each line of pattern onto corresponding square.

2| Refer to diagram and work freehand – or lay enlarged pattern flat on work surface for guide – to assemble wire tree, 1 piece at a time. With pliers, twist coil at end of wire, bend into shape by hand, then cut to required length, allowing approx 6.5 cm (2½ inches) at end for joining; wrap end tightly around adjacent wire, then crimp twisted wire to secure join. Repeat for each branch.

3| Hang tree on nail at each hanging point shown on diagram. Tuck each photo into 1 coil at branch end.

Tips:

• Preserve precious photos by scanning them into your computer, then use copies – not the originals – for your craft.

• Convert all the scanned photos to sepia or black-and-white (if desired), then size them to suit your family tree and print them out on glossy photo-quality paper.

• Mimic old-fashioned wavy white borders by trimming each photo, just beyond the edges, with decorative scalloped-blade scrapbooking scissors.

• If desired, increase the scale of the tree, then add more branch coils to accommodate even more photos.

Gilded Cache Pot

With gold leaf, it's easy to make household objects gleam anew.

YOU NEED:

- Cache pot, cleaned and dried

- Faux gold leaf, adhesive (also called gold size) and sealer (usually sold together as a kit)*

- Artist's small fine-tip, and medium and large broad-tip, soft-bristle paintbrushes*, for applying adhesive, gold leaf and sealer

- Clean, dry, soft cloth

Available at art supply, craft supply, and some hardware and home decor stores

Note:

Work on one small area at a time.

TO MAKE:

1| With medium brush and following manufacturer's instructions, apply thin, smooth coat of adhesive to pot. Wait until milky adhesive becomes clear and tacky (on porous surface, such as unglazed terra-cotta, it may take longer than specified).

2| Using large brush, ease sheet of gold leaf onto adhesive [A]; with dry, large brush and working out from centre, gently dab and stroke sheet to adhere [B]. It will crack and crease in places, adding highlights and texture. With small fine-tip brush, work into crevices.

3| Repeat Step 1 and Step 2, overlapping sheets slightly, to cover desired area (avoid aligning edges of sheets with edges on your pot; wrap sheets over edges for stronger bond).

4| When gilding is complete, brush off any excess leaf, then burnish with cloth.

5| With medium brush, apply thin, smooth coat of sealer; let dry.

Tips:

- Gold leaf adheres best to surfaces that have a slight tooth or texture, such as unglazed ceramic, plaster, metal and wood, rather than high-gloss surfaces.

- Gold-leafed items can't be submerged in warm, soapy water for a wash, so gild decorative items that will only need an occasional moist wipe.

- You can apply gold leaf to an entire surface, or use it to show off a selected area, such as an embossed band or motif.

- Gold leaf is fragile and may tear, so handle it sparingly, nudging it out of its protective tissue and onto the object with the tip of a large broad-tip, soft-bristle brush, not your fingers.

- Don't fret about small areas accidentally left uncovered (gilders call these holidays); they will lend an antique look.

- Save any leftover flakes (called skewings) for another project.

- Gold leaf was originally made from real gold; some of it still is, but the budget-friendly faux version looks almost as good. One caveat: The real stuff can be used outdoors, but the fake is for indoor use only.

- If gold isn't your colour, try aluminum, copper or silver leaf.

Repaired Chair Seat

With a little glue, some patience and a fresh coat of paint, it's easy to update your favourite old, cracked wooden chairs.

YOU NEED:

- Chair
- Trisodium phosphate (TSP)
- Sandpaper in grades from 80 to 120
- Paint scraper (optional)
- Tack cloth
- Putty knife, wooden plant marker, tongue depressor or wooden stir stick, for applying glue (or, for very narrow cracks, use a glue syringe)
- Wood filler
- Wood glue
- Bar clamps, long enough to span chair seat
- Small blocks of wood (optional)
- Clean rag moistened with water
- Paintbrush, primer and paint

Before

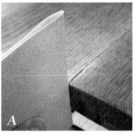

A

B

C

Note:

When using TSP, protect yourself by wearing rubber gloves and eye protection.

TO MAKE:

1| Wash chair with TSP; let dry. Sand all over and, if necessary, use scraper to remove any chipped paint or varnish. Wipe down with tack cloth.

2| With putty knife and wood filler, fill all small cracks and splits in back, rungs, legs and seat; let dry, then sand smooth.

3| Fold sandpaper in half, grit side out [A]. Carefully ease apart seat at any large cracks, if necessary, until they accommodate folded sandpaper. Holding sandpaper vertically to avoid rounding edges, sand inside surfaces of crack(s) to remove old glue.

4| Working quickly, generously squeeze line of glue along crack, then, with clean putty knife, spread onto both inside surfaces [B]. At right angles to crack, clamp seat to hold inside surfaces snugly against each other [C]. (To protect seat, if desired, place small block of wood between clamp and seat at each end.) With rag, wipe off any excess glue. Let dry overnight.

5| Sand glue seam smooth. Prime and paint chair as desired, letting dry after each coat.

Plate Shelf

Highlight your family treasures – or your favourite flea market finds – on this simple plate rack.

YOU NEED:

- 1 piece 1x3* pine, 6 feet long

- 1 piece 1x1* pine, 9 feet long

- 1 piece 1x2* pine, 9 feet long

- Brown paper

- Pencil, ruler, measuring tape and carpenter's square

- Drill and ⅛-inch bit, hammer, nail set and clamps

- Saw and coping saw, jigsaw or scroll saw

- Carpenter's glue

- 1½-inch finishing nails

- Wood filler and putty knife

- Sandpaper of various grades, fine steel wool and tack cloth

- Spray lacquer in cream or desired colour

- Furniture wax and clean rags

- ¼-inch eye hook

- Carpenter's level

- 3 screws, for installation (appropriate to type of wall)

Nominal sizes; actual dimensions will be somewhat smaller

Notes:

• Refer to diagrams (page 266) throughout.

• Before proceeding to next step, let glue, wood filler, lacquer and wax dry, according to manufacturers' instructions.

TO MAKE:

1| Enlarge pattern (page 266) by squaring method as follows: On brown paper, draw grid of horizontal and vertical lines 2.5 cm (1 inch) apart. Each square on diagram equals a square on brown paper. Enlarge by drawing each line of pattern onto corresponding square. Cut out pattern.

2| Measure actual thickness of 1x3 pine; multiply measurement by 2, then add 32 inches to determine total length. From 1x1, cut 3 rails, each having total length.

3| From 1x2, cut 3 shelf pieces, each 32 inches long.

4| From 1x3, cut 2 sides, each 32 inches long. Using pattern for each, trace top and bottom curve onto front edge of each side; with coping saw, cut out. Drill hole from front to back through each top curve as shown on Diagram 1 (page 266). On each back edge, mark shelf positions as shown on Diagram 1, then, using carpenter's square, mark position on inside of each side.

5| Lay sides, back edges down, on flat work surface. One rail at a time, apply glue to back edge from each end to ¾ inch along; position against front edge of each side as shown on Diagram 2 (page 266), check that rail is perpendicular to sides, then nail in place. Check that entire assembly is square. Measure diagonally from corner to corner; if measurements are equal, assembly is square. Clamp and let dry.

6| Stand assembly upright. One shelf at a time, apply glue along each end; position at marks between sides, check that shelf is perpendicular to sides, then nail in place. Let dry.

7| With nail set, countersink nails; with putty knife, smooth filler over holes. Let dry.

8| Sand smooth. Lightly spray shelf all over with lacquer; let dry. Smooth with steel wool to expose wood grain as desired; rub down with tack cloth. With rag, apply wax; let dry, then polish.

9| Screw eye hook into midpoint of bottom shelf as shown on Diagram 1 (page 266). At each top corner, screw levelled shelf to wall, then screw through eye hook to anchor bottom.

Upcycled Cups and Saucers

Let heirloom china cups and saucers shine – and serve a new purpose – by recycling them into beautiful displays for indoors or out.

YOU NEED:

Teacup Bird Feeder

- China teacup and saucer
- 1.2 m (4-foot) copper pipe with cap to fit*
- Exterior-grade epoxy
- Birdseed

*Available at hardware and plumbing supply stores

Teacup Candle

- China teacup and saucer
- Candle stubs
- Double boiler
- Candy or candle thermometer
- Tongs
- Candle wicks and wick tabs
- Bamboo or metal skewers
- Ruler and scissors

Teacup Bird Feeder
TO MAKE:

1| With epoxy, glue teacup to saucer, then centre and glue saucer on top of cap.

2| Push pipe 30 cm (11⅞ inches) into ground; cap top and fill cup with birdseed.

Teacup Candle
TO MAKE:

1| Melt candle stubs over simmering water in top of double boiler, clipping thermometer onto side and watching carefully to ensure temperature doesn't get higher than 85°C (185°F); overheated wax is a fire hazard.

2| With tongs, remove old wicks. Cut new wick 10 cm (4 inches) longer than cup depth; tie 1 end to wick tab and 1 end to skewer. Dip bottom end of tab into wax; adhere inside cup. With skewer suspended on cup rim, pour in wax to within 1.3 cm (½ inch) of rim.

3| Let harden; remove skewer and trim wick.

Tin Tile Hanging Pot

Curved into a cone, a vintage embossed ceiling panel presents a fresh or faux bouquet beautifully – and right at eye level.

YOU NEED:

- Textured tin ceiling panel, at least 51 cm (20⅛ inches) square

- Brass fasteners with 5 cm (2-inch) shanks*

- Metal primer and enamel in desired colour; paintbrushes and clean rags (all optional)

- 18-gauge wire

- Cut-glass or crystal chandelier pendant

- Three 30.5 cm (12-inch) lengths of No. 16 jack chain (or similar recycled chain)

- 1-inch harness ring

- Brown paper

- Pencil, ruler and set square

- Scissors, chalk and jar lid, approx 7.5 cm (3 inches) in diameter

- Tin snips

- Hammer

- Needle-nose pliers with wire cutters and/or spring clamp

- ¼-inch centre punch

- Drill and ³⁄₁₆-inch bit (for use with metal)

Available at office supply stores

Notes:

- Use soft wire brush to remove any flaking paint from panel before you start.

- Wear long sleeves and gloves as you work, and safety glasses while you drill.

- Before drilling, start each hole with a centre punch.

- To lengthen cone, draw longer side edges on triangle in Step 1 as desired, then, in Step 3, drill third hole through overlapped edges, halfway down, and fasten.

- The glossy paint on this model lets the texture really shine, but for a shabby-chic look, leave the surface as you find it.

TO MAKE:

1| With pencil, ruler and set square, on brown paper, draw isosceles triangle as shown on pattern (page 267). Cut out, then roll to form into cone with short edges overlapped at least 2 cm (¾ inch); trim so top edge is level all around, then open out and lay flat. Centring first scallop in middle of paper with top of curve at top edge of paper, trace around jar lid to draw shallow scallop. Working out to each side edge, continue tracing in same manner to complete scalloped top edge. Cut out pattern.

2| Ensuring panel motifs are oriented as desired, lay pattern on tin panel; with chalk, trace around pattern. With tin snips, cut out just inside chalk lines. Lay flat, wrong side up, and hammer all over to slightly flatten. With tin snips, cut straight across bottom point where indicated by broken line (see pattern, page 267).

3| Roll to form into cone, overlapping straight side edges as in Step 1 and matching scallops. With pliers or spring clamp, hold securely at top edge, then drill hole through overlapped layers, approx 2.5 cm (1 inch) from top edge and 1 cm (⅜ inch) from overlapped edge. From inside, push fastener through hole, then flatten shanks tightly against outside. Drill second hole through overlapped layers, approx 2.5 cm (1 inch) from bottom edge, then fasten. For longer cone, add third fastener (see Notes, above).

4| With pliers, flatten bottom edges together, then fold up edge approx 3 mm (⅛ inch) and crimp. Drill hole for pendant through bottom point, approx 6 mm (¼ inch) from folded edge, then drill 3 holes for hanging chains, approx 2.5 cm (1 inch) from top and evenly spaced around top edge.

5| If desired, brush on coat of primer, then 1 or 2 coats of enamel, letting dry after each coat. To highlight texture, rub paint off raised surfaces with clean rags after each coat, then let dry (see photo, opposite).

6| With pliers, cut short length of wire. Thread top end through bottom hole in cone and twist to secure; thread remaining end through top of pendant and twist to secure.

7| With pliers, open bottom link of each chain length; thread through hole at top edge, then close link to secure. Or cut short length of wire for each chain length; thread through bottom link, then through hole at top edge and twist inside cone to secure. Open top link of each chain length; thread through harness ring, then close to secure. Or cut short length of wire for each chain length; thread through top link, then harness ring and twist to secure.

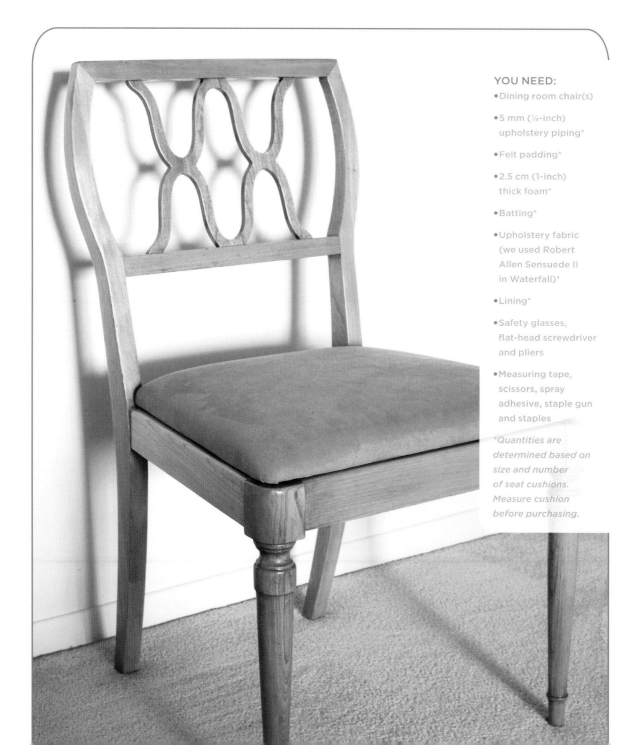

Reupholstered Dining Room Chair

Give your dining room a quick face-lift by reupholstering your chairs in a fresh new fabric.

YOU NEED:

- Dining room chair(s)
- 5 mm (¼-inch) upholstery piping*
- Felt padding*
- 2.5 cm (1-inch) thick foam*
- Batting*
- Upholstery fabric (we used Robert Allen Sensuede II in Waterfall)*
- Lining*
- Safety glasses, flat-head screwdriver and pliers
- Measuring tape, scissors, spray adhesive, staple gun and staples

*Quantities are determined based on size and number of seat cushions. Measure cushion before purchasing.

TO MAKE:

1| Remove all layers of fabric and old padding from seat cushion to expose wooden base. Wearing safety glasses, tap handle of flat-head screwdriver with pliers to drive flat end under each staple to loosen [A]. Use pliers to remove each staple.

2| Place base right side up on table. Staple piping around edge with flange on inside [B].

3| Cut piece of felt padding to fit inside piped edge; turn edges under neatly as you staple padding to base [C].

4| Cut piece of foam 1.3 cm (½ inch) larger than wood base on all 4 sides. Place base on foam, padding side down. Use spray adhesive to secure all 4 edges of foam to base.

5| Place base on piece of batting, foam side down. Glue all 4 edges of batting to foam. Trim excess batting [D].

6| Cut square of fabric approx 10 cm (4 inches) larger than base on all 4 sides. Centre base on fabric, batting side down. Mark centre on each edge of base and fabric. Pull 1 edge of fabric over base, being careful to match centre marks; staple with temporary staple at centre mark [E]. Repeat for 3 remaining edges, stapling opposite edges first [F].

7| Smooth fabric tightly over edges and corners [G].

8| Staple around edges, placing staples 1.3 cm (½ inch) from edges and 10 cm (4 inches) from each corner. Remove temporary centre staples as each edge is stapled.

9| Trim excess fabric from edges.

10| Pull fabric tightly over corners; smooth over each corner to remove folds or wrinkles in fabric, then staple fabric to base [H].

11| Cut piece of lining 7.5 cm (3 inches) larger than base on all 4 sides. Staple lining to base, folding edges under as you work and placing staples 6 mm (¼ inch) from edge, as close together as possible. Staple around edges first, then corners [I].

A

E

B

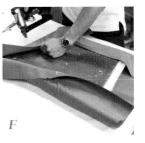

F

C

G

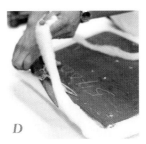

D

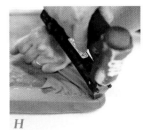

H

I

Vintage Shadow Boxes

Small vintage kitchen objects get a modern vibe when showcased in shadow boxes made from scraps of pine, moulding and a little paint. These pretty boxes are perfect for displaying favourite treasures or collectibles.

**YOU NEED
(FOR EACH):**

• Vintage kitchen utensil or other object

• Scraps of 1½- x 1¼-inch pine, for frame

• Scraps of ¼-inch bead board, for backing

• Scraps of ¾-inch moulding, for trim

• Measuring tape

• Handsaw and mitre box, or mitre saw

• Jigsaw

• Carpenter's glue

• Hammer and nail punch

• 1- and 1½-inch finishing nails

• Wood filler

• 120-grit sandpaper

• High-gloss paint and paintbrush

• Glue gun

TO MAKE:

1| Measure utensil to be framed. Add 6 inches to length and width to determine final dimensions for shadow box frame. (We used a 15 x 5 cm/6- x 2-inch utensil, so our frame is 30.5 x 20.5 cm/12 x 8 inches.) Use these dimensions to make cuts for frames.

2| Using mitre box and saw, cut pine into 2 length and 2 width pieces on a 45-degree angle for frame. (Position pine in mitre box so that thickness of frame will be 1¼ inches and width will be 1½ inches.) Set aside.

3| Using jigsaw, cut bead board backing to dimensions determined in Step 1.

4| Aligning edges, glue pine frame pieces to face of bead board and nail through the back of board using 1½-inch nails. Nail mitres using 1-inch nails.

5| Set nails on face and mitres with nail punch, then fill nail holes with wood filler. Let dry; sand lightly.

6| Mitre, glue and nail moulding to pine frame using techniques above.

7| Paint as desired.

8| Use glue gun to adhere utensil to bead board.

Tips:

• Scour flea markets, auctions, garage sales or Granny's attic for eye-catching or nostalgic objects to display in shadow boxes.

• Choose a theme for your shadow box displays, such as kitchen utensils or cutlery for the kitchen, seashells for the bathroom or cottage, or vintage toys for a kid's room.

• Use a durable semigloss or high-gloss paint for your shadow boxes so they're easy to clean – especially if you'll be displaying them in the kitchen.

• If you choose to make several shadow boxes all the same size, choose objects that have similar dimensions (see photo, opposite).

Designer Dog Bed

Rover deserves a bed of his own. Here's how to make one with easily available upcycled or salvaged wood.

around the house

CANADIAN LIVING | CREATE. UPDATE. REMAKE

YOU NEED:

- 2 pieces ½-inch plywood, each 31 x 3 inches, for box front and back

- 2 pieces ½-inch plywood, each 21 x 3 inches, for box sides

- 1 piece ½-inch plywood, 31 x 22 inches, for box bottom

- 1 piece panel cut from door, 32 inches wide x 16 inches high, for headboard

- New or salvaged quarter round or other narrow trim (optional)

- Paintbrush, primer and paint

- Cushion, approx 76 x 53.5 x 15 cm (30 x 21 x 6 inches)

- 1½-inch finishing nails

- Hammer

- 1¼-inch wood screws

- Drill with bits

- Jigsaw, or mitre box and saw (optional)

- Wood filler

- Fine-grit sandpaper

TO MAKE:

1| With top, bottom and side edges flush, nail box front and back to front and back edges of sides. With edges of bottom flush with outside surfaces, nail bottom in place to complete box.

2| Flip box over. With bottom and side edges flush, centre box back on headboard and screw in place.

3| If desired, nail trim along bottom edge of box front and sides, mitring front corners.

Then, nail trim along top edge of front and sides, mitring front corners. Nail overhanging trim to top edge of headboard.

4| Fill joints and nail holes; let dry, then sand smooth. Prime and paint as desired, letting dry after each coat. Fit cushion into box.

Tips:

• Prepare salvaged panels before assembling project: Fill holes with wood filler, let dry, and sand. Then wash to remove any dust and grease. Use an eco-friendly solution such as Natura Safe Prep to prepare surfaces for painting, and use a paint free of polluting volatile organic compounds (VOCs).

• To strengthen joints, apply carpenter's glue to adjoining surfaces before nailing or screwing together.

Cat Throne

This regal perch is the perfect hideout for your favourite kitty cat.

YOU NEED:

• 2 pieces 1- to 1½-inch thick panel cut from door, each 16 inches wide x 15 inches high, for throne sides

• 1 piece 1- to 1½-inch thick panel cut from door, 21 inches wide x 20 inches high, for throne back

• 1 piece ½-inch plywood, 21 x 3½ inches, for back support

• 2 pieces ½-inch plywood, each 14 x 3½ inches, for side supports

• 1 piece ½-inch plywood, 21 x 14½ inches, for seat bottom

• 1 piece ½-inch plywood, 21 x 5 inches, for throne front

• Paintbrush, primer and paint

• Cushion, approx 53.5 x 35.5 x 15 cm (21 x 14 x 6 inches)

• 1¼-inch wood screws

• Drill with bits

• Jigsaw (optional)

• 1½-inch finishing nails

• Hammer

• Wood filler

• Fine-grit sandpaper

TO MAKE:

1| With throne sides on either side of throne back, align bottom and back edges. Screw back edge of each throne side to 1 side edge of throne back.

2| With bottom edges flush, screw back support along inside bottom edge of back; repeat with side supports and sides. With back edge of seat bottom against throne back, screw seat bottom to top edges of supports.

3| If desired, use jigsaw to cut arch in throne front. With bottom edge of front flush with bottom edges of sides, nail throne front to front edges of seat bottom and side supports.

4| Fill joints and nail holes; let dry, then sand smooth. Prime and paint as desired, letting dry after each coat. Fit cushion into throne.

Tips:

• Find old doors at flea markets, from salvage suppliers or, if you're lucky, at the curb on garbage night.

• Prepare salvaged panels before assembling project: Fill holes with wood filler, let dry, and sand. Then wash to remove any dust and grease. Use an eco-friendly solution such as Natura Safe Prep to prepare surfaces for painting, and use a paint free of polluting volatile organic compounds (VOCs).

• To strengthen joints, apply carpenter's glue to adjoining surfaces before nailing or screwing together.

Rewired Table Lamp

If you spot a vintage lamp with great potential, don't let a bad colour or some damaged wiring put you off. Paint it with spray paint, then rewire it with an inexpensive lamp kit and let it shine again.

YOU NEED:

- Vintage lamp (repainted, if desired)
- Lamp kit*
- Wire cutters and wire strippers
- Masking, electrical or duct tape
- Screwdriver(s) that fits socket screws

*Available at hardware and lighting stores

TO MAKE:

1| Unplug lamp and remove bulb and shade. With wire cutters, cut off plug. Tape top end of new cord to bottom end of old cord.

2| Loosen screw below existing socket; twist socket off of lamp, then pull off shell and insulating sleeve. Pull old cord to draw new cord up through lamp. Remove tape and discard old plug, wire and socket.

3| Thread new socket cap onto cord, then twist onto lamp. Separate 15 cm (6 inches) of wire at end, then tie in underwriter's knot [A].

4| With wire strippers, strip 1.3 cm (½ inch) coating from end of each wire; at each end (separately) twist strands together clockwise. Following kit manufacturer's instructions, twist hot wire around and under gold-colour screw head on socket body and tighten, then twist neutral wire around silver-colour screw head on socket body and tighten.

5| Replace insulating sleeve on socket, then replace shell [B].

6| Replace bulb and shade.

Tip:

To be extra safe and prevent shorts, wrap newly wired socket screws with a layer of electrical tape before sliding into insulating sleeve.

A   B

Refinished Wood Table

If you have a piece of wooden furniture that needs a little DIY-style care, you'll be pleased to know it's easy. Read on to learn how to refinish a table in six simple steps.

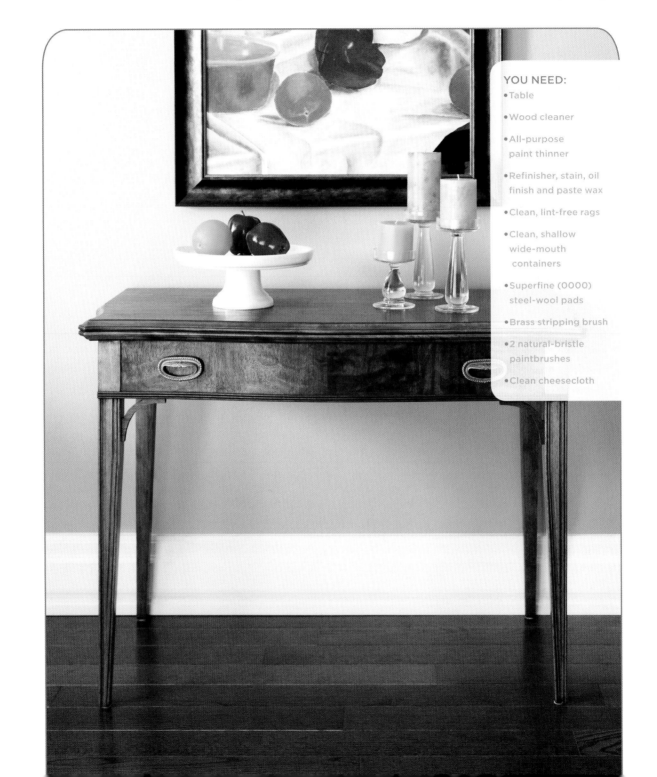

YOU NEED:

- Table
- Wood cleaner
- All-purpose paint thinner
- Refinisher, stain, oil finish and paste wax
- Clean, lint-free rags
- Clean, shallow wide-mouth containers
- Superfine (0000) steel-wool pads
- Brass stripping brush
- 2 natural-bristle paintbrushes
- Clean cheesecloth

Before

TO MAKE:

1| With wood cleaner and damp rag, rub down outside surface of table to remove dirt and grime.

2| Pour small amount of paint thinner into container; moistening rag with thinner as necessary, wipe down surface, wiping immediately with dry rag to remove built-up wax and cleaners.

3| Pour small amount of refinisher into each of 2 separate containers. Working in circular motion on 1 small area at a time, moisten steel-wool pad in refinisher and squeeze out excess, then apply to surface to soften and remove most of the old finish (use stripping brush in cracks and crevices). Moisten fresh pad in second container of refinisher and squeeze out excess, then reapply to surface, wiping immediately with dry rag to remove any residue. Repeat over entire surface, using fresh pad and refinisher. Let dry for several days.

4| Working along wood grain and moving from legs up to tabletop, brush on stain; let penetrate for 5 minutes, then, with clean rag, wipe off excess. Following manufacturer's instructions, let dry. Repeat until desired shade is achieved.

5| Brush on oil finish; let penetrate for 5 minutes, then, with clean rag, wipe off excess. Let dry for 24 hours, then repeat.

6| Wrap small ball of paste wax in 2 or 3 layers of cheesecloth; working in circular motion, apply thin uniform coat. Let dry for 30 minutes. Buff with clean rag to polish. Repeat to apply 3 or 4 more thin coats, polishing after each.

Tips:

• First, determine if refinishing will reduce the value of the furniture; if in doubt, consult a professional restorer.

• Remove hardware, such as drawer pulls, before you start.

• Work in a well-ventilated area. Protect workspace with drop cloths.

• Wear safety glasses, gloves and old clothes, and read all directions for safe use and proper waste disposal of each product.

• Test each product on a hidden area of the furniture first to check results.

around the house

Framed Pressed Flowers

Create instant botanical art with posies plucked from your own garden.

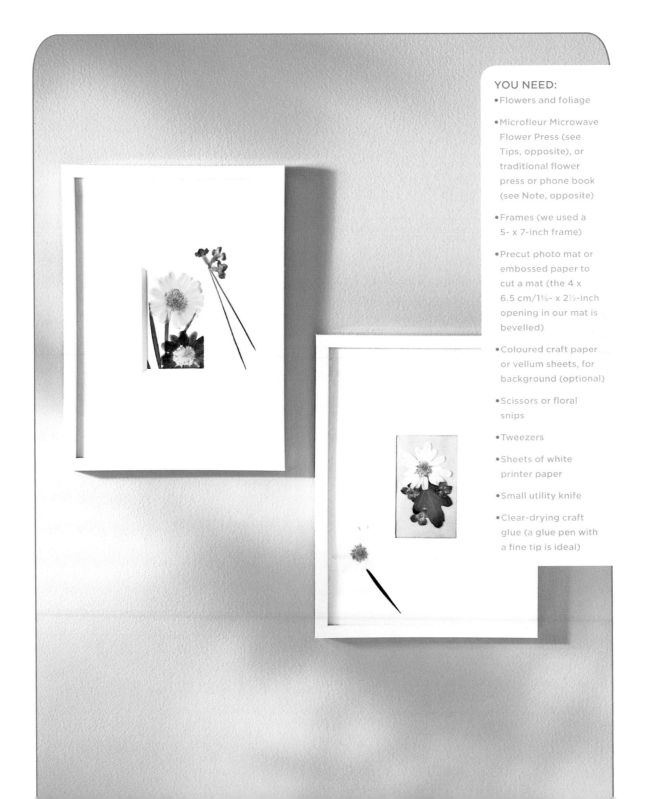

YOU NEED:

- Flowers and foliage

- Microfleur Microwave Flower Press (see Tips, opposite), or traditional flower press or phone book (see Note, opposite)

- Frames (we used a 5- x 7-inch frame)

- Precut photo mat or embossed paper to cut a mat (the 4 x 6.5 cm/1⅝- x 2½-inch opening in our mat is bevelled)

- Coloured craft paper or vellum sheets, for background (optional)

- Scissors or floral snips

- Tweezers

- Sheets of white printer paper

- Small utility knife

- Clear-drying craft glue (a glue pen with a fine tip is ideal)

Note:

You can also press flowers between cardboard layers of a traditional flower press (available at craft stores) or between the pages of a heavy book, such as a phone book, then leave them for 10 to 14 days to dry completely.

TO MAKE:

1| Gather dry, blemish-free flowers (we used marguerite daisies, violas and kalanchoe) and foliage; snip off stems close to bases of flower heads [A]. Press flowers immediately according to instructions on Microfleur Microwave Flower Press, placing flowers and foliage on felt pad and leaving space between each. Carefully place the second felt pad on top, followed by the microwaveable plate, and snap flower press closed using supplied clips.

2| Place flower press in microwave [B]; for best results, microwave in a series of short bursts on high. (We microwaved our flowers and foliage for 20 seconds, let them rest in microwave for 20 seconds, then microwaved them for 30 seconds.) Timing will vary depending on type and size of flowers and foliage. Microwave leaves and grasses separately from flowers; they will take longer to dry because they contain more water.

3| Remove flower press from microwave; let cool for a few seconds. Open carefully and gently remove flowers and foliage using tweezers, transferring to a sheet of printer paper [C].

4| Remove cardboard backing from frame. Cover with sheet of coloured paper, cut to size. Place mat on top and lightly trace opening of mat onto paper to use as a guide for placing flowers and foliage. Using tweezers, pick up 1 flower and dab craft glue onto back; arrange as desired to fit inside opening of mat [D]. Repeat with remaining flowers and foliage. Place mat on top (add flowers and foliage on the mat, if desired); assemble frame.

A

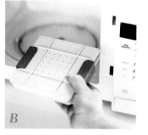
B

C

D

Tips:

•To buy a flower press online, visit elizabeths-flowers.com.

•Intensely hued blooms with flat bottoms, such as pansies, violets and verbena, make excellent pressed flowers. Queen Anne's lace, mini chrysanthemums, leaves and ornamental grasses are other good choices.

•Gather specimens on a sunny afternoon to ensure that they are not wet with rain or dew.

•Use tiny pressed flowers for gift tags, bookmarks and place cards. Protect them with clear adhesive sheets or take them to an office supply store to have them laminated.

•Store unused pressed flowers and foliage between two pieces of printer paper and slip them between the pages of a heavy book.

Salvage Table

Craft a graceful three-legged demi-table from salvaged vintage lumber and furniture parts. Choose pieces in good condition with finishes and patinas that will require minimum refinishing or painting.

around the house

CANADIAN LIVING | CREATE. UPDATE. REMAKE

YOU NEED:

- Salvaged dresser top (we used a 38-x 14-inch top)

- Approx 1- x 3-inch board(s) for skirting, such as an old bed rail

- 3 spindles or table legs, each approx 29 inches long

- Scrap of 1- x 1½-inch pine, for front leg supports

- Measuring tape and pencil

- Mitre box and saw

- Carpenter's glue

- Hammer, 1- and 1½-inch finishing nails, and nail punch

- Jigsaw

- Bar clamp

- 2 to 4 metal L-brackets

- Drill, and 1- and 1½-inch wood screws

- Wood filler and fine-grit sandpaper

- Refinishing wax

- Paintbrush and stain or paint (optional)

Note:

This project makes a
38- x 14- x 30-inch table.

TO MAKE:

1| The dimensions of your tabletop will determine the lengths to cut from 1- x 3-inch board to make 4-sided skirting. Measure length of top and subtract approx 6 inches; cut 1 piece to this measurement, mitring front corners. Measure width of tabletop and subtract 3 to 5 inches. Cut 2 pieces to this measurement for the 2 sides, mitring front corners.

2| Glue and nail mitred corners.

3| For skirting back, measure inside length of skirting front between sides; using jigsaw, cut a piece of 1- x 3-inch board to this measurement. Do not mitre ends. This piece can be butt-jointed to sides [A]. Apply glue to edges of board, then position between the 2 sides; nail from outside through sides. Use bar clamp to tightly secure joints.

4| Fill all nail holes with wood filler. Sand when dry, then patch with matching stain or paint, if necessary.

5| With tabletop face down on a clean flat surface, centre skirting on underside of tabletop, with back of skirting flush with back edge of tabletop.

6| Using 1 leg, mark positions of the 2 back legs with pencil. Remove and set aside. Using leg placement markings as a guide, fasten L-brackets to sides and tabletop on inside of skirting [A], using 1-inch wood screws.

7| Before fastening legs to inside of skirting, ensure they are identical in length. Trim with a saw if necessary, then sand smooth and flat. Apply glue to 2 sides of top of each leg and position in each back corner; fasten legs by screwing through back from outside, using two 1½-inch screws per leg.

8| Centre third leg on inside front face of skirting and mark position with pencil. Remove the leg and set aside.

9| Using jigsaw, cut 2 blocks of pine approx ½ inch shorter than depth of skirting. Glue 1 side of each block and, using two 1½-inch screws, fasten blocks to inside face of skirting on either side of markings.

10| Apply glue to 3 sides of leg and slip it in between the 2 blocks of pine. Drill 1 pilot hole on an angle through each block and into sides of leg. Use a 1½-inch screw to secure legs to blocks through each side.

11| Fill all nail and screw holes with wood filler; sand and stain or paint as required. Apply durable wax finish.

Tips:

- Give your demi-table a signature one-of-a-kind look by mixing styles, wood types and finishes.

- Always bring along a measuring tape when shopping for table parts. You may find pieces at different locations, and you'll want to make sure all the pieces match in size and scale. You don't want to run out of an unusual piece of material, so make sure you purchase a little extra.

- If you find that your table is a bit unstable, use an E-Z Ancor, found at hardware stores, to fasten it to the wall.

Mantel Headboard

This clever design starts with a salvaged mantel, then builds on a platform and adds a shelf for books, a clock, a light or whatever you want to keep within reach.

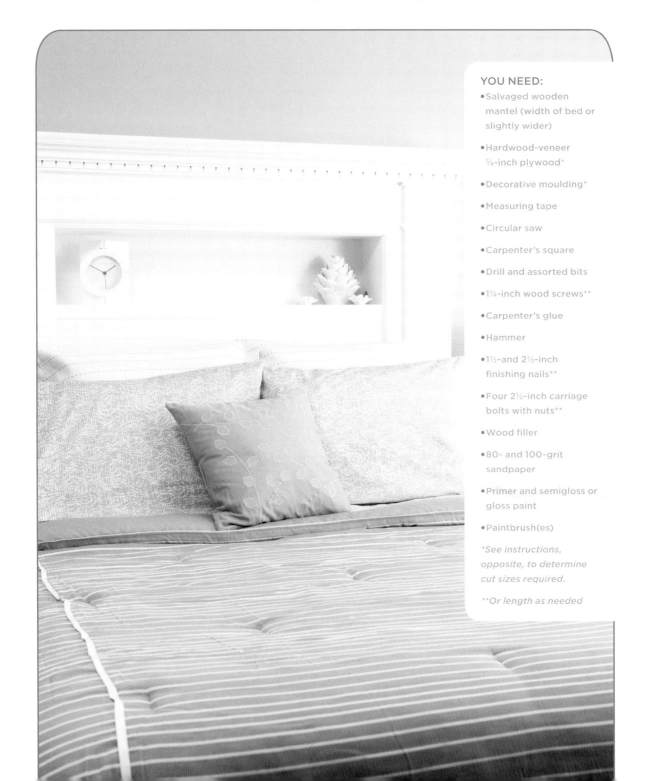

YOU NEED:

- Salvaged wooden mantel (width of bed or slightly wider)
- Hardwood-veneer ¾-inch plywood*
- Decorative moulding*
- Measuring tape
- Circular saw
- Carpenter's square
- Drill and assorted bits
- 1¼-inch wood screws**
- Carpenter's glue
- Hammer
- 1½- and 2½-inch finishing nails**
- Four 2½-inch carriage bolts with nuts**
- Wood filler
- 80- and 100-grit sandpaper
- Primer and semigloss or gloss paint
- Paintbrush(es)

*See instructions, opposite, to determine cut sizes required.

**Or length as needed

Notes:
- Use a carpenter's square as you work.
- During assembly, attach using glue and nails or screws, countersinking nails and screws, and predrilling screw holes.

TO MAKE:

1| Reinforcing base and panels: Measure overall inside width and depth (spanning hearth opening) of mantel base. From plywood, cut rectangle, width x depth (do not cut out hearth opening), for base. Place rectangle so bottom surface is flush with bottom of mantel, then attach. From plywood, cut 2 panels, each width x 15 inches; set panels aside.

2| Front panel: Determine desired height of bottom of shelf, then subtract ¾ inch for total height; measure width of mantel opening at front, then add 3 inches for total width. From plywood, cut rectangle, total height x total width, for panel. With bottom edge on base at mantel front and sides overlapping 1½ inches on either side of mantel opening, attach panel, from back, to mantel front.

3| Shelf box: Measuring from inside front of mantel, measure depth of remaining space above front panel in mantel opening, then subtract ¾ inch for total depth. Measure height and width of remaining space above front panel. For box top and bottom, from plywood, cut 2 rectangles, each total depth x width. To width, add 1½ inches for total width. For box back, from plywood, cut 1 rectangle, height x total width. From height, subtract 1½ inches for total height. For box sides, from plywood, cut 2 rectangles, each total depth x total height. Assemble box inside remaining space, from back, attaching to top of front panel, with sides between top and bottom, and back covering back edges of top, bottom and sides.

4| Reinforcing panels: Attach 1 panel (cut in Step 1) to mantel back at top (trimming to fit above shelf box, if necessary); attach the other halfway down.

5| Platform: Measure height from floor to top of mattress; measure outside width and depth of mantel at base. For platform top and bottom, from plywood, cut 2 rectangles, each width x depth. From height, subtract 1½ inches for total height. For platform front and back, from plywood, cut 2 rectangles, each width x total height. From depth, subtract 1½ inches for total depth. For platform sides, from plywood, cut 2 rectangles, each total depth x total height. Assemble platform, attaching sides between front and back, and attaching top and bottom to cover top and bottom edges of front, back and sides. Set head of bed against platform front; through metal bed frame, mark placement of bolt holes on platform front, then drill and attach.

6| Moulding: Attach mantel to platform. Where desired to cover rough edges of plywood, cut moulding to fit and attach.

7| Fill holes; let dry. Sand. Apply coat of primer; let dry. Paint as desired; let dry. Bolt bed frame to headboard.

Pediment Headboard

Hang up an elegant architectural castoff to make an impressive,
almost instant headboard.

YOU NEED:
- Pediment (finished as desired)*
- ¾-inch plywood (see Step 1 to determine sizes needed)
- Measuring tape and pencil
- Table saw
- Drill and bits
- 1½-inch and 3-inch wood screws
- Level
- Cup washers

*Paint on vintage pieces
may contain lead;
consult a professional
refinisher

Notes:

- Use level when attaching plywood.

- Predrill and countersink screw holes.

TO MAKE:

1| On back of pediment, mark each side edge one-quarter of the way down from top edge; from mark to mark, measure pediment length. From plywood, cut 2 strips, each 3 inches wide x pediment length; saw 45-degree bevel on 1 long edge of each.

2| With shorter face against pediment back and bevel angled down, securely attach 1 strip, between marks, using 1½-inch screws [A].

3| Using level, hold pediment against wall at desired height; mark low (outside) edge on either side of bevel, then remove pediment and, from mark to mark, draw line on wall. Locate studs and, just above line, mark each. With shorter face against wall, top edge along line and bevel angled up, securely attach second strip at each stud using 3-inch screws with washers [A].

4| Place pediment against wall, then lower pediment strip to interlock with wall strip [A].

Side View

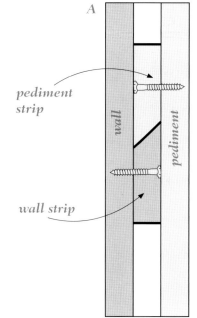

A

pediment strip

wall

wall strip

pediment

Style-Savvy Dresser

Give a dowdy dresser a second chance. After a little TLC and paint, it's bold and beautiful – and back in the bedroom.

YOU NEED:

- Old dresser
- Trisodium phosphate (TSP)
- High-adhesion primer
- Washable interior-grade semigloss paint
- Paint scraper
- Clean cloth
- Superfine (0000) steel-wool pad
- Tack cloth
- Paintbrushes
- Small sponge roller and tray
- Drawer knobs, handles or drop pulls in desired finish (optional)

Before

Note:

When using TSP, protect yourself by wearing rubber gloves and eye protection.

TO MAKE:

1| Remove drawer knobs, handles and/or drop pulls; set aside. With paint scraper, gently remove any loose paint or varnish. With TSP and damp cloth, wash exterior of dresser, including edges of drawer fronts, to remove old wax, grease and dirt, following manufacturer's instructions. Rinse thoroughly with clean water; let dry.

2| With steel wool, lightly rub down washed areas in direction of wood grain; rub down with tack cloth to remove any residue.

3| With brush, apply coat of primer to prepared areas; let dry. Brush on coat of paint; let dry. For smooth finish, roll on second coat of paint; let dry. Replace drawer knobs, handles or drop pulls, if desired (see Tips, right).

Tips:

• Before replacing metal hardware, gently clean it with superfine steel wool, then buff with a clean rag, using the appropriate metal polish.

• Don't be put off by missing or damaged hardware. Reproduction knobs and pulls are readily available, and, if you're missing only one or two items, you might get lucky and find a match at a salvage store or website that sells antique hardware.

• Look for smooth-sliding drawers with sturdy sides and bottoms, and strong joints at the front edges.

• Many dressers were built using a cheaper, unfinished secondary wood for the hidden parts, such as the drawer backs, sides and bottoms. Basswood was a common choice; unfortunately, it develops a musty smell as it ages. You can eliminate this odour by sealing all of the unfinished interior surfaces with one or two coats of shellac.

Updated Mirror

Transform an old wooden frame into a stunning silver-studded mirror. It's easy when you use crackling, a simple weathered paint-finish technique.

YOU NEED:

- Wooden frame in desired size (with mirror inside or with mirror cut to fit)

- Painter's tape (optional)

- Primer

- Latex interior paint with flat or eggshell finish in black and white

- Crackle-finish medium*

- Satin-finish polyurethane

- Upholstery tacks

- 220-grit sandpaper

- Tack cloth or rags

- 2- and 3-inch foam brushes

- Hammer

*Available at craft and art supply stores

TO MAKE:

1| If frame contains mirror, remove mirror or protect it by covering with painter's tape.

2| Sand entire frame; wipe with tack cloth or damp rag to remove dust.

3| Using 2-inch foam brush, apply primer to frame; let dry.

4| Using 2-inch foam brush, paint frame black for base coat; let dry.

5| Using 3-inch foam brush, apply crackle medium over entire frame. The thicker the application, the larger the cracks. Let dry for about 1½ hours.

6| Working quickly and using 3-inch brush to cover a large surface area, apply thin coat of white paint over crackle medium for topcoat. Wait for crackle effect to appear.

7| Remove any painter's tape from mirror before paint is completely dry. When frame is dry, seal finish with 2 coats of polyurethane.

8| Hammer in upholstery tacks around border of frame [A].

9| Replace or insert mirror, if necessary.

Tips:
• Choose two contrasting paint colours for a dramatic effect. For a larger piece, such as a dresser, choose two colours with less contrast for a more subtle finish.

• To master the paint technique, practise on a scrap of wood or on the back of the frame.

• Experiment with the amount of topcoat applied over the crackle-finish medium. A thin coat of paint will result in fine cracks; apply a thicker coat for wider cracks.

• Apply crackle medium in one direction with a continuous stroke and using a wide foam brush that will cover the area quickly.

DIY Message Centre

This multipurpose message centre delivers both fun and function. Closing the windows enables you to display photos and souvenirs; open the windows to reveal a chalkboard and corkboard.

YOU NEED:

- Pair of 2-foot-square framed windows

- 2 pieces ¼-inch plywood for chalkboard and corkboard inserts (we used pieces of scrap bead board)

- Chalkboard paint in desired colour*

- Cork (we used adhesive-backed 3 mm/⅛-inch thick cork)**

- Mirror clips

- Pair of hinges (salvage from windows if possible)

- Window latch, or hook and eye

- Framing square

- Circular saw or jigsaw

- Orbital sander or 120-grit sandpaper

- Measuring tape

- Paintbrush

- Screwdriver

- Drill

- Nails, picture hangers, 1-inch screws and plugs

- Hammer

- Paint for front display panel and frame (optional)

*Available at craft supply and hardware stores

**Available in rolls at office and craft supply stores

TO MAKE:

1| Lay windows on a flat work surface. Carefully remove pane of glass from 1 window; set aside.

2| If windows are not square, use framing square to measure and mark square lines on window frames; trim using a circular saw or jigsaw.

3| Smooth rough edges with sander.

4| Place window with glass face down on work surface. This window will be front of message board when closed and mounted on wall (see photo, opposite). Measure inside opening of window frame; cut plywood panel to fit inside. Paint 1 side of plywood panel with chalkboard paint; let dry. Paint other side (front) in desired colour.

5| Secure painted plywood panel in place with mirror clips [A]. This will allow for easy removal of panel to change photos behind glass.

6| Measure inside opening of window frame without glass; cut plywood panel to fit. Nail panel to frame. Cut a piece of cork to cover plywood panel; adhere to surface.

7| Paint frame, if desired.

8| To assemble, fasten hinges [B] and latch windows [C] with cork and chalkboard panels facing each other.

9| Fasten 2 picture hangers on back of window with cork panel insert. To mount on wall, use appropriate screws and plugs to support weight of message centre.

A

B

C

Tiny Emergency Kits

Use these tricks to assemble a tiny emergency kit to stash in your purse or desk drawer, and you'll never have to paper-clip your shirt closed or give someone a birthday card made out of Post-It notes again.

YOU NEED:

- Small tin with hinged lid, such as an Altoids tin

- Self-adhesive paper for inkjet printers

- Decorations such as stamps, buttons, stickers, coloured paper, scrapbooking decorations and glitter

- Ruler, scissors and craft glue

- Decoupage medium, such as Mod Podge (optional)

- Supplies for mini mail kit: stamps, air mail stickers, address labels, folded-up writing paper and envelope, and pen or pencil

- Supplies for small sewing kit: straight pins, safety pins, sewing needles, spare buttons, thread, seam ripper or scissors, and iron-on patches

- Supplies for impromptu birthday kit: balloon, candle and matches, birthday-themed confetti, stickers and coffee-shop gift card (just add a cupcake!)

- Supplies for tiny first-aid kit: alcohol wipes, cotton swabs, adhesive bandages, tweezers, safety pin, needle and thread, acetaminophen, ibuprofen, Gravol and Imodium

TO MAKE:

1| Wash and dry tin.

2| Measure length and width of tin. Print or draw designs (see photo, opposite) for tin top and bottom on sheet of self-adhesive paper.

3| Cut out labels to fit tin measurements; carefully matching corners, apply stickers to front and back of tin.

4| Decorate as desired. For mini mail kit, decoupage stamps to the tin using craft glue or a decoupage medium. For small sewing kit, use craft glue to affix button to top of tin. For impromptu birthday kit, apply birthday-themed stickers or scrapbooking decorations. For tiny first-aid kit, apply thin layer of craft glue to red cross; sprinkle with red glitter.

5| Fill tin with supplies.

Tip:
If desired, use indoor-outdoor spray paint to paint tin. Apply sticker after paint is dry, or use stencil and contrasting colour of spray paint to create your own design.

Handmade Memory Book

This handmade book is a versatile, easy-to-make gift. However you fill this little accordion-style book, it's sure to be a treasured keepsake.

YOU NEED:

- 1 strip heavy plain paper, such as watercolour paper*, 16.5 x 45.8 cm (6½ x 18 inches)

- 1 strip heavy plain paper, such as watercolour paper*, 16.5 x 47 cm (6½ x 18½ inches)

- 2 pieces grey board (or other 3 mm/⅛-inch thick cardboard, such as matte board)*, each 12.5 x 18 cm (5 x 7 inches)

- 2 sheets decorative paper, such as wrapping paper*, each 23 x 28 cm (9 x 11 inches),

- Pencil

- Cork-backed metal ruler

- Bone folder*

- Paintbrush

- Polyvinyl acetate (PVA) glue*

- Flat weight, such as heavy books

- X-acto or small utility knife

- Waxed paper and printer paper

- Glue stick or adhesive photo corners (if desired)

- Ribbon, string or decorative trim

Available at specialty paper or art supply stores

TO MAKE:

1| Lay shorter strip of heavy plain paper lengthwise on work surface. Using pencil and ruler, mark top and bottom of strip at halfway point (23 cm/ 9 inches from left side). Flip and repeat, marking sheet at 11.5 cm (4½ inches) and at 34 cm (13½ inches) from left side. Repeat with longer strip of paper, adding second set of marks on first side, 45.8 cm (18 inches) from left side, for joining flap.

2| Align ruler with first set of marks on 1 strip; lightly score fold line by running tip of bone folder along edge of ruler [A]. Repeat for each set of marks on first side, then flip paper and repeat. Carefully fold paper (with score marks on inside of folds) to form accordion-style folds. Repeat with second strip.

A

3| Using paintbrush, apply thin layer of PVA glue to inside of joining flap on longer strip. Join strips, positioning joining flap behind 1 end of shorter strip. Set aside, stacking flat weight on top of paper; let dry for 10 minutes.

4| Centre 1 piece of grey board on 1 sheet of decorative paper; with pencil, trace around board. Set board aside. With ruler, measure diagonally 6 mm (¼ inch) from each corner point of inner rectangle. Draw a diagonal line across each corner at mark. Using X-acto knife, cut at lines to remove corners. Repeat with second sheet of decorative paper.

5| Working on sheet of waxed paper and using paintbrush, apply thin, even layer of PVA glue to 1 sheet of decorative paper; place piece of grey board in centre. Using ruler to help lift edges, fold 2 short sides of paper over grey board and press firmly. Tuck in corners [B], then fold over remaining 2 sides, pressing firmly. Repeat

B

with second sheet of decorative paper and second piece of grey board. Stack covers between sheets of printer paper (to absorb excess moisture) and let dry under flat weight for 20 minutes.

6| Place sheet of waxed paper under top sheet of accordion-folded pages and, using paintbrush, apply thin, even layer of glue to top sheet. Using both hands, pick up inner pages and carefully centre glued sheet on wrong side of 1 of the covers; press firmly in place [C]. Repeat with back sheet and back cover. Let dry under flat weight for 20 minutes.

7| Fill book as desired, using glue stick or adhesive photo corners to attach pictures and souvenirs. Wrap with ribbon and tie closed.

C

Tip:
Make your book any size or shape by adjusting the dimensions of your materials. A good general rule is to allow a 6 mm to 1.3 cm (¼- to ½-inch) border all the way around your photos; size pages and covers accordingly.

outdoors

planters • lights • birdhouses • garden art • stepping stones • wreaths

Lush Strawberry Pot

Made from porous clay, which soaks up moisture and heat, strawberry pots are the ideal environment for drought-loving sedums and sempervivums.

YOU NEED:

- 9-hole terra-cotta strawberry pot

- Small amount of latex paint, preferably brown or black

- Small paintbrush

- Piece of tightly woven cloth, approx 15 cm (6 inches) square

- Styrofoam chunks, approx golf ball size

- Large bucket

- Potting soil

- Coarse sand

- 13 or 14 hardy dwarf succulent plants

TO MAKE:

1| Brush inside of pot with thin coat of paint; let dry for 24 hours.

2| Lay cloth over drainage hole in base of pot. Fill pot with Styrofoam to approx 5 cm (2 inches) below lowest row of openings.

3| In bucket, mix 3 parts potting soil with 1 part sand. Add soil mixture to pot until level with bottom of lowest row of openings. Tamp down, forming mound in centre.

4| Choose a mat- or cushion-forming plant for each of the lowest openings and transplant, gently angling root-balls downward onto soil mixture [A]. Tamp soil around roots.

5| Add layer of soil mixture to pot until level with next row of openings. Tamp down, mounding in centre. Transplant trailing plant into each remaining side opening [B].

6| Add soil mixture to pot until approx 4 cm (1⅝ inches) below rim. Transplant 4 to 6 plants into top [C].

7| Water sparingly. Until roots are established, use spray bottle for plants in pockets to avoid spilling soil. Thereafter, water only after 1 or 2 rainless weeks, or when leaf edges begin to brown. During long hot spells, soak soil mixture occasionally.

Tip:
To protect from winter weather, let soil dry out completely before the first frost, then store pot where it will get natural light in a dry, unheated garage or shed. Do not water. Move back outdoors in spring and trim off dead flowers and foliage to make room for new growth.

Versailles Latticework Planter

This classic planter shows off a formal boxwood, an asymmetrical shrub or flowering perennials beautifully. The inset mirror adds a little sparkle.

YOU NEED:

- 1 piece ¾-inch pine shelving, 15½ inches square, for base

- 2 pieces ¾-inch pine shelving, each 15½ x 17 inches, for front and back

- 2 pieces ¾-inch pine shelving, each 17 inches square, for sides

- 2 pieces 1x3 pine, each 15 inches long, for reinforcement pieces

- 2 pieces 1x3 pine, each 17 inches long; and 2 pieces 1x3 pine, each 12 inches long, all for mirror frame

- 4 drapery finials, each approx 3 inches tall

- Fine-grit sandpaper

- Exterior-grade semigloss latex paint

- 1 piece lattice, 12 inches square

- Mastic adhesive for mirrors

- Mirror tile, 12 inches square

- Exterior-grade carpenter's glue

- Hammer, 1¼-inch finishing nails and ½-inch brads

- 1-inch wide paintbrush

- Drill and ⅜-inch spade bit (optional)

A

B

1| Referring to assembly diagram (page 268): Set base flat on work surface. Apply glue along 2 opposite edges. With side edges flush, position 1 short (bottom) edge of back against 1 glued edge and nail in place. Repeat with front and remaining glued edge. Apply glue along both remaining edges of base and along side edges of front and back; position, then nail each side piece, to form box. Let dry for at least 1 hour.

2| Apply glue to back of each reinforcement piece. With top edges flush, position 1 inside against each box side; nail in place.

3| Turn box so front faces up. Apply glue to back of each mirror frame piece. With outside edges flush, lay 1 long piece on front along bottom edge and the other along top edge. Lay 1 short piece along each side edge. Adjust, if necessary, to ensure that mirror tile will fit snugly inside; nail frame in place. Let dry for at least 1 hour.

4| Turn box right side up. Screw finial into each top corner. Sand box; paint inside and out. Paint both sides of lattice in contrasting colour, if desired [A]. Let dry. Apply second coat if desired. Let dry.

5| Turn box so front faces up. Apply adhesive to back of mirror tile; press firmly onto front inside frame [B]. Position lattice on top; with brads, carefully nail outside edges of lattice to edges of frame. If desired, dab nail heads with matching paint to conceal. Let dry. Turn box right side up.

Tip:
If you intend to plant directly in box, use spade bit to drill centred drainage hole through base.

outdoors

Leftover Lattice Window Box

Chances are, if you've built a deck, you have leftover lattice, lumber and trim.
This window box is a quick, creative way to use it up.

YOU NEED:

- ½-inch plywood*

- Scraps of
  standard lattice

- Scraps of 1x2*

- 2-inch and 1½-inch
  finishing nails

- ¾-inch common nails

- Hammer

- Pencil, set square
  and tape measure

- Sandpaper in various
  grades

- Paintbrushes, and
  exterior-grade primer
  and paint, or stain,
  as desired

*Nominal size; actual
size will be smaller

Notes:

• Refer to step-by-step diagrams (page 269) as guide during assembly.

• Trim off and discard small triangle at each corner of base, for drainage holes.

CUT:

From plywood:
• Base, 29 x 8 inches
• 2 sides, each 8 x 5½ inches

From lattice:
• 2 panels, each 7½ x 29 inches

From 1x2:
• 4 pieces A, each 27 inches long
• 4 pieces B, each 10 inches long

TO MAKE:

1| With top edges flush and using 2-inch nails, assemble front and back frames with pieces A and B.

2| With top edges flush, centre each lattice panel on inside surface of 1 frame; using ¾-inch nails, attach.

3| With top edges flush and lattice to inside, assemble window box with 2 sides between front and back frames; using 1½-inch nails, attach.

4| Slide base up inside window box; using 1½-inch nails, attach.

5| Sand and paint or stain finished window box as desired.

Tip:

Cut lattice panels so vertical and horizontal centre of each piece aligns with points of latticework, as shown on diagrams (page 269).

outdoors

Hypertufa Planters

These faux-stone bowls are easy to form into shapes and sizes that perfectly suit your space. Reinforced with wire mesh, they'll stand up to winter frost.

YOU NEED:

- Container, for mould (see Tips, page 122)

- Coating or covering for mould, such as vegetable oil, nonstick cooking spray or petroleum jelly, for nonpermeable mould; or plastic wrap or bag, for permeable mould

- Portland cement*

- Sharp builder's sand*

- Peat moss (or vermiculite or perlite, or a combination)*

- Cement colourant (optional)*

- Fine-mesh chicken wire or hardware cloth, cut in strips approx 4 to 7 cm (1⅝ to 2¾ inches) wide*

- Waterproof gloves, safety goggles and fine-dust mask

- Large board or tray covered in sturdy plastic, for work surface

- Mixing container, such as large metal or plastic bucket or tub

- Mixing tool, such as hand hoe, trowel or large wooden spoon

- Measuring scoop, such as coffee can or yogurt container

- Wire cutters

- Plastic bags or drop sheet

- Drill and ⅜-inch masonry bit*

Available at building supply and some hardware stores

Caution:

Cement is caustic. Work outdoors and wear safety mask when mixing dry ingredients (avoid raising dust as you stir), and wear safety goggles and waterproof gloves throughout. Keep mixture out of reach of children, pets and wildlife.

TO MAKE:

1| Coat or cover mould as appropriate, then position right side up (to form container inside mould) or upside down (to form container around mould) on work surface.

2| In mixing container, mix equal parts cement, sand and peat moss. Add water, stirring thoroughly, until mixture can be formed into patties that hold their shape. Add colourant if desired.

3| With gloved hands, form mixture into patties; working up sides, press patties together over mould to evenly cover entire surface, approx 2 cm (¾ inch) thick.

4| Lay mesh strips, side by side and approx 4 cm (1⅝ inches) apart, over entire surface, using wire cutters to trim even with edges and corners and pressing lightly to adhere. Repeat, laying second series of strips perpendicular to first.

5| Follow Step 3 to cover entire surface with second 2 cm (¾-inch) thickness of mixture, ensuring strong rim (if forming inside mould, flute or otherwise decorate rim, if desired; if forming outside mould, create flange around rim, if desired) and levelling base.

6| Shroud with plastic bags, weighing down edges of plastic; let cure in shady, frost-free spot for 2 or 3 days. Unmould, then cover again and continue to cure for 2 or 3 weeks (the longer, the better). Drill drainage holes through base. Scrub container with soap and water, rinsing well with hose, before planting.

Tips:

- You can use moulds of various sizes and shapes. Use a wooden or sturdy cardboard box, a metal or plastic bowl, a pan or tub, or even an old cooler.

- A container formed over the mould will have larger outside dimensions than the mould; one formed inside will have smaller inside dimensions.

- Whatever you use – and whether you form the mixture around the inside or outside – the mould must have straight sides, or sides that angle outward up to the rim, so the hardened shape can slide out or off. The exception to this rule? An inflated ball. Wrap it with strips of mesh left open at the top, pat on the mixture and let it cure; deflate the ball and pull it out the opening, then coat the wire inside with a slurry of cement and let that cure.

- Experiment to make decorative pagodas, plinths or finials.

- With permanent marker, draw two 2 cm (¾-inch) increments, up from tip, on bamboo or metal skewer; use to check thickness.

Planting Ideas:

- Perennial alpine plants, dwarf shrubs and hardy succulents are good choices for hypertufa planters.

- Use a good-quality soil mix, then mulch with pebbles, pea gravel or fine wood chips.

- Nestle a piece of driftwood, a rock, a shell, a sculpture or a tiny basin (for a pool) into the soil.

Turning an Old Container into a New Planter:

• Remember that chips, dents and flaky paint lend a welcome, well-worn look.

• Clean watertight containers with a solution of one part bleach to 10 parts water.

• Line leaky containers with heavy-gauge plastic.

• Add a layer of terra-cotta pot shards to absorb excess water.

• When planting, run a knife around each plant pot to loosen the root-ball. Turn the pot over, then gently tap and squeeze it to release the plant. Adding a layer of potting soil to the container, if necessary, so the plants sit at the proper height (the soil surface of the root-balls should sit about 1 cm/⅜ inch below the rim), arrange your plants in the container as desired, filling any holes with more potting soil and gently tamping it down.

• Alternatively, if the pot fits neatly inside your container, simply slip it in, then hide the pot rim and soil with a layer of moss (available at floral supply shops).

• Many spring plants can be enjoyed indoors, then planted in the garden for a return next year. Let all the leaves of bulbs (such as daffodils) die back naturally, and harden off other plants (such as primulas), before planting them outside when the weather warms up.

Giving New Life to Vintage Containers:

Search flea markets and garage sales, or take a peek in your attic or basement, for containers that are inexpensive or free. Then put them to work in every corner of your home.

• Fill cut-glass vases and jugs with silverware, then display them in the kitchen or dining room so they can sparkle in the sunlight [A].

• Pierced with decorative patterns, colanders are great for holding balls of yarn and preventing them from rolling across the floor as you knit [B].

• Their old fridges may be long gone, but aluminum ice-cube trays can keep going as handy office-supply organizers [C].

• You can never have enough containers in your craft room. A jadeite mug and a vase become brush holders, and an amber glass floral frog serves as the perfect pencil holder [D].

• Old mismatched china saucers are great for corralling car keys and loose change just inside the front door.

• Cut-glass salt and pepper shakers with corroded or missing lids make delightful mini-vases for dainty spring blossoms.

Sugar-Bowl Garden Lights

Glass sugar bowls are inexpensive and a cinch to find at garage sales and flea markets. And they're even easier to turn into sparkling votive holders to hang in a sheltered spot on balmy summer nights.

YOU NEED
(FOR EACH):
• 14-gauge galvanized wire
• Sugar bowl with handles
• Votive candle or tea light
• Pliers with wire cutters

TO MAKE:

1| With pliers, cut 2 lengths of wire, each 70 cm (27⅝ inches) long. One at a time, thread end of 1 wire through each handle. With pliers, bend end up and tightly twist 3 or 4 times, securing wire close to rim. Trim ends.

2| Holding wires together and centred approx 28 cm (11 inches) above rim of bowl, bend top ends down to form hanging loop (see photo, opposite). Holding 3 wires together at bottom of loop, tightly twist fourth wire 3 or 4 times around them, to secure. Curl ends decoratively as desired or trim.

3| Set votive in bowl.

Tips:

• Choose sugar bowls with faceted glass to boost the sparkle and shine.

• Thread nonflammable beads or crystals onto the wire, if desired.

• For safety's sake, ensure hanging loop is at least 28 cm (11 inches) above candle flame, and never leave burning candles unattended.

Boxy Birdhouses

These pretty birdhouses will help you attract your favourite local songbirds.

outdoors

YOU NEED (FOR EACH):

• 1 piece, 1x8* cedar, 4 feet long

• Exterior wood solid-hide stain

• $^3/_{16}$-inch diameter stainless-steel rod

• Wooden clothespins

• 2 heavy-duty screw hooks

• $^1/_{16}$-inch diameter stainless-steel cable (length will be determined by location)

• Two $^1/_8$-inch wire rope clips

• Measuring tape, pencil and carpenter's square

• Compound mitre saw or table saw

• Drill with ¼- and $^1/_{32}$-inch bits, and 1½-inch Forstner bit

• Paintbrush and tray

• Exterior-grade carpenter's glue

• 1½-inch finishing nails

• Hammer, nail set, corner clamps and small clamp

• Wood filler

• 220-grit sandpaper

• 1¼-inch wood screws

• Hacksaw and wire cutters

• File or rasp (to smooth edges of steel rod)

• Exterior-grade clear epoxy

*Nominal size; actual size will be smaller

Note:

Refer to assembly diagrams (page 270) as you work.

TO MAKE:

1| Using compound mitre saw or table saw, cut 6 pieces from 1x8 cedar as follows: Two 7½-inch squares for top and bottom, two 7½- x 6-inch pieces for front and back, and two 6-inch squares for sides.

2| Drill entry hole in front (see Diagram 2, page 270) using Forstner bit. Drill ventilation holes in sides (see Diagram 3, page 270) and drainage holes in bottom using ⅟₃₂-inch bit. Drill holes for stainless-steel rod in sides (see Diagram 3, page 270) using ¼-inch bit.

3| Paint exterior and edges of all pieces with 2 coats of exterior stain. Let dry overnight. Do not paint interior.

4| Glue then nail top to front, bottom to front, and both side pieces to top and bottom of box (see Diagram 1, page 270). Ensure all pieces are flush.

5| Countersink all nails. Fill holes with wood filler and let dry.

6| Dry-fit back panel in position. Mark hole in each corner of back panel and transfer marks to edges of side panels. Remove back panel and set aside.

7| Carefully predrill the 4 marked holes in back panel. Predrill ½ inch into edges of 2 side panels using ¼-inch bit.

8| Sand box, including edges and access hole.

9| Attach back panel to box with wood screws.

10| Using hacksaw, cut stainless-steel rod to 12 inches and smooth cut ends with file. Thread rod through holes in sides of box. Using toothpick, carefully apply epoxy around rod at points where it meets hole. Let dry thoroughly.

Tip:

Clean birdhouse after each nesting season by removing back panel and shaking out debris.

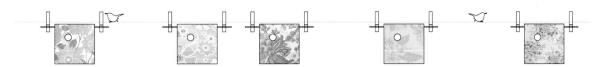

11| Using a pencil, mark 1.3 cm (½ inch) in on each end of rod. Apply epoxy to insides of clothespins, 1 at a time, and clamp to rod as shown. Let dry thoroughly. (Epoxy dries quickly and cannot be easily removed. Once you have clamped peg to rod, do not adjust location.)

12| Screw hooks into desired locations. Measure stainless-steel cable to fit between hooks, adding 51 cm (20 inches) to length; cut cable. Loop 1 end of cable around wire rope clip [A]; secure according to manufacturer's instructions. Thread other end of cable through metal spring loop on each clothespin. Loop remaining end of cable around wire rope clip; secure according to manufacturer's instructions.

13| Have a friend support the weight of the box while you hang birdhouse.

Tip:

For a colourful finish, glue wallpaper over outside surfaces of birdhouse.

A

Build It Right:

A little research can help you design the house that's right for the birds in your area. Here are a few easy modifications for three specific species.

- Purple martins: Group houses together. These birds like to live in colonies.

- Screech owls: Make a generous entrance hole (about 7.5 cm/3 inches in diameter).

- House wrens: These tiny fellows require a scant 3 cm (1⅛-inch) opening.

Good Materials, Safe Homes:

The main goal is to make a house that's durable, weather-resistant and safe. Start with the right materials: Natural cedar weathers well and is untainted by preservatives; the exterior may be painted white to reflect heat, but never paint the interior.

To keep the inside dry, allow the roof to overhang the walls. Recess the floor and add drainage holes to prevent rainwater from seeping under the nest. Also, be sure to drill holes for ventilation – birds need to breathe!

Incorporate a removable roof or wall, too, to make it easy to access the box to clean out old nests before the next breeding season.

To discourage predators, extend the roof beyond the face to make it difficult for raccoons and other marauding animals to climb on top and reach into the entrance hole.

Where to Place Your Birdhouse:

The best location depends on the type of bird you want to attract; bluebirds, for example, like wide open spaces, while barn owls prefer their abodes on lofty tree limbs. Wherever it's situated, your birdhouse should be installed before the breeding season begins, typically from late March to early May, depending on the species. And be patient – it might take time for birds to find their new home.

Recycled Silver Wind Chimes

This project makes great use of slightly battered silver plate – a steal at flea markets and vintage shops. Hung outside, these simple chimes will weather to a lovely verdigris.

YOU NEED:

- 5 mismatched silver-plated spoons or forks

- 14-gauge wire

- Strip of ¼-inch cedar, 2 to 3 inches wide (see Step 4 to determine length)

- Unpainted wire coat hanger

- Small block of softwood and scrap of thick fabric, such as synthetic fleece

- Hammer, clamp and handsaw

- Needle-nose pliers with wire cutters

- Pencil and ruler

- Drill with ⅛- and ³⁄₁₆-inch bits

TO MAKE:

1| One at a time, lay each spoon on wooden block; cover with fabric scrap and hammer to flatten, beginning with bowl and working up handle to tip.

2| Sandwiching wooden block, firmly clamp each spoon handle to work surface; with ³⁄₁₆-inch bit, drill centred ho le approx 1 cm (³⁄₈ inch) from tip of handle.

3| With pliers, cut short lengths of wire, each 30.5 to 56 cm (12 to 22 inches) long; thread end of each through hole in spoon and twist to secure.

4| On work surface, arrange spoons as desired, right side up and with bowl edges almost touching (spoons should hang freely but clink together in the wind), to determine desired length of cedar strip. Strip should extend about 2 cm (¾ inch) beyond outside edges of spoons. With handsaw, cut, angling ends if desired. Lay strip on work surface above spoons and mark corresponding drill holes for spoon wires, approx 1.5 cm (⅝ inch) up from bottom edge. With ⅛-inch bit, drill at each mark. Drill 1 hole at each top corner, approx 1.5 cm (⅝ inch) from side and top edges.

5| Thread top end of each spoon wire through corresponding hole in strip and twist to secure.

6| With pliers, remove hook and 1 "shoulder" from hanger; discard. With remaining "shoulder" at top, trim to desired hanging height, leaving approx 7.5 cm (3 inches) extra on each end; thread 1 end through each top hole in strip and twist to secure.

Bejewelled Silver Wind Chimes

Give old silver dishes and flatware new life as a work of garden art.

outdoors

CANADIAN LIVING | CREATE. UPDATE. REMAKE.

YOU NEED:

- Silver-plated item, such as wineglass, candlestick or candy dish

- Silver-plated flatware, including 3 teaspoons, 3 forks, and 1 dessert or soup spoon

- Jump rings

- Tigertail jewelry wire

- Nylon-coated stainless-steel crimping beads

- Beads from 1 or 2 necklaces

- Seed beads (optional)

- New or recycled metal chain, such as recycled necklaces (3 to 6 mm/ ⅛- to ¼-inch diameter)

- S-hook or split key ring

- Ruler and fine-tip marker

- Drill and ³⁄₁₆-inch bit

- Silver polish

- Lumber scraps

- Hacksaw or bandsaw with metal cutting blade

- Vise, emery paper, needle-nose pliers, wire cutters and hammer

- Clear alkyd antioxidant spray-on sealer, such as Tremclad Clear protective coating

TO MAKE:

1| Using ruler and marker, measure and mark 4 evenly spaced hole positions around base edge of silver-plated item; drill for hangers.

2| Measure, mark and drill 6 evenly spaced holes around top rim of item, approx 3 mm (⅛ inch) from edge, for danglers. Polish article and flatware.

3| Sandwich each piece flatware between lumber scraps; flatten in vise. Approx 9 cm (3½ inches) up from bottom edge of teaspoons and forks only, saw straight across handle with hacksaw (set aside ends for other chimes). Approx 3 mm (⅛ inch) up from bottom edge of dessert spoon and down from cut edges of forks and teaspoons, drill centred hole. Using emery paper, smooth cut edges. One at a time, place dessert spoon and forks in vise; using pliers, twist spoon handle and curl fork tines as desired.

4| Thread jump ring through hole in each fork, teaspoon and dessert spoon, and close.

5| Assemble six 23 to 30.5 cm (9- to 12-inch) beaded dangler wires and 1 beaded tinkler wire that's 2.5 cm (1 inch) longer than danglers as follows: For each beaded wire, with wire cutters, cut tigertail wire 10 cm (4 inches) longer than finished length. Thread 1 end of wire through crimping bead, then through ring on fork or teaspoon (for danglers), or dessert spoon (for tinkler). Thread end back through crimping bead; using pliers, crimp bead to secure. String necklace beads onto wires, separating large beads with seed beads, if desired.

6| Thread end of each beaded wire through crimping bead, then through jump ring, and back through crimping bead; using pliers, crimp bead to secure. Trim wire end and thread tail through beads to hide. Turn item upside down. Thread jump ring on each dangler through drilled hole in top rim of item, alternating forks and spoons, and close.

7| Cut chain into four 10 to 20.5 cm (4- to 8-inch) lengths. Using jump rings, attach bottom end of each hanger wire to 1 hole in base. Attach top end of all chains to jump ring; slip ring into S-hook.

8| Measure diameter of rim; cut piece of chain to this length plus 2.5 cm (1 inch). Attach jump ring to each end, then stretch chain across rim and attach to 2 opposite holes. Attach tinkler to centre of chain, adjusting height so tinkler spoon strikes tines of forks and bowls of teaspoons.

9| To weatherproof, spray with 2 or 3 light coats of sealer; let dry after each coat.

Tips:

• To prevent drill bit from skittering, use hammer and nail to make depression at each hole position before drilling.

• All attachments must swing freely to make music.

• If desired, hang with ribbon (see photo, opposite).

Cement Stepping Stones

No need to buy and fit heavy stones into your landscape. Make the perfect size and shape "stones" from less-expensive concrete.

YOU NEED:

• 10 cm (4-inch) wide plastic garden edging*, cut in 50.5 cm (20-inch) lengths for each mould

• Crushed gravel*

• Sand

• 30 kg (65 lb) bag rapid-setting concrete* (1 bag will make 3 to 4 stones)

• Decorations, such as pebbles or glass marbles (optional)

• Pencil and paper

• Scissors, duct tape, spade, level, hoe, trowel, and sheet of plastic or piece of burlap

*Available at garden centres or home improvement stores

Note:

Each stone is approx 25.5 x 30.5 x 5 cm thick (10 x 12 x 2 inches thick).

TO MAKE:

1| Draw pattern on paper in shape of the stone you'd like to make (we used a leaf pattern). Using your hand-drawn pattern as a guide, bend 1 length garden edging into shape [A], and cut to fit. Tape ends together using duct tape and set aside.

2| With spade, cut out and remove a section of sod approx the size of mould.

3| Gently loosen soil inside cut-out section to a depth of about 5 cm (2 inches).

4| Insert the mould into loose earth about 1.3 cm (½ inch) deep, tamping earth inside mould so that it's level but slightly lower on 1 edge for water runoff [B].

5| For extra support, push soil tightly up against outside wall of mould.

6| Pour in 1.3 cm (½-inch) layer of gravel for drainage. Tamp with garden hoe or trowel. Pour in 1.3 cm (½-inch) layer of sand to help level stone [C]; tamp lightly.

7| Mix concrete with water according to package directions (mixture should have the consistency of runny oatmeal). Pour concrete into mould to about 1.3 cm (½ inch) below top. Spread carefully into crevices. Use a stick to remove air pockets.

8| Using trowel, smooth concrete evenly, embedding aggregate below surface [D]. Tap sides of mould lightly to release any air bubbles.

9| While mix is still soft, add details and decorate as desired: Score veins, make leaf impressions, or sink pebbles or glass marbles into surface of concrete [E].

10| Let cure for 24 hours. Cover with plastic or damp piece of burlap to keep concrete from curing too quickly and cracking.

11| When cured, remove moulds from stones. Fill space between stones with soil, sod, pebbles or creeping plants.

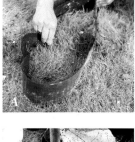

Autumn Glory Wreath

Dress up your door in beautiful fall hues. This straightforward wreath is gorgeous and simple to create using your favourite flowers and leaves.

YOU NEED:

- Floral-foam wreath base, 16 inches in diameter*

- 5 cm (2-inch) wide ribbon or several strands of raffia, approx 1 m (39⅜ inches) long

- 1 or 2 bundles fresh salal* and, if available, bay laurel*, with stems cut to 12.5 to 20.5 cm (5 to 8 inches) with 2 to 4 leaves each

- Floral material, with stems trimmed approx 12.5 cm (5 inches) down from flowers, including:

    Approx 5 dozen stems each of safflower, sage, tansy and yarrow

    Approx 3 dozen stems each of bearded wheat, lady's mantle and oregano

- Wired wooden floral picks, each 4 inches long*

- Approx 12 red peppers

- Approx 9 hydrangea flowers

- Approx 3 garlic bulbs

- 3 to 4 dried quince slices

- 1 sunflower on 12.5 cm (5-inch) stem

- Secateurs, for cutting stems

Available at floral supply stores

TO MAKE:

1| With ends even, tie ribbon around wreath base at top, then tie ends together with overhand knot to make hanging loop [A].

2| Working counterclockwise from top, push stems of salal and bay laurel, held at sharp angle, into base to cover front and sides [B].

3| With each type of floral material, form 9 small bundles of 3 to 7 stems each. One at a time, hold wooden pick, point down, against stem ends of each bundle and wire stems together [C].

4| Push picks firmly into base, combining 2 or 3 picks of each material into 3 to 5 vignettes, at more or less regular intervals around base [D].

5| One at a time, wire red peppers, hydrangeas, garlic bulbs, quince and sunflower onto picks, then push into base where desired [E].

Tips:

• Your wreath will look its best if you limit your choice of floral material to about seven different types, selecting pleasing colour combinations and varied textures – then add the accents!

• Boxwood can stand in for the bay laurel.

• Replace or complement the floral material and accents with: stems of the dried seed heads of clematis, coneflowers or poppies; grasses or barley; rose hips, silver dollars or straw flowers; sprigs of rosemary or thyme; Chinese lanterns; crab apples; tiny gourds; dried lemons or pomegranates; or grapevine.

A

B

C

D

E

outdoors

Nest Shelf

Phoebes and robins will happily build their nests in this simple, beautiful wood shelf – safe, snug and away from predators and bad weather.

YOU NEED:

- 1 piece, 1x10* pine, 3 feet long

- Pencil, ruler and set square

- Handsaw

- Plane or table saw

- Drill, No. 6 countersink bit (optional), ¼-inch and ⁹/₆₄-inch bits, and bits for screwing

- 15 No. 6 1½-inch wood screws

- Wood filler and fine-grit sandpaper (optional)

- Spar varnish and paintbrush (optional)

Nominal size; actual size will be smaller

Notes:

- Refer to diagrams (page 271) as you work.

- Use pencil, ruler and set square to measure and mark cutting lines on pine; cut out all pieces with saw.

- Predrill and countersink all screw holes.

TO MAKE:

1| Measure and mark pine as shown in cutting diagram (page 271); cut out. With plane, bevel 1 long (back) edge of C as shown in assembly diagram (page 271).

2| With 1 long (back) edge of A flush with back edges of Bs, fasten A to Bs with 2 screws at each edge. With underside of A 1½ inches from 1 short (bottom) edge of D, fasten D to A and Bs with 2 screws at each edge. Using 3 screws to fasten back edge and 1 screw to fasten each side edge, fasten C to D and Bs.

3| If desired, fill screw holes; let dry and sand. Following manufacturer's directions, apply 1 or 2 coats of varnish, if desired.

Tips:

- If desired, replace pine with rough barn board and leave unfinished (don't use pressure-treated lumber, which can be toxic to young birds).

- If you prefer a painted box or shelf, choose nontoxic paint in muted green, grey or brown.

- Don't add a perch or platform; these make it easier for predators to get at the nest.

- Securely mount box or shelf at least 1.8 m (6 feet) above ground and facing away from the prevailing wind, on a post, tree trunk or wall (ensure it's accessible for fall cleanup). And choose a spot that's sheltered from direct sunshine for some of the day (mount the shelf under the eaves on an exterior wall, for example).

- Other birds need different-size openings. Research bird species to determine what kind of modifications to make for other types of birds you want to attract (or see Build it Right, page 129).

Porch Daybed

Revive a castoff cast-iron bedstead with a cushy foam topper – covered in a cheery print – and create the perfect place to snooze away long summer afternoons.

YOU NEED:

- Cast-iron bed frame

- High-density foam of desired thickness, cut to fit bed frame, for mattress

- High-loft polyester quilt batting (optional)

- Upholstery fabric (see Step 1 to determine required amount), for mattress cover

- Matching thread

- Long upholsterer's needle, heavy-duty thread and 1-inch diameter 2-hole buttons in desired number and colour

- Scraps of coordinating felt

- Measuring tape, dressmaker's chalk pencil, yard stick, set square and compass

Notes:

- Machine-stitch with right sides together, using matching thread and 1 cm (⅜-inch) seam allowance throughout.

- Backstitch at beginning and end of seams, then stitch again to reinforce.

- Inexpensive, sturdy bed frames are common at flea markets, often separated into head, foot, sides and springs.

TO MAKE:

1| Measure foam length, width and depth; to each measurement, add 2 cm (¾ inch) for seam allowance to determine total length, total width and total depth. If desired, for added softness, wrap foam with layer of quilt batting, trimming so edges butt without overlapping, then handstitch in place.

2| On wrong side of fabric and using chalk pencil, yard stick and set square, measure and mark cover top and bottom, each total length x total width, then mark 2 cover sides, each total length x total depth, and 2 cover ends, each total width x total depth. Cut out. Mark midpoint of each edge on each piece.

3| Alternating them, stitch sides to ends, along short edges, to form loop. Aligning corresponding midpoints and matching seam lines to corners, stitch 1 edge of loop to edges of top, pivoting at seam lines. In same manner, stitch remaining edge of loop to bottom, beginning approx 7.5 cm (3 inches) from corner on 1 side, then stitching along end, remaining side and end, and finishing approx 7.5 cm (3 inches) from last corner to leave opening for foam. Clip seam allowance at corners. Turn right side out. Press under 1 cm (⅜ inch) around opening.

4| Insert foam, aligning edges with seams; slipstitch opening closed.

5| Determine desired number of buttons (each top button pairs with 1 on bottom), then mark desired button positions on top and bottom. On felt and using compass, mark 4 cm (1⅝-inch) circle for each button; cut out. Attach each button pair as follows: Centre button on felt circle over mark on bed top. Using upholsterer's needle and 2 or more long strands of heavy-duty thread, push needle into 1 hole of button, straight through bed top and out corresponding bottom mark, then through felt circle and 1 hole of bottom button; repeat in reverse, pushing needle through remaining buttonholes and out top. Holding each group of strands together and pushing down firmly on foam, tie in reef knot to secure [A]. Finish with overhand knot and trim 2 cm (¾ inch) from knot.

Tips:

- If you find a daybed you like at a flea market, assemble it on the spot – to ensure that all the pieces fit securely – before you buy it.

- On furnishings for a covered porch or for indoors, any sturdy upholstery fabric will do, but if the mattress will be exposed to lots of direct sun and humidity, you may want to choose weatherproof fabric.

outdoors

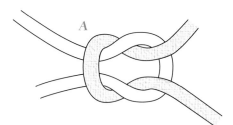

A

kids

puppets • marionettes • kites • baskets • totes • wind chimes • toys

Clothespin Butterflies

Hang up artwork and pictures with these cute-as-a-bug pins. Let kids' imaginations run wild as they decorate them.

YOU NEED (FOR EACH):

• Wooden clothespin, for body

• 2 small googly eyes*

• Small pom-pom or wooden bead, for nose*

• Pipe cleaner, for antennae

• Crayons and markers

• Stickers (optional)

• Coloured card stock or heavy paper, for cutouts and wings

• Self-adhesive magnets (optional)

• White craft glue or Tacky glue

• Hole punch (optional), pencil and scissors

*If you don't have these, you can draw on the eyes and nose

TO MAKE:

1| About 1 cm (⅜ inch) from top edge of front of clothespin, glue on eyes, then glue nose below. Let dry.

2| Push 1 end of pipe cleaner through clothespin spring until you have equal lengths of pipe cleaner at each side. Tightly twist lengths around each other, between 2 halves of clothespin, for about 2.5 cm (1 inch), then open them out and curl each end to make antennae.

3| Decorate body by drawing on dots, lines or squiggles; by adding stickers; or by gluing on paper cutouts (use hole punch to cut out dots).

4| Lay body, face up, on a piece of card stock and draw a wing at each side. Leaving wings attached down the centre, cut them out, then decorate the front and back. Glue the wings, down the centre, to the back of the body. Let dry.

5| If you want to use your bug on the fridge or a locker, stick a magnet onto the back.

Tip:
Before you start, test your markers on an extra clothespin. Some make a neat line or dot, while others bleed into the wood and make a mess.

Woven Finger Puppets

Craft a simple loom and let little hands help weave the cloth for these tiny friends.
Parents should help make and set up the loom, and sew and stuff the puppet.

kids

**YOU NEED
(FOR EACH):**

Loom
• Six 15 cm (6-inch)
  squares corrugated
  cardboard

• Masking tape

• 4 straight pins

• 14 glass- or plastic-
  head pins, 3 cm
  (1⅛ inches) long

Puppets
• 85 g (approx) bulky
  weight polyester
  chenille yarn in
  desired colour

• Small amount
  of stuffing

• Embroidery floss in
  black and/or pink

• 2 shiny black "E"
  beads

• Tapestry needle and
  sewing needle

Loom

TO MAKE:

1| Alternating direction of corrugations, stack cardboard squares so edges are even, then tape around entire stack 3 mm (⅛ inch) inside each edge.

2| Photocopy loom top diagram (page 272). Cut out 3 mm (⅛ inch) outside outline; centre on stack and, with straight pins angled toward centre, pin in place at each corner. Insert glass-head pins – angled away from bottom edge on bottom row and top edge on top row – through dots in each row as directed in puppet instructions.

Notes:

• Read all instructions before you begin.

• To start each weaving, make slipknot (see page 149, [A] and [B]) in yarn and loop over first pin, as directed; wind yarn down and around pin below, up and around next pin above, and so on, until you've wound around every pin, then trim yarn end to correct length – all as directed on pages 148 and 149. These vertical threads are called warp threads.

• To weave, thread trimmed end through tapestry needle, then slip needle under first thread (at far right), over second, under third, and so on, until you reach left-hand side of loom. Gently pull woven yarn through warp threads (not too tight or side edges will be wobbly), then use needle tip to straighten and push newly woven thread toward bottom of loom. To weave second row, slip needle over first thread (at far left), under second, over third, and so on, until you reach right-hand side of loom. These horizontal threads are called weft threads. In the same manner, weave up to first pin, then finish by threading yarn end through slipknot loop (leave end untrimmed to sew with).

• To remove weaving from loom, pull out pins.

• To sew up, use tapestry needle and yarn end; finish with knot to secure, then weave in yarn ends and trim.

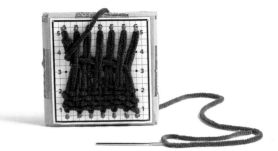

Puppets

TO MAKE:

1| Body: Insert pin in each dot in Row 1 and Row 5. Starting at 5A (first pin), wind warp to 1G; trim end to 1 m (39⅜ inches), then weave 13 rows to finish at 5A. Remove square from loom. Gently pull yarn end to gather top edge (neck edge), then sew side edges together down centre back of body.

2| Head: Reinsert pins A through D in Row 1 and Row 5. Starting at 5A (first pin), wind warp to 1D; trim end to 60 cm (23⅝ inches), then weave 13 rows to finish at 5A. Remove rectangle from loom. Repeat to make a second rectangle. Stack rectangles so edges are even, then stitch together up 1 short edge and knot at corner. Stitch together across long edge (top of head), pull gently to gather and knot at corner; stitch down remaining short edge and knot at corner. Separate layers and sew line of straight stitches all around bottom edge; stuff, pull yarn end to gather, then sew onto neck edge of body.

3| Arms: Reinsert pins A through C in Row 1 and Row 3. Starting at 3A (first pin), wind warp to 1C; trim end to 30 cm (11⅞ inches), then weave 7 rows to finish at 3A. Remove rectangle from loom. Gently pull yarn end to gather short edge (paw), then fold in half so long edges are even; sew long edges together up arm. Sew open end to body approx 6 mm (¼ inch) from neck. Repeat for second arm.

4| Bear's muzzle: Reinsert pins at A and B in Row 1 and Row 4. Starting at 4A (first pin), wind warp to 1B; trim end to 30 cm (11⅞ inches), then weave 11 rows to finish at 4A. Remove rectangle from loom. Fold in half so short edges (top of muzzle) are even and sew sides together. Separate layers and stuff; sew open end to face.

5| Bear's ears: Reinsert pins A through C in Row 1 and Row 2. Starting at 2A (first pin), wind warp to 1C; trim end to 25 cm (9⅞ inches), then weave 5 rows to finish at 2A. Remove rectangle from loom. Gently pull yarn end to gather long edge (tip of ear); weave needle tip, in and out, back across gathered edge to secure, then down short side edge (don't pull to gather). With ear facing front, stitch remaining long edge to 1 side of head. Repeat for second ear.

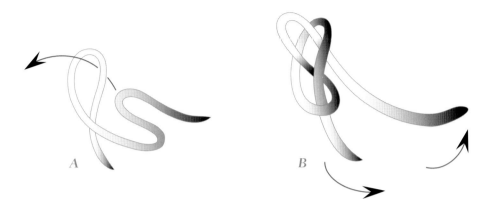

A

B

6| Rabbit's ears: Follow Step 3 until rectangle is removed from loom, then proceed as follows: Gently pull yarn end to gather short edge (tip of ear); weave needle tip, in and out, back across gathered edge to secure, then down long side edge (don't pull to gather). With ear facing front, stitch remaining short edge off-centre at top of head. Repeat for second ear.

7| Cat's ears: Reinsert pins A and B in Row 1 and Row 2. Starting at 2A (first pin), wind warp to 1B; trim end to 20 cm (7⅞ inches), then weave 5 rows to finish at 2A. Remove rectangle from loom. Gently pull yarn end to gather short edge (tip of ear); weave needle tip, in and out, back

across gathered edge to secure, then down side edge. With ear facing front, stitch remaining short edge to side of head. Repeat for second ear.

8| Rabbit's tail: Reinsert pins A through C in Row 1 and Row 5. Starting at 5A (first pin), wind warp to 1C; trim end to 40 cm (15¾ inches), then weave 13 rows to finish at 5A. Remove rectangle from loom. Fold in half so short edges are even, then stitch sides together. Separate layers and sew line of straight stitches all around top edge; gently pull yarn end to gather, then sew just above bottom edge of body at centre back.

9| Cat's tail: Follow Step 8 until rectangle is removed from loom, then proceed as follows: Gently pull yarn end to gather short edge (tip of tail), then fold in half so long edges are even and sew together up centre back; sew open end to bottom edge of body at centre back.

10| To finish: With sewing needle and 3 strands of black floss, securely stitch bead eyes onto face. With 6 strands of black floss for bear or 6 strands of pink floss for cat or rabbit, stitch X-shape for mouth, then make 2 tiny stitches over centre of X.

The Five-Minute Kite

This kite is a fantastic way to recycle plain old paper into a fun toy.
It's a bit delicate, so enjoy flying it in light winds.

YOU NEED:

- 8½- x 11-inch paper (recycle a piece of artwork or correspondence, or print a photo from your computer)

- Bamboo barbecue skewer

- Large plastic recycling bag

- Spool of strong thread

- 15 cm (6-inch) length of ¼-inch dowel*, or pencil that fits through hole in spool

- 2 wide elastic bands

- Scissors, small hole punch and ruler

- 2 cm (¾-inch) wide clear tape

Available at art and craft supply stores and lumberyards

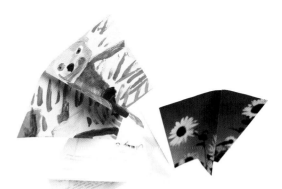

Note:
Refer to step-by-step diagrams (page 273) as you work.

TO MAKE:
1| With blank side to inside, fold sheet in half so short edges are even; run thumb along fold to crease.

2| Fold again where shown by broken line on diagram, so corner is even with edge, to shape long triangular keel.

3| Check that your folded paper matches Step 3 of the diagram.

4| Turn over, so second fold is right-hand edge.

5| Open out top layer along second fold. With scissors, clip sharp end off skewer to make 14 cm (5½-inch) spar; with 1 long strip, tape spar across kite where shown by broken line. Cutting vertically through both layers and leaving bottom fold intact, cut 5 cm (2-inch) wide strip from recycling bag for tail; tape 1 end of tail where shown by dotted line.

6| Turn kite over. About 1 cm (⅜ inch) from folded edge, punch small hole through keel where shown (reinforce with piece of tape, if desired). Bend keel back and forth until it stands straight up. Push thread end through hole, then tie to make loop for bridle. Slip spool (will act as reel for kite line) onto dowel, then secure by wrapping each dowel end with elastic.

Recycled Paper Baskets

Fun to make – and nearly free – these containers put a whole new slant on the name "wastepaper baskets."

YOU NEED:

- Even number of paper strips (see To Cut Strips, opposite, to determine dimensions)

- Flat ½- or ¾-inch artist's paintbrush and acrylic varnish or decoupage medium, such as Mod Podge (all optional)

- Ruler

- Clothespins

- Low-temperature glue gun

TO CUT STRIPS:
Brown paper
For large basket (approx 19 cm/7½ inches square and high): Cut off and discard bottom of large paper bag(s), then slit down side along glue seam. Across width, cut twenty 95 x 9 cm (37⅜- x 3½-inch) strips.

Newspaper
For medium basket (approx 12 cm/4¾ inches square and high): Cut thirty-six 56 x 7.5 cm (22- x 3-inch) strips.

For large basket (approx 15 cm/6 inches square and 13 cm/ 5⅛ inches high): Cut thirty-six 56 x 9 cm (22- x 3½-inch) strips.

Magazine paper
For small basket (approx 6 cm/2⅜ inches square and high): Tear out 12 pages.

For medium basket (approx 10 cm/4 inches square and high): Tear out 32 pages.

TO FOLD STRIPS:
Brown paper
Fold each strip in half so long cut edges are even; firmly press fold to crease. Open out, then fold each long edge to centre crease. Refold along centre crease, enclosing long cut edges; firmly press folds to crease, creating folded strip 4 layers thick.

Newspaper
For strength, stack 3 strips so edges are even, then treat as single strip and fold in same manner as for brown paper, above, creating folded strip 12 layers thick.

Magazine paper
Fold each page in half so long edges are even. In same manner, fold in half again, then again; firmly press to crease. Open out last fold, then fold each long edge to centre crease. Refold along centre crease, creating folded strip 16 layers thick.

For medium basket only, join folded strips in pairs (see To Join Folded Strips, right).

TO JOIN
FOLDED STRIPS:
Overlap 1 strip end approx 2 cm (¾ inch) over another and glue.

A

Note:
Use clothespins to temporarily secure weaving where noted.

TO MAKE:

1| Weave base: Divide even number of strips into 2 equal groups. Placing long open edges of strips to centre, and keeping strip ends even and 1 group perpendicular to the other, weave strips, alternating 1 over and 1 under. Slide strips tightly together into centred base [A]. Secure at each corner.

2| Begin sides: Alternately weaving next right-hand strip, then next left-hand strip, weave 1 side at a time as follows: Fold strips straight up from base and divide into 2 equal groups.

At 45-degree angle to woven edge, cross 2 centre strips [B], then weave each strip out to nearest side edge and gently pull strips to tighten [C]. Repeat, weaving in all remaining strips, to complete diamond-shaped side [D]. Secure with clothespin at tip of diamond. Repeat, starting with 2 centre strips from each remaining side, to complete 4 sides (strip ends from adjacent sides will cross at corners).

3| Join sides: Alternately weaving next right-hand, then next left-hand strip, weave crossing strips from 1 side into strips from adjacent side edge, so each strip crosses from 1 basket side to nearest side [E]. Secure.

4| Finish sides: Continue weaving as in Step 3 to complete all 4 corners.

5| Finish rim: Fold any 2 crossing strips, 1 over the other, down inside basket; trim even with second woven strip down and glue in place. Repeat around edge.

6| Varnish (optional): Invert basket. Brush varnish onto base and exterior; let dry. Turn basket upright. Brush varnish onto interior and rim; let dry.

Tips:
- For your first basket, avoid using slippery, shiny magazine paper.

- Weave with the outside facing you.

- The trickiest step is making the bottom corners, which may take a few tries; once they're done, the strips cross over in the direction you will weave them to finish the sides. The rest is easy.

- Before finishing the rim, gently pull strips to tighten all the weaving.

- Gluing down the strip ends in Step 5 is quick and easy. For a traditional finish, diagonally fold each end into a point (trim the end even with the side of the strip); fold it over the rim and weave it over and under 4 strips down the inside, then trim.

B

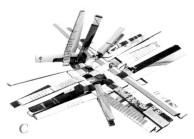

C

D

E

Plastic Spoon Crocuses

Celebrate the first flowers of spring with a craft that's easy for little hands. These cheerful blooms are great on an Easter table or a sunny windowsill.

TO MAKE:

1| Fold over end of pipe cleaner 2.5 cm (1 inch) and twist together; repeat on other end. Repeat 3 more times, for total of 4 pipe cleaners. Gather pipe cleaners together and bend in half, twisting centres loosely to form single unit.

2| Apply hot glue to top of handle of plastic spoon; adhere pipe cleaner bundle to handle, overlapping loose pipe cleaner ends with bowl of spoon.

3| Repeat with 3 more spoons to form flower (see photo, right).

4| Cut two 20.5 cm (8-inch) lengths of twist tie; twist around spoon handles and curl as desired.

5| Make more crocuses. Bundle together and arrange in pot. Fill in spaces around crocuses with moss.

YOU NEED:
- Pipe cleaners
- Plastic spoons
- Green plastic twist ties (on spool)
- Decorative pot or urn
- Moss
- Low-temperature glue gun
- Scissors

Puppet Theatre

A puppet theatre offers hours of creativity for children. And with cute dragon (page 158) and princess (page 160) sock puppets, the story possibilities are endless.

YOU NEED:

- 1.2 m x 91 cm (4- x 3-foot) tri-fold foam or cardboard display board*

- 1 sheet red bristol board*

- 1 package gold bulletin board trim, approx 1 m (3 feet) long*

- 2.5 m (8-foot) length 1 cm (⅜-inch) diameter yellow nylon rope (optional)

- Pencil, ruler and scissors

- Painter's tape, glue stick and craft glue

Available at office supply stores

For best results, test trim layout (taping pieces down if necessary) before gluing.

TO MAKE:

1| With pencil and ruler, draw 61 x 40.5 cm (24- x 16-inch) rectangle, centred, with short sides parallel to bottom, on centre panel of display board. Using scissors, cut out rectangle and discard.

2| With pencil, and using photo as guide, draw curtains on bristol board. Draw 1 top curtain, 51 cm (20⅛ inches) long and 7.5 cm (3 inches) wide at widest point. Draw 2 side curtains, 61 cm (24 inches) long and 8 cm (3⅛ inches) wide at widest points. Cut out curtains.

3| Align straight edge of top curtain with top edge of opening, curved edge up. Position side curtains with straight edges overlapping side edges of opening and bottoms of curtains hanging above bottom of board.

4| Cut two 61 cm (24-inch) lengths of bulletin board trim. Place 1 length trim on either side of opening, aligning straight edges of trim with edges of opening, and underlapping curtain (see photo, opposite).

5| Positioning so 1 "bump" hangs in centre of opening and edges are symmetrical (cut off excess if necessary), place third strip of trim across top of opening, aligning long straight edge of trim with bottom of top curtain and aligning short straight edges with ends of vertical pieces of trim. Centre second, smaller piece above, as accent (see photo, opposite).

6| To create decorative moulding around top curtain, place small sections of trim just under top edge of curtain, starting in centre and angling and overlapping as needed to match curve of curtain. Add a horizontal row of trim above, tucking under edge of curved trim. Repeat above with final short row of trim.

7| Apply trim to topmost edge of each panel of display board, matching long straight edges and centring trim on centre panel to match long horizontal strip from Step 5.

8| Apply symmetrical sections of trim to bottom edge of each of the panels.

Tip:

To set the scene, hang scenery (such as a painting or a large photo cut from a magazine) on wall behind theatre.

9| Using trim scraps and cutting as necessary to create symmetrical pieces, place small pieces of trim on upper and lower edges of side panels to create decorative moulding.

10| Using glue stick, glue bristol board and trim pieces in place (removing tape if necessary). Glue trim along straight edges only, tucking next layer of trim in behind.

11| If desired, arrange nylon rope as shown. Working with 1 short section of rope at a time, apply craft glue beneath rope, then secure rope with painter's tape. Let dry completely before removing tape. Fray ends of rope if desired.

Dragon Puppet

Don't worry – he's not the fire-breathing kind.
This adorable googly-eyed dragon will steal your heart – and the show!

YOU NEED:

- 1 green sock

- 10 x 12.5 cm
  (4- x 5-inch) piece
  cardboard

- Scraps red and
  black felt

- 23 x 30.5 cm (9- x
  12-inch) piece each
  yellow and green felt

- Scraps purple, green
  and black craft foam

- Large googly eyes

- Fabric scrap or
  disposable dishcloth

- 8 large green
  pom-poms

- 6 small green
  pom-poms

- 2 pieces fabric, approx
  30.5 cm (12 inches)
  square, such as tulle
  (we used gold) or
  organza for wings

- Brown paper, pencil,
  scissors, paper clips
  and straight pins

- Craft glue

- Low-temperature
  glue gun

TO MAKE:

1| Enlarge templates (page 274) by squaring method as follows: On brown paper, draw grid of horizontal and vertical lines 2.5 cm (1 inch) apart. Each square on diagram equals a square on brown paper. Enlarge pattern by redrawing each line of pattern onto corresponding square. Cut out.

2| Turn sock inside out. Using template, cut dragon mouth shape out of cardboard. Fold mouth along dotted line. Put sock on your hand, with heel over your wrist. Push fabric in between upper fingers and lower thumb to make mouth opening; fit cardboard mouth shape into place. Trim where necessary to make a good fit.

3| Use fitted cardboard mouth shape to cut an identical mouth shape out of red felt; set aside.

4| With craft glue, glue cardboard mouth shape into place on wrong side of sock. Use paper clips to hold in place while drying.

5| Meanwhile, use templates to cut: interior mouth shape from black felt; spikes, large wings and belly from yellow felt; and small wing supports and nostrils from green felt.

6| Cut assorted-size teardrop shapes from craft foam. Glue together to make fan shape (see photo, opposite). Glue googly eyes to craft-foam pieces to create dramatic eyes.

7| Turn sock right-side out. Arrange mouth shape so puppet's mouth works, then glue red felt mouth into place over top. Position and glue black felt piece onto red felt to create mouth interior. Hold both pieces in place with paper clips while drying.

8| Tie knot in centre of strip of fabric scrap to form padding for forehead. Put puppet on your hand and fit padding into place. Adjust as necessary; glue in place with glue gun. Let dry.

9| With puppet on hand, position 2 large green pom-poms for eyes. Use glue gun to glue in place.

10| Using template as guide, make fringe along yellow felt spikes as follows: Make short perpendicular cuts along straight edge every 1 cm (3⁄8 inch), beginning about 4 cm (1⅝ inches) in from front tip. For convenience, slip puppet onto a bottle or tube so it stands upright. Centre spikes along back of puppet, starting just behind eyes. Using straight pin, bend tabs of fringe in opposite directions to make 2 alternating rows of tabs. Using glue gun, dab small amount of glue on first tab, then on centre of puppet's back. Repeat on second tab. Press to adhere to back. Repeating on remaining tabs, 2 at a time, to end of spikes.

11| Using glue gun, glue eyes to pom-poms on head.

12| To make wings, gather large yellow felt wings at base, leaving bottom point free. Glue gathered felt together with glue gun; set aside. Fold fabric squares in half and gather at base; hold against yellow wings to determine placement. Using glue gun, glue tulle gathers together. Attach tulle wings behind yellow wings at base with glue gun. Glue wings to back of puppet at base of spikes, with gathers facing forward. Press to adhere to body. Glue green wing supports over wings and body to conceal seams.

13| Using glue gun, glue remaining pom-poms alongside spikes, using small pom-poms on either side of upper spike and larger pom-poms below.

14| Glue belly to sock with glue gun, adding green felt stripes, if desired.

15| Glue nostrils in place.

Princess Puppet

A princess dressed in frothy frills is the perfect heroine
for a puppet theatre show.

YOU NEED:

- 1 buff-colour sock

- 10 x 12.5 cm (4- x 5-inch) piece cardboard

- Scraps red and pink felt

- Fabric scrap or disposable dishcloth

- 1 pink sock

- 2 large white pom-poms

- Scraps blue and black (optional) craft foam

- Large googly eyes

- 2 pieces fabric, such as tulle (we used pink) or organza: one 30.5 cm x 91.5 cm (12 inches x 3 feet), for skirt; and one 30.5 cm (12 inches) square, for hat

- Pink stretchy lace

- Decorations, such as sequins, strings of beads or earrings

- 4.5 m (5 yards) golden wired ribbon, for hair, and matching pom-poms (optional)

- 30.5 cm (12-inch) square aluminum foil

- Brown paper, pencil, scissors, straight pins, stapler and paper clips

- Craft glue

- Low-temperature glue gun

TO MAKE:

1| Enlarge template (page 274) by squaring method as follows: On brown paper, draw grid of horizontal and vertical lines 2.5 cm (1 inch) apart. Each square on diagram equals a square on brown paper. Enlarge pattern by redrawing each line of pattern onto corresponding square. Cut out.

2| Turn buff-colour sock inside out. Using template, cut princess mouth shape out of cardboard. Fold mouth along dotted line. Put sock on your hand, with heel over your wrist. Push fabric in between upper fingers and lower thumb to make mouth opening; fit cardboard mouth shape into place. Trim where necessary to make a good fit.

3| Use fitted cardboard mouth shape to cut an identical mouth shape out of red felt; set aside.

4| With craft glue, glue cardboard mouth shape into place on wrong side of sock. Use paper clips to hold in place while drying.

5| Turn sock right-side out. Arrange mouth shape so puppet's mouth works, then glue red felt mouth into place over top. Hold in place with paper clips while drying.

6| Tie knot in centre of strip of fabric scrap to form padding for forehead. Put puppet on your hand and fit padding into place. Adjust as necessary; glue in place with glue gun. Let dry.

7| Cut toe area off pink sock and set aside for hat. Slide remaining pink sock tube over the buff-colour sock to make dress. Glue socks together, making the back of the dress higher than the front.

8| With puppet on hand, position white pom-poms for eyes. Use glue gun to secure in place.

9| For convenience, slip puppet onto a bottle or tube so it stands upright. Cut circles from blue craft foam, slightly larger than googly eyes, adding long eyelashes cut from black craft foam if desired. Using glue gun, glue googly eyes onto foam, then foam onto pom-poms.

10| To make skirt, fold 1 fabric piece in half and gather, securing with a straight pin. Put skirt on puppet (all around pink sock) to check fit. Staple gathers to secure in place. Affix skirt to dress with glue gun. Glue on lace where body of dress and skirt meet (see photo, opposite). Trim bodice with lace. Decorate dress with sequins or strings of beads as desired.

11| To make hair, fold lengths of ribbon to desired length. Gather at crown and secure with glue gun. If desired, attach earrings to hair-colour pom-poms; glue onto sock, concealing pom-poms with hair as much as possible.

12| To make hat, form foil into cone shape. Slip reserved sock toe over foil and glue in place. Glue hat to head using glue gun. Decorate by attaching small piece of fabric to point of hat; add sequins and lacy cutouts as desired.

13| To make lips, cut desired shape from pink felt (see photo, opposite). With glue gun, attach lips just above mouth.

Pom-Pom Chicks

Cute, cuddly and full of personality, these little chicks are a cinch to make.
And you probably already have all the craft supplies on hand.

**YOU NEED
(FOR EACH):**

•Yarn in desired colour

•Card stock

•Pipe cleaner

•Bottle cap

•Decorations, such as
  beads, buttons
  or ribbon

•Felt scraps

•Googly eyes

•Compass, pencil,
  scissors, markers and
  craft glue

•Tapestry needle

TO MAKE:

1| Cut two 30.5 cm (12-inch) lengths of yarn; set aside.

2| With compass, on card stock draw two 4 cm (1⅝-inch) diameter circles and two 5 cm (2-inch) diameter circles; centred inside each, draw 1.3 cm (½-inch) diameter circle. With scissors, cut out each outer circle. Cut 1 slit straight in from outer edge; cut out each inner circle and discard. With edges even and slits aligned, hold 2 small circles together. Holding yarn in other hand, and beginning and ending at slit, wind yarn evenly and thickly counterclockwise around circle through centre hole, until hole is full. Holding yarn firmly in place at centre, slip scissors between circles at outside edge and cut yarn all around; still holding yarn firmly in place at centre, slip 1 length of yarn (cut in Step 1) between circles and around yarn at centre, then tightly knot. Do not trim tie ends. Repeat with large circles to make second, larger pom-pom.

3| Carefully push pipe cleaner through centre of large pom-pom; bend in half at midpoint. Form legs and feet by bending pipe cleaner (see photo, opposite). To make spiral legs, twist pipe cleaner around pencil.

4| Thread tie ends from small pom-pom onto tapestry needle; push through centre of large pom-pom, tie securely and trim. Trim tie ends from large pom-pom.

5| On card stock, draw bill (for cap) or brim (for hat or bonnet) to fit bottle cap; cut out. With marker, colour as desired, then glue to bottle cap; decorate cap as desired. Let dry. Cut triangle of felt for beak.

6| Using craft glue, affix cap to head; glue on googly eyes and beak (see photo, opposite).

Tip:

To make your chick into a key ring, after attaching small pom-pom in Step 4, thread tie ends from large pom-pom onto tapestry needle; push up through centre of large pom-pom and out at centre of back of bird. Tie securely around key ring; trim.

In Like a Lion,
Out Like a Lamb Totes

Master one (or both) of these easy fabric-printing techniques.

YOU NEED:

In Like a Lion Tote Bag

• Canvas tote bag*

• Freezer paper

• Card stock

• Heat-set fabric paint* (we used Pebeo Setacolor Opaque in 19 Black Laque and 47 Shimmer Light Copper)

• Stencil brushes*

• X-acto knife, cutting mat and iron

• Masking tape and paper towels

• Paper plates or plastic lids

Out Like a Lamb Tote Bag

• Canvas tote bag*

• Card stock

• 2 or 3 large potatoes

• Heat-set fabric paint* (we used Pebeo Setacolor Opaque in 10 Titanium White, 19 Black Laque and 24 Spring Green)

• Paper towels, paper plates or plastic lids and wooden stir sticks

• Pencil and paring knife or cookie cutters in desired shapes

Available at craft and art supply stores

Note:

The lion bag is suitable for older teens or adults.

In Like a Lion Tote Bag

TO MAKE:

1| Enlarge lion template (page 275) to desired size.

2| Using masking tape, affix template to matte side of freezer paper with image face up.

3| On cutting mat, using X-acto knife, cut out image, cutting through both layers of paper and leaving bridges intact. Discard printed template.

4| Iron tote bag; steam if necessary to remove wrinkles. Line with card stock.

5| Place freezer paper stencil, shiny side down, on bag, smoothing to ensure edges don't curl or fold. Place medium-heat no-steam iron on stencil and slide slowly all over stencil, ensuring all air bubbles are removed, until stencil adheres to bag.

6| Place bag on work surface. With X-acto knife, carefully trim off bridges.

7| Pour small amount of black paint onto paper plate. Dip brush straight down into paint until bristles are coated; blot on paper towel to remove excess.

8| Holding brush perpendicular to bag and masking face details and mane with scraps of paper if necessary, paint inner ears, eyes, nose and mouth black by dabbing brush onto surface until coated. (If necessary, reload brush with paint.) Let dry.

9| Repeat Step 7 with copper paint and clean brush, masking black areas with scraps of paper if desired and painting remaining areas of face and mane copper. Let dry completely.

10| Carefully peel off freezer paper stencil and discard. Heat-set paint with iron according to manufacturer's directions.

Tip:

Any line drawing can be converted into a stencil. Print or photocopy several copies of the image; colour in the pictures with pencil crayons to determine which areas you'll cut out and what paint colours you'll use.

Note:

This lamb tote is better suited to children, but make sure to carefully supervise little ones when they're using sharp knives or hot irons.

Out Like a Lamb Tote Bag

TO MAKE:

1| Iron tote bag; line with card stock. Place on work surface.

2| Halve potatoes lengthwise; blot with paper towel to remove excess moisture. Trace shapes for lamb body, head and feet, and grass (see photo, opposite) on cut sides of potatoes; using paring knife, cut out. (Or, if using cookie cutter to make shapes, place potato flat side down on work surface and press cookie cutter through potato, discarding cutaway flesh.)

3| Pour small amount of white paint onto paper plate; using stir stick, spread thin layer of paint over plate. Dip lamb body stamp in paint to evenly coat. Wipe excess paint from edges of stamp.

4| Press stamp onto fabric, pressing firmly for 5 seconds; lift straight up. Repeat until desired number of lamb bodies have been printed, reloading stamp with paint as necessary. Let dry completely.

5| Repeat Steps 3 and 4 with black paint and stamps for lambs' heads and feet, and with green paint for tufts of grass. Let dry completely.

6| Heat-set paint with iron according to manufacturer's directions.

Pop Bottle Wind Chimes

Sparkles, snowflakes, shiny jingles and shimmery pop-bottle bells –
together they'll make music in the chilly winds.

YOU NEED:

- 2 midsize translucent plastic pop or water bottles in cool colours

- 3 gold preserving-jar screw bands

- Silver, gold or coloured glitter*

- Scraps of narrow metallic ribbon*, to match

- 3 precut craft foam snowflakes*

- Approx 3 m (10 feet) clear sparkle plastic lacing*

- ⅜-inch dowel, 28 cm (11 inches) long, painted as desired

- Six 1-inch diameter and eight ½-inch diameter gold jingle bells*

- Wide metallic or coloured wired ribbon*, approx 1.5 m (5 feet) long (optional)

- X-acto knife, hammer, and awl or nail

- Tacky glue*

*Available at craft supply stores

Note:

Adults should assist with all cutting and hole piercing with sharp tools.

TO MAKE:

1| Cut around each pop bottle with X-acto knife to make 3 bells (use both top and bottom of 1 bottle and only the top or the bottom of the other). With hammer and awl, pierce hole through centre of each base or cap, and through each jar band. Decorate bells by gluing on glitter, narrow ribbon and snowflakes; let dry.

2| From lacing, cut 1 m (39⅜-inch) length; fold in half at midpoint, then tie overhand knot, approx 20 cm (7⅞ inches) down, for hanging loop. About 2.5 cm (1 inch) from each dowel end, tie 1 lacing end, ensuring that dowel hangs level.

3| Cut and tie together lengths of remaining lacing and narrow ribbon to create a chime for each bell. Thread lengths through jar bands, jingle bells and snowflakes, as desired, tying on each.

4| Finish each by tying large knot (leave 20.5 to 25.5 cm/8- to 10-inch end at top of lacing), then pushing lacing up through hole in bell. Adjusting to desired height, tie around dowel. If desired, add wide ribbon bow to hanging loop.

Door Organizer

Corral lunch money, permission slips, bus passes and more in this simple doorknob organizer, made with household items in under 30 minutes.

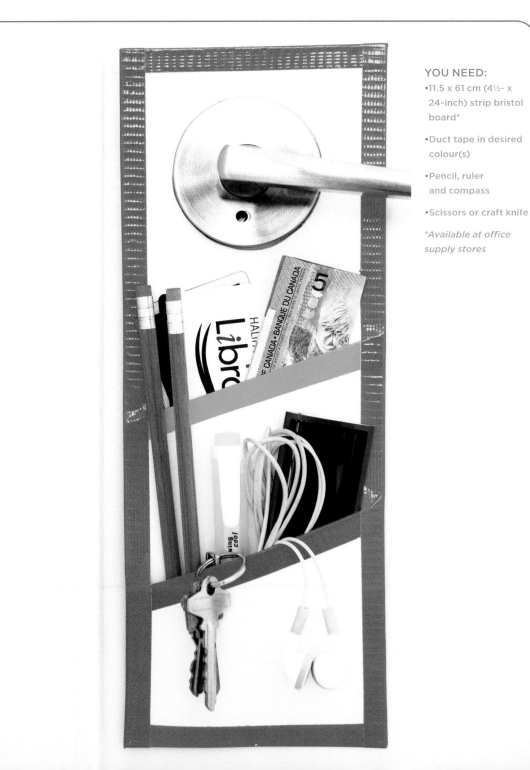

YOU NEED:

•11.5 x 61 cm (4½- x 24-inch) strip bristol board*

•Duct tape in desired colour(s)

•Pencil, ruler and compass

•Scissors or craft knife

Available at office supply stores

TO MAKE:

1| From bristol board, cut one 11.5 x 30.5 cm (4½- x 12-inch) strip for base. Using pencil and ruler, and working on right side of board, mark line 1.3 cm (½ inch) in from edge on top and sides. With compass, mark 6.5 cm (2½-inch) diameter circle, centred near top of rectangle. Carefully cut out and discard circle.

2| Measure 7.5 cm (3 inches) from top of remaining strip of bristol board and mark on left-hand edge; measure and mark 10 cm (4 inches) from top on right-hand edge. Join marks with diagonal line; cut to divide into 2 pocket pieces. Mark line 1.3 cm (½ inch) in from edge on top and sides on both pockets, and from bottom of smaller pocket as well.

3| Aligning edge of tape with pencil line, tape top edges of pocket pieces. Trim tape even with edges.

4| In same manner, apply tape to top edge of base; trim.

5| Stack pocket pieces and base, aligning bottom edges. Aligning edge of tape with pencil line, apply tape to bottom edge of small pocket piece; wrap tape to bottom, securing all pieces together. Trim tape even with edges.

6| In same manner, apply tape to long sides, securing pocket pieces to base and trimming tape ends.

Tips:
•If desired, decorate with stickers or drawings.

•Add additional pockets if you have more to organize.

Caterpillar Marionette

This colourful caterpillar puppet might be hatched from an ordinary egg carton – and other odds and ends you have around the house – but he will worm his way into your heart.

YOU NEED:

- Cardboard egg carton

- Cord or yarn, cut in 10 lengths, each 15 cm (6 inches) long, for legs

- Gesso (optional)

- Acrylic paints, ½-inch paintbrush and fine-tip artist's paintbrush

- Pom-pom, for nose

- 2 pipe cleaners

- Two ¼-inch dowels, each about 25 cm (9⅞ inches) long, or 2 unsharpened pencils

- Clear monofilament and needle

- Scissors and Tacky glue

- Clothespins, for clamping

- Compass, for piercing holes

TO MAKE:

1| Cut lid and flap off egg carton. Turn base upside down, then cut in half lengthwise, between the bumps, to make 2 strips. Glue 1 strip inside the other to make body; let dry.

2| From carton lid, cut 20 loonie-size circles. Apply glue to 1 side of 10 circles. Lay 1 end of each leg cord on 1 glued circle, then, sandwiching the end, stick an unglued circle on top to make a foot; clamp each with a clothespin until dry.

3| If desired, brush gesso onto body and feet; let dry. Paint body and feet in desired colours; let dry. Paint desired details, such as eyes, dots, squiggles and stripes; let dry. Glue on pom-pom nose; clamp in place with a clothespin until dry.

4| Using compass point, carefully pierce holes through base of body, between bumps, along each long side edge. Thread 1 leg through each hole, then knot it so foot dangles about 5 cm (2 inches) below body. Trim excess cord. Dab knots with glue; let dry. Carefully pierce a hole through top of head at each side. Thread the ends of 1 pipe cleaner up through holes, then twirl to make antennae.

5| Crisscross the dowels perpendicular to each other; tightly wrap remaining pipe cleaner around centre to hold dowels together.

6| From monofilament, cut ten 60 cm (23⅝-inch) lengths. One at a time, thread 1 end of each through needle, then poke needle through a foot, near edge opposite the leg, and tie end in an overhand knot to secure. Even up remaining ends of all 5 lengths on 1 side; knot ends together, then tie them around 1 of the dowels, about 2.5 cm (1 inch) from 1 end. Repeat with remaining lengths of monofilament and the opposite end of the same dowel.

7| From monofilament, cut 50 cm (19¾-inch) length. Tie large knot at 1 end, then thread remaining end through needle and poke needle up through centre of bump behind head; tie remaining end around dowel above head. Repeat to tie last bump onto opposite end of same dowel.

8| Dab all knots with glue; let dry.

Tip:

You could paint the nose, glue on googly eyes or tie on a big wooden bead for each foot, instead.

seasonal

paper crafts • gift bags • linens • bookmarks • toys • wreaths• ornaments

Folded Fish

Start off the new year by recycling last year's Christmas cards into clever little fish to string into a mobile or use as place cards at a special dinner.

YOU NEED (FOR EACH):

- Christmas card(s)
- Small scrap of aluminum foil
- Scraps of gold or silver cards
- 25.5 cm (10-inch) length of monofilament or fine metallic cord (optional)
- Pencil, ruler, scissors and hole punch
- Tacky glue and toothpick, or glue stick
- Fine-tip permanent black marker
- Darning needle or thumbtack (optional)

Notes:
- Refer to step-by-step photos (right) as you work.

- Work with strips right side up, unless otherwise indicated.

- Glue strips together at each overlap as follows: Carefully lift top strip, dot bottom strip with glue, then press top strip back into place.

TO MAKE:

1| With pencil and ruler, mark 6 strips on front of card: each 12 cm x 6 mm (4¾ x ¼ inch) for small fish, 15 x 1 cm (6 x ⅜ inch) for medium, or 16.5 x 1.5 cm (6½ x ⅝ inch) for large. Cut out.

2| Lay 1 strip horizontally on work surface; lay second strip on top, perpendicular to first, forming uneven cross with 2 short, 5 cm (2-inch) arms [A]. Glue.

3| Slide another vertical strip under horizontal strip at each side, keeping top and bottom ends even with first strip [B]. Glue.

4| Weave in another horizontal strip at top and bottom, keeping side ends even [C]. Glue. Turn over so wrong side is up.

5| Fold each set of 3 long, loose ends across top so right side is up [D], then weave over and under each other [E]. Glue. Trim loose end of each centre strip even with edge of woven square; turn over and repeat to trim all 4 centre-strip ends, leaving fins and tail [F].

6| Form marble-size ball of foil; push inside woven fish to fatten it up, then, leaving fins and tail unglued, glue unwoven edges of fish together.

7| Diagonally trim fin and tail strips. Cut slits along each tail strip (1 for small fish, 2 for medium and 3 for large), then curl outward.

8| With hole punch, punch out 2 eyes from shiny gold or silver card scraps; with marker, draw pupil on each, leaving tiny highlight. Glue onto fish.

9| To use as place card: Write name on top fin, then open out bottom fin and tail so fish stands up.

To hang on tree or mobile: Push needle through top corner near fin; through hole, push monofilament, then tie (for ornament, form 2.5 cm/1-inch loop at other end and tie to make hanging loop).

To use as gift tag: Write name on each side. Push needle through top corner near fin; through hole, push cord, then tie.

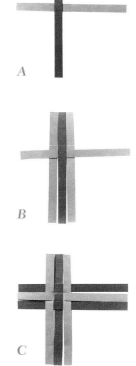

A

B

C

D

E

F

seasonal

CANADIAN LIVING | CREATE. UPDATE. REMAKE.

Sweet Valentine Packages

This Valentine's Day, deliver treats in personalized packages to your favourite people.

YOU NEED:

- Lightweight and medium-weight card stock, in desired colours

- Decorations, such as scraps of patterned and plain paper, scraps of foil and fabric, beads, buttons, charms, cut-out photos and words, markers, stamps and stamp pads, stickers, or paint and paintbrush

- Scraps of raffia, ribbon or string, for ties

- Pencil

- Glue stick and/or Tacky glue

- Scissors and X-acto knife (optional)

- Ruler and letter opener or dull butter knife, for scoring lines

TO MAKE:

1| Trace templates (page 276) or photocopy to enlarge to desired size; cut out along solid lines. Using glue stick, adhere pattern to medium-weight card stock to make box pattern and scoring guide; cut out.

2| Trace box pattern onto card stock; cut out and place, wrong side up, on work surface. Position ruler where indicated by each dotted line on pattern; with point of letter opener, score line on wrong side. Lay scoring guide on each curved end of box, top and bottom, so outside edge is aligned, then score folding line on wrong side where indicated by broken line.

3| Decorate package as desired.

4| Fold box in half along centre dotted line so wrong sides are together; apply glue to flap A where indicated by shading, fold over edge B and adhere. Fold in ends along scored lines, folding C flaps, then D flaps.

5| Fill package and tie with raffia.

Tip:
Use lightweight card stock for small boxes and medium-weight for large ones.

seasonal

"Be Mine" Decorations

Make your feelings known with these simple declarations of love.

YOU NEED:

"Be Mine" Bunting

- Red and white card stock
- Grosgrain ribbon
- Pencil and plain white paper
- Scissors
- X-acto knife or small sharp pointed scissors
- Glue stick and clear tape
- Paper clips

Valentine Holder

- Pink card stock
- Scissors
- Craft glue
- Glitter glue, markers, buttons or sequins

"Be Mine" Bunting

TO MAKE:

1| Using a word-processing program, type your message; style in desired font and type size (we used Book Antiqua at 144 points), and print.

2| Photocopy or trace heart template (page 277) and cut out.

3| Trace cutout onto red and white card stock, making 1 white heart and 1 red heart for each character (including spaces). Using scissors, cut out hearts; set white hearts aside.

4| Centre each letter, printed side down, on wrong side of a red heart and trace, using sharp pencil and pressing heavily. For a space, draw smaller heart on wrong side of red heart.

5| Using X-acto knife, cut out letters and heart shapes.

6| Using glue stick, glue red hearts to white hearts. With tape, affix large loop of paper clip to wrong side of each white heart, just below centre dip.

7| Clip hearts to ribbon to join letters; hang up.

Valentine Holder

TO MAKE:

1| Fold 21.5 x 28 cm (8½- x 11-inch) piece card stock in half so long edges meet; crease fold.

2| Using scissors, trim corners from 1 end of rectangle to form rounded end.

3| Unfold paper and lay flat on work surface with rounded ends at top. Fold bottom edge up so untrimmed edge is approx 5 cm (2 inches) from top; crease. Fold bottom left corner in to meet crease in middle of page; crease. Repeat for right corner. Fold top (untrimmed) edge of paper down to overlap; secure with craft glue.

4| Decorate as desired with glitter glue, markers, buttons or sequins.

Easter Gift Bag

Decorate a plain paper bag with a small bunny, then fill it with sweet treats.

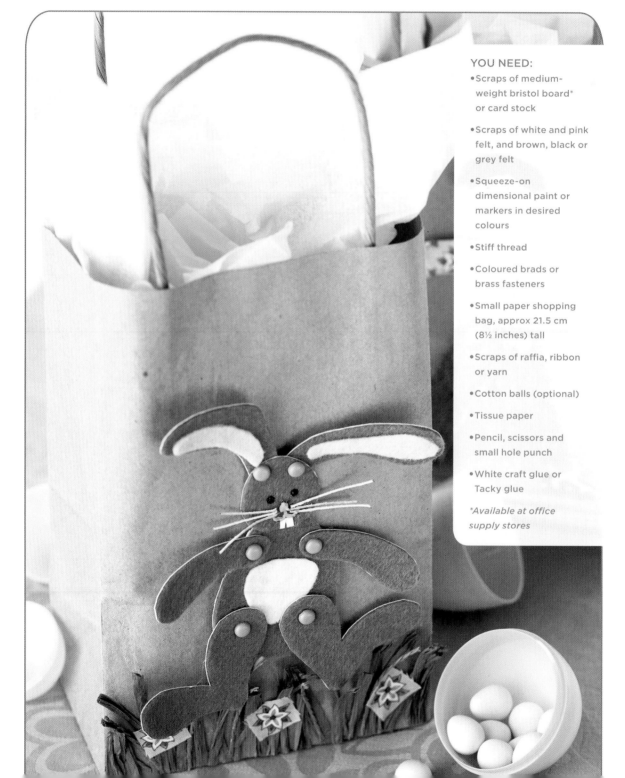

YOU NEED:

- Scraps of medium-weight bristol board* or card stock

- Scraps of white and pink felt, and brown, black or grey felt

- Squeeze-on dimensional paint or markers in desired colours

- Stiff thread

- Coloured brads or brass fasteners

- Small paper shopping bag, approx 21.5 cm (8½ inches) tall

- Scraps of raffia, ribbon or yarn

- Cotton balls (optional)

- Tissue paper

- Pencil, scissors and small hole punch

- White craft glue or Tacky glue

*Available at office supply stores

TO MAKE:

1| Trace pattern pieces (page 278) or photocopy to enlarge pieces to desired size.

2| Cut out pattern pieces along solid black lines, then punch hole at each grey dot.

3| From bristol board, cut out 1 body, 2 arms, 2 ears and 2 legs. From white felt, cut out 1 belly. From pink felt, cut out 2 inner ears.

4| Apply glue to right side of each cut-out piece of bristol board; lay it flat, glue side down, on brown felt, then smooth down and let dry. Turn over and trim felt even with edges of board. Lay pattern on each piece and mark a dot at each hole; remove pattern and punch hole at each dot.

5| Glue on belly and inner ears where indicated by broken lines; let dry.

6| Using red lines as guide, paint or draw face, or cut from scraps of felt and glue on. Cut short lengths of thread and glue on at either side of nose for whiskers.

7| Matching lettered dots, push brad through body and each arm (or leg), then open ends against back to secure. In same way, push brad through head and each ear, then secure.

8| Glue assembled bunny onto bag front, attaching head and body only, so arms, ears and legs are free to move. Decorate bag front as desired, gluing on raffia grass, a ribbon path or cotton-ball clouds; let dry.

9| Line bag with tissue paper, then fill with Easter treats.

Canada Day Pinwheel

Take a spin in the summer wind with a fun, easy-to-make homemade pinwheel.

**YOU NEED
(FOR EACH):**
- Red or white origami paper*, 15 cm (6 inches) square
- Pushpin and map pin
- Two 6 mm seed beads in red or white
- ¼-inch wooden dowel
- Pencil and ruler
- Scissors

*Available at art and craft supply stores

Note:

To make your pinwheels larger or smaller, use different size squares of paper.

TO MAKE:

1| Place paper, wrong side up, on work surface. Matching opposite corners, fold in half diagonally and crease [A]; open up. Repeat with other corners to form X through centre of paper.

2| With pencil and ruler, mark each fold line 2.5 cm (1 inch) from centre point [B]. With scissors, cut along each fold, stopping at mark, to divide each corner into 2 points [C].

3| Using pushpin, pierce hole in every other point, about 6 mm (¼ inch) from end; pierce hole in centre of pinwheel [D].

4| Slide seed bead onto map pin. Push map pin through holes in points from wrong side, starting at 1 point and working clockwise until all points have been gathered onto pin [E]. Push map pin through centre hole.

5| Slide second seed bead onto map pin, behind pinwheel. Push pin into dowel, approx 1.3 cm (½ inch) from end, being careful not to push map pin through back of dowel.

Tiny Pinwheels

With scissors, cut origami paper into 5 cm (2-inch) squares. Follow Steps 1 through 4, cutting diagonal lines to within 6 mm (¼ inch) of centre and pushing pin into, but not through, top of bamboo fork (available at kitchen supply or dollar stores). Fit fork over rim of glass.

Tips:

• For ease in pushing pins into dowel or bamboo forks, soak wood for 10 minutes first.

• If making this craft with very young children, use a pencil instead of a dowel; push the pin into the eraser.

A

B

C

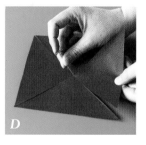

D

E

Canada Day Maple Leaf Birds

String your birds into a garland to drape across your front window, porch or picnic table.

YOU NEED (FOR EACH):
- 15 cm (6-inch) square card stock, for templates
- 15 cm (6-inch) square each stiff red and white paper
- Black, blue, green and red fine-tip markers
- Glue stick

TO MAKE:

1| Colour-photocopy patterns (page 279) and cut out along solid black lines. With markers, transfer markings. Fold card stock in half. Place leaf pattern on folded card stock as indicated; trace and cut out. Fold large card stock scrap in half; place beak pattern on card stock scrap as indicated, trace and cut out.

2| Using templates, trace and cut 1 leaf from red paper, cutting slit along red line, then fold in half along broken line. Cut 1 beak from red paper, then fold in half along broken line. Cut 1 leaf from white paper, then fold in half along broken line and cut slit along blue line (just to where it turns green), to make triangular flap.

3| With black marker, draw eyes on front of white leaf where shown by big black dots. Then, using glue stick, glue beak to underside of white leaf where shown by dotted lines.

4| To turn leaves into a bird, pinch folded white leaf (body) together at eyes, then, with folds lined up, slide slit edges of red leaf (wings) under triangular flap, and down body, along green lines.

Autumn Table Runner and Accessories

These felt place card holders, napkin rings and table runner are easy to make, and kids will love helping you with this colourful fall craft.

YOU NEED:

Autumn Table Runner
- 0.25 m (9⅞ inches) felt in each of several fall colours
- 1 m (39⅜ inches) linen or linen-look fabric
- Embroidery floss to match felt
- All-purpose thread to match linen
- Straight pins
- Small, sharp scissors
- Tapestry needle
- Fabric shears or rotary cutter, acrylic ruler and cutting mat

Quick Place Card Holders
- Scraps of felt (each at least 7.5 cm/3 inches square) in fall colours
- Wooden clothespins (1 per place card holder)
- Straight or safety pins
- Small, sharp scissors
- Scrap paper or newspaper
- Heavy-duty white craft glue

Five-Minute Napkin Rings
- Pieces of felt, 7.5 x 25.5 cm/ 3 x 10 inches, in fall colours (1 per napkin ring)
- Straight or safety pins
- Small, sharp scissors

Notes:

- To make eight place card holders, eight napkin rings and the table runner, you need about 0.25 m (9⅞ inches) felt in each of several fall colours (such as red, orange, yellow, green and brown).

- Enlarge all patterns (pages 280 and 281) by squaring method as follows: On brown paper, draw grid of horizontal and vertical lines 2.5 cm (1 inch) apart. Each square on the pattern equals a square on brown paper. Enlarge pattern by redrawing each line onto corresponding square. Cut out pattern pieces.

Autumn Table Runner

TO MAKE:

1| Enlarge larger table runner pattern pieces (page 280) as directed in Notes, above. Cut out pattern pieces.

2| Centre pattern pieces on felt and secure with pins. With scissors, cut out felt around each pattern. Remove pins and pattern pieces. Repeat to make 16 beech leaves, 2 oak leaves and 2 maple leaves.

3| From linen, cut two 45.8 x 91.5 cm (18- x 36-inch) rectangles. Set 1 aside. Fold remaining rectangle in quarters and finger-press folds. Unfold; lay right side up on work surface. In each quadrant, arrange 4 beech leaves in arc (see photo, opposite). Place 1 maple leaf in centre at each short side of oval; place 1 oak leaf in centre at each long end of oval. Pin leaves in place.

4| With coordinating embroidery floss and using backstitch, stitch down centre of each leaf and through linen backing, securing stitching with knot on wrong side.

5| Place linen rectangles right sides together; align edges and pin together, leaving 15 cm (6 inches) unpinned in centre of 1 short end.

6| Stitch around rectangle, using 1.5 cm (⅝-inch) seam allowance, backstitching at beginning and end of stitching and leaving unpinned gap unsewn. Trim seams and threads, clip corners and turn right side out.

7| To finish, turn under edges of opening; pin closed. Beginning and ending at 1 corner, edgestitch around runner. Press (avoiding felt with iron) if desired.

Quick Place Card Holders

TO MAKE:

1| Enlarge smaller place card holder pattern pieces (page 280) as directed in Notes (page 187). Cut out pattern pieces.

2| Centre pattern pieces on felt and secure with pins. With scissors, cut out felt around each pattern. Remove pins and pattern pieces.

3| Repeat Step 2 to make 2 or 3 leaves per holder. Arrange leaves in desired pattern for each holder.

4| Lay scrap paper over work surface. Spread glue thinly and evenly on 1 flat side of 1 clothespin. Carefully press leaves onto glue, keeping bottom edges of felt flush with bottom edge of clothespin and adding small amount of extra glue where felt pieces overlap. Let dry completely.

Five-Minute Napkin Rings

TO MAKE:

1| Enlarge napkin ring pattern pieces (page 281) as directed in Notes (page 187). Cut out pattern pieces.

2| Centre pattern pieces on felt and secure with pins. With scissors, cut out felt around each pattern. Remove pins and pattern pieces.

3| Fold felt horizontally at centre and make 1.3 cm (½-inch) cut through fold, about 1.3 cm (½ inch) in from base of right-hand leaf to make 2.5 cm (1 inch) opening when unfolded. Repeat to make desired number of napkin rings.

4| To use, place napkin ring on flat surface with slit at right. Fold or roll napkin and place on top. Carefully push left-hand leaf through slit in felt.

Marilyn

Halloween Treat Buckets

Dole out sweets to little ghouls and goblins from this fun bucket.

**YOU NEED
(FOR EACH):**
- Twigs
- Artificial leaves
- Black spray paint
- Black and orange construction or tissue paper
- Bucket (such as ice cream container or plastic pail)
- Assorted decorations, such as trims, ribbon, pom-poms, lace or beads
- Black and/or orange pipe cleaners
- Scissors
- Craft glue

TO MAKE:
1| Working on protected surface, spray paint twigs and artificial leaves black. Let dry.

2| Cut construction or tissue paper to fit around bucket; glue in place. Cut out decorative shapes from contrasting colour. Glue twigs, leaves, shapes and assorted decorations onto bucket as desired.

3| Poke holes in opposite sides of bucket with scissors. Thread pipe cleaners through holes, twisting ends to join and secure handles.

Halloween Loot Bags

Personalized pillowcases mean there won't be any mix-ups when it comes time to stash the Halloween candy.

YOU NEED:
- Plain pillowcase
- Fabric scraps, felt or self-adhesive felt
- Pink grosgrain ribbon and yellow and green rope
- Assorted trims, such as lace, netting, cord or yarn
- Card stock, paper or thin cardboard
- Assorted stickers (optional)
- Stick-on decorations, such as glittered foam decorations, jewels or sequins (optional)
- Felt-tip markers or fabric paint
- Aluminum and gold foil
- Paper towel roll, grey paint and paintbrush
- Scissors, ruler, pencil and compass
- Needle, thread or embroidery floss, and pins
- Tacky glue or glue gun and clear tape

Notes:

- If the pillowcase is too long for your child, shorten it by moving the end seam. Have your child hold the pillowcase so you can determine the ideal length; mark with pin. On wrong side of pillowcase, using straight edge and fabric marker, mark new seam line; sew along marked line and trim, leaving 1.3 cm (½-inch) seam allowance and clipping corners. Or, adjust the length of the handles accordingly, attaching them with safety pins when trying out different lengths.

- If you like, use your child's costume to inspire the decorations on the trick-or-treat bag. Use different colours and whatever decorations you have on hand.

Princess Trick-or-Treat Bag

TO MAKE:

1| For decorative band: Measure width of pillowcase hem; double and add 1.3 cm (½ inch) for total width. Measure short side of pillowcase; double and add 2.5 cm (1 inch) for total length. Cut scrap of pink fabric, total width x total length. Fold under and press 6 mm (¼ inch) on all but 1 short edge; press in half lengthwise. Pin fabric strip around opening of pillowcase, with fold at outside edge and overlapping raw short edge of strip with folded short edge at 1 side seam. Edgestitch both layers of pink fabric to pillowcase. Cut length of pink grosgrain ribbon for handle (see Notes, left, for help determining length). Pin 1 end of ribbon at each side seam and sew to pillowcase, backstitching for added strength. Pin length of lace to bottom of pink fabric, overlapping by 6 mm (¼ inch), and stitch.

2| For crown: Draw crown as desired on card stock or paper (see photo, opposite) and cut out. Trace shape(s) onto wrong side of felt; carefully cut out. Position crown pieces on pillowcase as desired; lightly mark placement with pencil. Pin felt pieces to pillowcase and stitch by hand. Or, if using self-adhesive felt, remove paper backing and stick felt to pillowcase.

3| Decorate crown as desired, gluing or sewing assorted trim onto crown, or adding stickers and other stick-on decorations.

Pirate Trick-or-Treat Bag

TO MAKE:

1| For drawstring: From red felt, cut four 6.5 x 7.5 cm (2½- x 3-inch) rectangles. Measure and mark faint line 6.5 cm (2½ inches) from open end of pillowcase. Place 2 felt rectangles, evenly spaced (see photo, page 190) on pillowcase front and back, aligning top edge of each rectangle with pencil line. Pin felt to pillowcase; stitch across long ends of rectangles. Cut length of yellow rope for drawstring (see Notes, page 191, for help determining length) and feed through all 4 felt tubes; tie rope with overhand knot.

2| Draw skull-and-crossbones design on paper or card stock and cut out (see photo, page 190). Trace templates onto wrong side of felt (or pin securely) and cut out. Position skull-and-crossbones pieces on pillowcase as desired; lightly mark placement with pencil. Pin felt pieces to pillowcase and stitch by hand. Or, if using self-adhesive felt, remove paper backing and stick felt to pillowcase.

3| For gold coins: With pencil and compass, draw four 5 cm (2-inch) diameter circles on card stock or cardboard; cut out. Draw eight 5 cm (2-inch) circles on wrong side of gold foil; cut out. With glue, affix 1 gold circle to each side of the 4 cardboard coins. With heavy-duty needle, pierce hole in each coin. Cut two 30.5 cm (12-inch) pieces yarn; thread each through felt tube on front of pillowcase. Tie 1 coin onto each end of each piece of yarn.

Monster Trick-or-Treat Bag

TO MAKE:

1| For eyeball: On paper, using compass and pencil, draw 3 circle templates, one 16.5 cm (6½ inches) in diameter, one 6.5 cm (2½ inches) in diameter and one 3.5 cm (1⅜ inches) in diameter. Trace or pin circles onto wrong side of felt, using white felt for largest circle, orange felt for medium circle and black felt for small circle. Cut out circles and stack according to size, with largest circle on bottom. Pin felt pieces together and stitch by hand or using machine. Or, if using self-adhesive felt, remove paper backing and stick together. Outline white circle using black marker; draw veins in white part of eye using purple marker. Position eyeball on pillowcase; stitch on by hand or using machine. Or remove paper backing from self-adhesive felt and stick to pillowcase.

2| For netting and handle: Cut netting open to make flat sheet. Lay netting on top of pillowcase with long edge of netting parallel to open edge of pillowcase; tack down using needle and thread. Rip, tear and overlap netting as desired (see photo, page 190). Cut length of green rope and place around open edge of pillowcase; tack down using needle and thread at regular intervals to secure. Tie second length of green rope (see Notes, page 191, for help determining length) to other rope at edges of opening for handle.

3| For chain links: Paint paper towel roll grey inside and out; let dry. Cut into 2.5 cm (1-inch) rings; snip through each ring to make a "C." Link rings together; join cuts with clear tape to make 2 chains. Attach to green handle by looping 1 link at either end around handle.

Spooky Pencil Toppers

Who needs sweets when you have these treats for Halloween?

YOU NEED:

- Scraps of felt: black and pink for cat, black and bright green, for pumpkin and witch

- Strips of felt, each 30.5 x 3 cm (12 x 1⅛ inches): 1 black for cat, 2 orange for pumpkin and 1 pale green for witch

- 3 pencils

- 2 green pom-poms, each 5 mm in diameter, and 1 black pom-pom, 10 mm in diameter, for cat; and 2 yellow and 1 green pom-pom, all 5 mm in diameter, for witch

- Heavy-duty black thread, for cat

- 6 tiny googly eyes

- Embroidery floss: orange, for pumpkin, and lime green, for witch

- Fine-tip permanent red marker, for witch

- Pencil, scissors and ruler

- Low-temperature glue gun

TO MAKE:

1| Photocopy patterns (page 282) and cut out. Trace patterns onto felt scraps as indicated on pattern pieces; cut out and set aside.

2| Beginning at 1 end, wrap each felt strip around eraser end of 1 pencil just until it overlaps; squeeze line of glue just inside end and press felt layers together. Continue rolling strip, gluing in same manner approx every 2 cm (¾ inch), then glue down end (to make fat pumpkin, repeat to roll on second strip); pull roll off pencil.

3| Cat: With edges even, glue ears together in pairs; centre and glue inner ear onto front of each ear. Glue along bottom edge and stick on top of roll. Centred between ears, glue black pom-pom nose onto front of roll, one-third of the way up. From black thread, cut two 3.5 cm (1⅜-inch) lengths; at midpoints, tie together, then form X with ends. Glue knot to centre top of nose; glue nose tip over knot. Glue 1 googly eye to each of 2 green pom-poms, then glue on pom-poms above nose.

4| Pumpkin: From orange floss, cut three 20.5 cm (8-inch) lengths. One at a time, wrap each around roll from top, around bottom, back to top and tie tightly to shape lengthwise ridges. Tuck ends into hole; squeeze in dab of glue to secure. Fold stem along bold line; glue together, then dab straight end with glue and tuck into hole. Cut 6 mm (¼-inch) slit in centre of pumpkin top; slip over stem. Glue top to roll, then trim edge even with ridges. Glue felt eyes, nose and mouth onto pumpkin

front; glue googly eyes onto eyes.

5| Witch: Wind green floss 12 times around all fingers of 1 hand and slip off. With loops at either side, glue to top of roll, then cut loops for hair. Run line of glue along 1 straight edge of hat, overlap with other straight edge and press together to form cone; fold under 6 mm (¼ inch) around bottom edge, then centre and glue onto brim. From green felt, cut strip, 9 cm x 6 mm (3½ x ¼ inch), for hat band; glue in place. Glue green pom-pom nose onto front of roll, about one-third of the way up. Glue 1 googly eye to each yellow pom-pom, then glue on pom-poms above nose. With red marker, draw smile.

6| Slide pencil topper over eraser end of each pencil.

Bookmarks

These Halloween-themed bookmarks make a sweet
(but not sugary) treat.

YOU NEED:
- Scraps of medium-weight card stock in orange, black, white, yellow and green
- Fine-tip permanent black marker
- Pencil and scissors
- Low-temperature glue gun

TO MAKE:

1| Photocopy patterns (page 283) and cut out along solid lines. Trace pattern pieces onto card stock; cut out.

2| Using broken lines as guide: With marker, draw eyes and mouth on ghost. Glue eyes, nose and stem on pumpkin and eyes on bat; with marker, draw pupils in all the eyes, leaving tiny highlight at top of each.

seasonal

CANADIAN LIVING | CREATE. UPDATE. REMAKE

Homemade Gift Tags

Homemade gift tags give your presents added panache.

- Find vintage postcards and photos at flea markets; add glitter, decorative edges and ribbon ties.

- Dollar-store white gift tags (100 for $2), trimmed with a decorative punched edge and tied with various ribbons and bows, are fast, fun and inexpensive to make.

- Cut shapes from salvaged Christmas cards and trim with fancy edges using decorative hole punches or scissors; add glitter and pretty ties.

- Make paper snowflakes and glue them to plain gift tags for a multidimensional look.

- Wire together miniature orphaned ornaments and beads to add luxe to a simple gift tag. Recycle the tags next year.

- Photocopy family pictures (don't forget Fido) in black and white and glue them to scraps of construction paper for personalized gift tags.

Upcycled Glass Ornaments

A collection of contemporary and heirloom ornaments – suspended on jewelled ribbons and wires – simply sparkles.

YOU NEED:

- Narrow ribbon

- Glass, ceramic, crystal, plastic and metal beads (new or vintage), and clip-on metal letter tiles

- 28-gauge wire

- New or vintage Christmas tree ornaments

- Pliers with wire cutters and/or scissors

TO MAKE:

1| For ribbon hangers: Thread ribbon through beads, 1 at a time or in groups (or along entire length), knotting above and below each bead or group of beads to secure. Or clip on letter tiles to spell out a holiday message.

2| For beaded wire hangers: Thread wire through beads, 1 at a time or in groups, twisting above and below each bead or group of beads to secure.

3| For wire hangers with beaded branches (see photo, right): Using single length of wire (3 to 4 times desired finished length), thread wire through bead, then tightly twist wire ends together for 1 to 2.5 cm (⅜ to 1 inch); thread 1 wire end through second bead and twist wire ends together in same manner. Repeat to add desired number of beads on branch. At bottom of branch, separate wire ends, using top end to continue hanger and form remaining branches as desired.

4| To attach ornaments: Tie or twist top end of ribbon or wire to add hanging loop to finished hanger; thread bottom end of ribbon or wire through ornament loop, then tie or twist to secure. Trim ends.

Tips:

• Use faceted beads, such as cut crystal or glass, instead of smooth ones for more sparkle.

• If desired, make wire tendrils by twisting wire ends around skewer or pencil to shape.

seasonal

Simple Temari Ball

This pretty Japanese craft is simple but elegant as a Christmas ornament.

**YOU NEED
(FOR EACH):**

• 5 or 6.5 cm (2- or 2½-inch) diameter Styrofoam ball

• Small amount of red 3-ply yarn

• Spool (approx 200 m/ 220 yards) red thread

• White and metallic gold or silver embroidery floss

• Needle and multicolour glass-head pins

Notes:

- If desired, replace Styrofoam ball with crumpled paper or aluminum foil rolled into tight ball.

- Keep yarn, thread and floss taut as you wind around ball.

TO MAKE:

1| Overlapping yarn end to secure, wind yarn randomly around ball, continuously turning ball while you wind, to cover entire surface with several layers. With needle tip, poke loose end under strands to secure. In same manner, wind thread around ball to cover entire surface with several layers, concealing yarn and using entire spool of thread.

2| Push pin into ball to mark "North Pole"; push pin of second colour into opposite end, or "South Pole." Thread needle with 3 strands of gold floss; knot 1 end. Approx 2.5 cm (1 inch) from North Pole, push needle into ball, then out at North Pole. Pull through, easing knot into ball. Wind floss around ball in north-south direction 4 times, crossing at poles and dividing ball into 8 equal sections. To finish, push needle in at North Pole and out approx 2.5 cm (1 inch) away, then trim floss at surface.

3| Halfway down 1 line of longitude, push pin into ball. In same manner as for Step 2, push prepared needle through ball and out at pin; wind floss around ball to mark "equator." Continue, winding floss around "Northern Hemisphere" at 45-degree angle from equator, across equator at opposite side, then around "Southern Hemisphere" and back to starting point; repeat, winding floss in opposite direction around Southern Hemisphere at 45-degree angle from equator, across equator at opposite side, then around Northern Hemisphere and back to starting point. To finish, push needle in at starting point and out approx 2.5 cm (1 inch) away, then trim floss at surface. Remove pins.

4| Preparing needle, then starting and finishing as for Steps 2 and 3, proceed as follows: With 6 strands of white floss (or 12 strands for larger ball), embroider large snowflake, in 3 cm (1⅛-inch) diameters, over each pole, then over equator at 2 points where floss crosses at 45-degree angle, to make a total of 4 large snowflakes. With 6 strands of white floss, embroider small snowflake over intersection centred between large snowflakes on each side, to make a total of 2 small snowflakes. With 3 strands of silver floss (or 6 strands for larger ball), embellish each snowflake with stitches (see photo, opposite). With 6 strands of white floss, stitch crisscross over each remaining intersection of gold floss.

5| Thread needle with 40 cm (15¾-inch) length of 6 strands of gold or silver floss, then take small stitch under snowflake at North Pole and pull through until ends are even. Knot floss close to ball, then tie ends in overhand knot for hanging loop.

Origami Gift Box

This origami gift box makes perfect reusable packaging for small gifts – and looks smashing under the tree.

YOU NEED:

• Medium-weight wallpaper or other heavy paper

• Ruler and pencil

• Scissors or X-acto knife

• Bone folder or other thin, blunt tool

Note:

This makes a 10 x 10 x 4 cm (4- x 4- x 1⅝-inch) box, but it's easy to adjust the size to fit the present – just use different-size squares.

TO MAKE:

1| Using ruler and pencil, measure and mark 25 cm (9⅞–inch) square for box bottom and 18.5 cm (7¼-inch) square for box lid; with scissors, cut out.

2| Fold corners of each square toward centre, using bone folder to make precise creases.

3| Fold 1 side of box bottom 4 cm (1⅝ inches) toward centre; crease, then unfold. Repeat for other 3 sides. Repeat for lid, folding each side in 1.3 cm (½ inch). At each corner of bottom and lid, fold toward centre the diagonal crease that bisects small square created by previous folds.

4| Unfold 2 opposite sides of box bottom. Refold remaining 2 sides of square along creases so they stand upright and form 2 walls of box. Fold up third side, tucking diagonal corner folds inward against it. Wrap third side over corner folds; lay in place. Repeat for fourth side. Glue together at the centre. Repeat to make box lid.

Bejewelled Wreath

Cover a basic wreath form with a dazzling array of vintage jewelry and pile on the glamour for the holidays.

YOU NEED:

- 35.5 cm (14-inch) diameter Styrofoam wreath form
- Styrofoam food trays, cleaned and broken into small pieces
- Gold acrylic spray paint
- 1.5 to 2 m (60- to 79-inch) length 5 cm (2-inch) wide gold satin ribbon
- Assorted costume jewelry
- Faux pearls (optional)
- Low-temperature glue gun

A

TO MAKE:

1| Onto front of Styrofoam wreath, adhere small pieces of clean Styrofoam food trays with glue gun to form gently undulating surface. With gold paint, spray wreath all over to conceal Styrofoam, using multiple coats and letting dry after each coat.

2| Loop ribbon through wreath; with ends even, tie at top, then glue loop at back of wreath. Tie ends in bow to make hanging loop or simply shape as desired.

3| With wreath flat on work surface, glue costume jewelry – such as brooches, button earrings and pendants – all over wreath front. Glue faux pearls into crevices, if desired [A].

Hand-Knit Stockings

Candy cane–striped and stitched with stars, these hand-knit stockings
are bound to be treasured for a lifetime.

YOU NEED:

- 1 ball (100 g/205 m) each Patons Classic Wool, 100% wool, in white (A) and red (B), for striped stocking

- 2 balls (100 g/205 m each) Patons Classic Wool, 100% wool, in blue (A); and 1 ball (100 g/205 m) Patons Classic Wool, 100% wool, in gold (B), for starry stocking

- Set of four 4.5 mm double-pointed needles (DPN), or whichever needles you require to produce the tension given

- Stitch markers

- Tapestry needle

Note:

Standard abbreviations are used (see page 284).

SIZE:

Each finished stocking is approx 30.5 cm (12 inches) from cuff to heel, and is worked from top to toe.

TENSION:

20 sts and 26 rows = 10 cm (4 inches) in st st. Work to exact tension with specified yarn to obtain satisfactory results.

To save time, take time to check tension.

Striped Stocking

TO MAKE:

*With B, loosely cast on 60 sts, then divide evenly among 3 needles. Being careful not to twist, join in rnd, placing marker on first st.

Rnd 1 (WS of cuff): Purl.
Rnd 2: [P2, k1] to end of rnd.

Repeat Rnds 1 and 2 (to form garter ribbing) until work from beg measures 12.5 cm (5 inches), ending on Rnd 2; break B.*

Work even in rnds as follows:
With A, k 6 rnds.
With B, k 6 rnds.
With A, k 6 rnds.
With B, k 6 rnds.
With A, k 6 rnds.
With B, k 6 rnds.
With A, k 6 rnds.
With B, k 6 rnds.
With A, k 6 rnds.

.

**To make heel:
Slip last 15 sts from third needle and first 15 sts from first needle onto 1 needle for heel, placing marker at centre (leave rem 30 sts on 2 needles for instep); break A.

Turn so that WS is facing and rejoin B. With B, work back and forth across heel sts as follows:
Row 1 (WS):
Sl1, p to end of row.
Row 2: Sl1, k to end of row.

Repeat Rows 1 and 2 until heel from beg measures 5 cm (2 inches), ending with WS facing for next row.

To shape heel:
Row 1: P19, p2tog, p1, *turn* (leave rem sts unworked).
Row 2: Sl1, k9, sl1, k1, psso, k1, *turn.*
Row 3: Sl1p, p10, p2tog, p1, *turn.*
Row 4: Sl1, k11, sl1, k1, psso, k1, *turn.*
Row 5: Sl1p, p12, p2tog, p1, *turn.*
Row 6: Sl1, k13, sl1, k1, psso, k1, *turn.*
Row 7: Sl1p, p14, p2tog, p1, *turn.*
Row 8: Sl1, k15, sl1, k1, psso, *turn.*

Row 9: Sl1p, p16, p2tog, p1, *turn.*
Row 10: Sl1, k17, sl1, k1, psso, *turn.*
Row 11: Sl1p, p to end of row; break B. 20 sts now on needle.

With A and RS facing, pick up and k12 sts along left-hand side of heel; with second needle, k across 30 sts of instep; with third needle, pick up and k12 sts along right-hand side of heel. K first 10 sts of heel onto third needle, then slip rem 10 sts of heel onto beg of first needle. 74 sts now on needles: 22 sts on first needle, 30 sts on second needle and 22 sts on third needle.

Rnd 1:
Needle 1: K to last 3 sts, k2tog, k1.
Needle 2: Knit.
Needle 3: K1, sl1, k1, psso, k to end of needle.
Rnd 2: Knit.
Rnd 3: With B, as given for Rnd 1.
Rnd 4: With B, k.

Repeat Rnds 1 and 2 as follows: With B, work twice more; with A, work 3 times. 60 sts now on needles: 15 sts on first needle, 30 sts on second needle and 15 sts on third needle.**

Work even in rnds as follows: With B, k 6 rnds; with A, k 6 rnds; with B, k 6 rnds; with A, k 6 rnds; break A.

To shape toe:
***Rnd 1:
Needle 1: With B, k to last 3 sts, k2tog, k1.
Needle 2: K1, sl1, k1, psso, k to last 3 sts, k2tog, k1.
Needle 3: K1, sl1, k1, psso, k to end of needle.
56 sts now on needles.
Rnd 2: Knit.

Repeat Rnds 1 and 2 8 times more. 24 sts now on needles.

Next: K sts from first needle onto third needle.

Graft tog 2 sets of 12 sts each for toe; fasten off.

To finish:
Make hanging loop:
With B, cast on 20 sts, CO.

Fold cuff to RS, then sew loop securely to folded top edge at centre back. Weave in ends on WS of work. With desired yarn colour, backstitch [A] name on cuff. Block; do not press.***

Starry Stocking
TO MAKE:
With B, work from * to * as given for Striped Stocking.

With A, k even in rnds until work from beg of A measures 25.5 cm (10 inches).

With B, work from ** to ** as given for Striped Stocking.

With A, k even in rnds until work from pickup rnd at instep measures 15 cm (6 inches).

With B only, work from *** to *** as given for Striped Stocking. With B, embroider stars as desired.

A

Spirited Paper Ornaments

These simple paper ornaments make good use of last year's holiday greeting cards.

YOU NEED:
- Recycled greeting cards, scrapbooking paper or card stock
- Embroidery floss
- Beads, crystals and bells
- Pencil and scissors
- Glue
- Darning needle

TO MAKE:

1| Draw and cut out 2 copies of a simple holiday motif, each about 10 cm (4 inches) high, from cards.

2| Cut a 46 cm (18⅛-inch) length of floss; fold it over at the top to create a hanger, leaving 1 end longer as desired. Glue the 2 motifs together with floss in between, catching 1 end between pieces of card and leaving about 12.5 cm (5 inches) of floss extending from bottom.

3| Thread floss end through darning needle and string with beads, crystals, bells and bits of paper cut into small holiday shapes. Tie knot to secure.

Needle-Felted Festive Snow Folk

Once you get the hang of this fascinating technique, you'll be felting up an entire village of these cute, fuzzy creatures.

YOU NEED:

- Natural white pure wool roving (avoid very long or curly fibres), for bodies

- Small amounts of coloured pure silk or pure wool roving, and unravelled pure wool knitting or tapestry yarn (optional), for eyes, noses, buttons and clothing

- Natural white and coloured curly wool fleece (optional), for hair

- 40-gauge felting needle(s)

- Sharp embroidery scissors

- Felting mat (optional)

Notes:

• Needle felting, also called dry felting, is a method of sculpting loose unspun wool (called roving) using a barbed felting needle that locks, or felts, the fibres together. It's an inexpensive, portable craft, but be careful – the needles are too sharp for very young children to use.

• Since needles are brittle and may break, purchase several.

• Separate roving by gently pulling apart along fibres; do not cut.

• To make a three-dimensional shape, start by roughly forming roving into similar shape that's about 25 per cent larger than desired finished size.

• To felt roving and form shape, hold loose roving in your nonworking hand and, taking care not to prick that hand, repeatedly jab needle into roving, "woodpecker style," bending your needle hand at wrist.

• Use deep jabs to produce dense felting inside shape to firm and define form. Concentrate jabs over small areas to make concave shapes, or along lines to make narrow grooves.

• Use light, shallow jabs to add details by attaching fine strands or thin layers of contrasting colour fibres, or to smooth out lumps by attaching matching fibres.

• For triple-snowball body, start with 18 to 20.5 cm (7- to 8-inch) lengths of roving and follow Steps 1 through 3. About one-third of the way down from neck, form waist and add hips, if desired, in same manner as for shoulders. Follow Steps 4 through 6.

• Loosely shape coloured roving into small cones, cups or cylinders, then needle to form hats or top-hat crowns. Shape small discs for caps and hat brims.

• To create flat fabric, such as a tiny scarf, lay roving on a felting mat (which resembles an upside-down flat brush) or dense foam, then lay contrasting colour fibres on roving to create dots, stripes or plaid pattern, and needle to felt into fabric and attach details.

• To avoid skin pricks and nicks, work with patience and care.

TO MAKE:

1| Double-snowball body: Arrange enough 15 to 18 cm (6- to 7-inch) lengths of roving, side by side, to make bunch about 10 cm (4 inches) in diameter, then grasp centre, as if holding bunch of flowers, in nonworking hand. Working around protruding top ends, felt top together into loose dome; turn roving bunch, loose ends up, and repeat. Holding at 1 end, work from end to end along side, turning roving, to form loose sausage-shaped body.

2| Neck and shoulders: About one-quarter of the way down from top end (head), needle in line around body, turning as you work, to tighten felting and shape neck. If desired, wrap thin layer of matching roving around body just below neck, then needle all around to attach to body and form shoulders.

3| Head: Gently needle head all over, turning as you work, to shape firm sphere.

4| Lower body and base: Needle around side to shape firm lower body. From base, needle deeply into body, straight up, shrinking body to about 10 cm (4 inches) tall, then closely needle quarter-size spots centred on base, to flatten base so body stands upright.

5| Eyes and buttons: For each, needle midpoint of very few short black fibres to attach, then coil fibre ends into tiny knot around needle tip and jab in place.

6| Carrot nose (make 2 at a time, as follows): Between fingers, roll pea-size clump of loose roving into 3 cm (1⅛-inch) length, tapering ends. Needle lengthwise, then crosswise to firm up. Between fingers, reroll each end to firm up taper. At midpoint, cut in 2. With scissor tips, cut small slit in face. Insert cut nose end into slit, then needle through face into nose to attach.

7| Add hair, clothing and other details as desired.

Paper Luminaria

Wrap glass candleholders in paper pierced with festive patterns and illuminate the season.

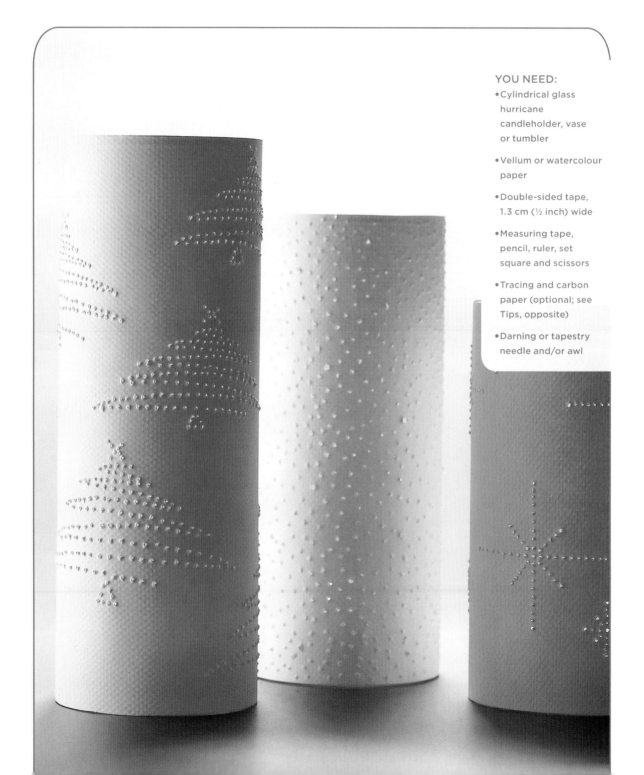

YOU NEED:

• Cylindrical glass hurricane candleholder, vase or tumbler

• Vellum or watercolour paper

• Double-sided tape, 1.3 cm (½ inch) wide

• Measuring tape, pencil, ruler, set square and scissors

• Tracing and carbon paper (optional; see Tips, opposite)

• Darning or tapestry needle and/or awl

TO MAKE:

1| With measuring tape, measure candleholder circumference, then add 2 cm (¾ inch) for total circumference; measure candleholder height, straight up from base to rim (or just below lip). On vellum with pencil, ruler and set square, mark rectangle, total circumference x height; cut out.

2| Working freehand with needle, pierce patterns of dots through vellum from wrong side, spacing dots 3 to 6 mm (⅛ to ¼ inch) apart.

3| Wrap vellum around candleholder, right side out. Apply double-sided tape to starting edge; overlap other edge 2 cm (¾ inch) and adhere.

Tips:

• To make handle for needle, push end with eye into wine-bottle cork.

• If you don't want to work freehand, lay tracing paper over desired motif – such as your own design, or a pattern from a magazine or colouring book – and trace the lines with a series of dots. Then, with carbon paper, transfer onto wrong side of vellum and pierce.

• For no-flame candlelight, use battery-operated LED votives and pillar candles, which produce a soft, flickering glow just like the real thing.

seasonal

gifts and food

pretty packages • candies • liqueurs • pet treats • cookies • teas

Cupcake Toppers

Top off your desserts with a touch of fun. Or turn these cute toppers into place markers or party favours.

gifts and food

YOU NEED:

• Craft foam in white, yellow, green, orange, black and/or pink

• Bamboo skewers

• Small googly eyes

• Pencil and ruler

• Pinking shears and scissors

• Craft glue

Yellow Daisy

TO MAKE:

1| With pencil, draw or trace 4 cm (1⅝-inch) diameter circle on white craft foam and 7.5 cm (3-inch) diameter circle on yellow craft foam. Using pinking shears, cut out white circle; using scissors, cut out yellow circle. With pencil and ruler, divide yellow circle into 8 wedges; round corners of wedges to form petals. Cut around and between petals, almost but not all the way into centre. Draw two 4 cm (1⅝-inch) long and two 5 cm (2-inch) long leaf shapes on green craft foam; cut out small shapes with pinking shears and large shapes with scissors.

2| Using thin layer of craft glue, adhere white circle to centre of yellow petals; glue leaves together (see photo, opposite). Spread craft glue on top 5 cm (2 inches) of bamboo skewer; adhere skewer to backs of flower and leaves. Let dry.

Yellow Ranunculus

TO MAKE:

1| With pencil, draw or trace one 2.5 cm (1-inch) diameter circle and two 5 cm (2-inch) diameter circles on yellow craft foam; draw or trace one 4.5 cm (1¾-inch) diameter circle on orange craft foam. Using pinking shears, cut out circles; set 1 large yellow circle aside.

2| Centre and stack circles together (see photo, opposite), adhering with thin layer of craft glue. Spread glue on wrong sides of large yellow circles, then adhere, sandwiching them around top 5 cm (2 inches) of bamboo skewer. Let dry.

gifts and food

Busy Bee

TO MAKE:

1| With pencil, draw 5 cm (2-inch) long oval on yellow craft foam, tapering one end slightly, for body. Draw 3.5 cm (1⅜-inch) high heart shape on white craft foam for wings. Draw three 6 mm (¼-inch) wide arcs on black craft foam for stripes. Using scissors, cut out; trim inner curve of heart for wing shape.

2| With craft glue, adhere stripes to body; trim if necessary. Adhere wings to wrong side of body. With dabs of glue, attach googly eyes (see photo, left). Spread craft glue on top 5 cm (2 inches) of bamboo skewer; adhere to back of bee. Let dry.

Pink Daisy

TO MAKE:

1| With pencil, draw or trace 2 cm (¾-inch) diameter circle on orange craft foam, 2.5 cm (1-inch) diameter circle on yellow craft foam and 7.5 cm (3-inch) diameter circle on pink craft foam. Using scissors, cut out orange and pink circles; using pinking shears, cut out yellow circle. With pencil and ruler, divide pink circle into 12 wedges; round corners of wedges to form petals. Cut around and between petals, almost but not all the way into centre.

2| Centre and stack foam circles together (see photo, opposite), adhering with thin layer of craft glue. Spread thin layer of craft glue on top 5 cm (2 inches) of bamboo skewer; adhere skewer to back of flower. Let dry.

Vanilla Cupcakes

Makes: 12 cupcakes

These treats are a beautiful backdrop to your colourful toppers.

2 cups (500 mL) sifted **cake-and-pastry flour**

1 cup (250 mL) **granulated sugar**

2 tsp (10 mL) **baking powder**

½ tsp (2 mL) **salt**

½ cup (125 mL) **butter,** softened

½ cup (125 mL) **milk**

2 **eggs**

1 tsp (5 mL) **vanilla**

In large bowl, whisk together flour, sugar, baking powder and salt. Using electric mixer on low speed, mix in butter, milk, eggs and vanilla; beat on high speed until smooth, about 2 minutes.

Spoon into 12 paper-lined or greased muffin cups, filling each about three-quarters full. Bake in 375°F (190°C) oven until cake tester inserted in centre comes out clean, about 18 minutes. Transfer to rack; let cool completely. (Store in airtight container for up to 1 day or freeze for up to 2 weeks.)

PER CUPCAKE: about 216 cal, 3 g pro, 9 g total fat (5 g sat. fat), 32 g carb, trace fibre, 56 mg chol, 233 mg sodium. % RDI: 4% calcium, 11% iron, 9% vit A, 11% folate.

MIX IT UP
Chocolate Cupcakes:

Reduce flour to 1 cup (250 mL) and baking powder to ½ tsp (2 mL). Add ½ cup (125 mL) cocoa powder and 1 tsp (5 mL) baking soda to dry ingredients. Sift before adding butter and wet ingredients.

Vanilla Buttercream Icing

Makes: about 3⅔ cups (900 mL), enough for 12 cupcakes

1 cup (250 mL) **butter,** softened

5 cups (1.25 L) sifted **icing sugar**

½ cup (125 mL) **whipping cream**

½ tsp (2 mL) **vanilla**

In large bowl, beat butter until light and fluffy. Alternately beat in sugar and cream, making 2 additions of sugar. Beat in vanilla. (Refrigerate in airtight container for up to 24 hours; let come to room temperature, about 1 hour. Beat lightly before using.)

PER 2 TBSP (30 mL): about 139 cal, trace pro, 8 g total fat (5 g sat. fat), 18 g carb, 0 g fibre, 25 mg chol, 66 mg sodium. % RDI: 7% vit A.

gifts and food

Dog Cookie Tins

Even Rover deserves homemade cookies. Package them in a handy tin – with a doggie ID tag – for the perfect dog lover's gift.

YOU NEED:

- Printer or fine-tip permanent marker
- Self-adhesive label small enough to fit on tag
- Blank dog ID tag
- S-hook
- Large lidded tin

Dog's Breath Biscuits

TO MAKE:

1| Using printer or marker, print dog's name on label. Embellish as desired.

2| Centre and press label onto dog ID tag.

3| Insert S-hook into hole in top of ID tag and hang from side of tin so that tag hangs out when lid is on.

4| Decorate top or side of tin as desired.

Tip:

A laser printer is the best choice for making the labels. Labels made with inkjet printers may bleed or smear when handled.

Dog's Breath Biscuits

Makes: about 12 biscuits

For a small dog, use a smaller cutter.

1 cup (250 mL) **rolled oats** (not instant)

¾ cup (175 mL) **cornmeal**

½ cup (125 mL) **whole wheat flour**

½ cup (125 mL) **all-purpose flour**

¼ cup (60 mL) packed **brown sugar**

2 tsp (10 mL) **baking powder**

½ tsp (2 mL) **salt**

¼ cup (60 mL) **butter,** softened

¼ cup (60 mL) **peanut butter**

2 **eggs**

¼ cup (60 mL) minced **fresh mint**

¼ cup (60 mL) minced **fresh parsley**

In bowl, whisk oats, cornmeal, whole wheat flour, all-purpose flour, brown sugar, baking powder and salt. In separate bowl, beat butter with peanut butter; beat in eggs, 1 at a time. Stir in flour mixture, mint and parsley to make soft dough. Divide in half; wrap and refrigerate until firm, about 1 hour or up to 2 days.

On floured surface, roll out dough to ½-inch (1 cm) thickness. Using 4-inch (10 cm) bone-shaped cookie cutter, cut out shapes.

Arrange on parchment paper–lined baking sheets; bake in 325°F (160°C) oven until golden and firm, 35 to 40 minutes. Transfer to racks; let cool.

Classic Canine Cookies

Makes: about 36 biscuits

This much-requested recipe, which first appeared in 1984, is still a hit.

1½ cups (375 mL) **whole wheat flour**

1 cup (250 mL) **all-purpose flour**

1 cup (250 mL) **skim milk powder**

⅓ cup (75 mL) melted **meat fat** (beef, lamb or bacon)

1 **egg,** lightly beaten

1 cup (250 mL) **cold water**

In bowl, whisk together whole wheat flour, all-purpose flour and skim milk powder; drizzle with fat. Add egg and water; mix well. Gather dough into ball.

On floured surface, roll out dough to ½-inch (1 cm) thickness. Using dog bone or other shape cookie cutter, cut out shapes.

Arrange on ungreased baking sheets; bake in 350°F (180°C) oven until dark brown and crisp, 40 to 50 minutes. Transfer to racks; let cool.

Birdseed Treats

These simple treats will bring songbirds galore to your backyard. Peanut butter and suet are both the sort of high-fat energy boosters that birds need in the winter.

YOU NEED:

Peanut Butter Pinecone

- Waxed paper
- Peanut butter
- Birdseed
- Pinecone, 12.5 cm (5 inches) long
- Twine

Suet Cakes

- Double boiler
- Suet
- Birdseed
- Other treats, such as raisins, peanut butter, nuts, seeds and/or crushed eggshells
- Muffin tin and paper muffin cup liners
- Skewer
- Twine

Peanut Butter Pinecone

gifts and food

CANADIAN LIVING | CREATE. UPDATE. REMAKE

Peanut Butter Pinecone
TO MAKE:

1| Lay 2 pieces of waxed paper on work surface. In centre of 1, spoon about 1 tbsp (15 mL) peanut butter; on the other, sprinkle about 3 tbsp (45 mL) birdseed.

2| Roll pinecone in peanut butter until coated; roll in birdseed. Spoon extra birdseed onto any remaining uncovered spaces.

3| Tie twine around stem end of cone; tie other end around tree branch just outside a window.

Suet Cakes
TO MAKE:

1| In top of double boiler, melt 2 cups (500 mL) suet. Stir in ¼ cup (60 mL) each birdseed and other treats.

2| Divide among 6 paper-lined muffin cups. Refrigerate until hard.

3| Remove from paper cups. Using skewer, poke hole through centre of each and thread twine through hole. Tie to secure around cake; tie other end around tree branch just outside a window. Freeze any leftover cakes to use later.

Spooky Cookie Tin

This tin is a fun way to bring sweets to share in the classroom or at a Halloween party. Pack it full of homemade Dancing Skeleton Cookies (recipe, page 227) for a spook-tacular treat.

YOU NEED:

• Black cookie tin

• 1 m (39⅜ inches) lightweight aluminum chain*

• Acrylic paint (orange, brown and/or rust, as desired)

• Old combination lock or padlock

• Foam paintbrush

• Black self-adhesive hook-and-loop tape

• Craft glue, hot glue gun

• Twigs

• Polyester batting, for spiderweb

• Flour (optional)

• Scary Pom-Pom Spider (page 226)

• Scissors and wire cutters

Available at home improvement stores

TO MAKE:

1| Measure top and sides of cookie tin and cut 2 pieces of chain long enough to stretch from bottom edge of 1 side, across top, to bottom edge of other side, allowing a little extra for overlap on top.

2| On newspaper-covered work surface, paint chains and lock with acrylic paint to make them look old and rusty, allowing time for paint to dry between colours; let dry completely.

3| Cut 4 pieces of hook-and-loop tape, each the length of 1 link in chain. Attach 1 piece of hook-and-loop tape to each end of painted chains, securing adhesive side of tape to chain link with dot of hot glue. When hot glue is dry, arrange chains, crisscrossed, on tin; adhere other halves of hook-and-loop tape to sides of tin.

4| Lock chains together on top of tin with painted combination lock.

5| Place twigs on top of tin as desired; stretch batting around twigs and chains to make spiderweb. If desired, dust decorated tin with flour (see photo, opposite).

6| Fasten Scary Pom-Pom Spider to top of tin using hot glue gun.

Tips:
• If you can't find a black cookie tin, make your own using an old cookie tin and two or three coats of black spray paint. Let dry completely before adding the decorations.

• To make your cookie tin even spookier, tangle plastic spiders, flies or worms in the spider web.

gifts and food

CANADIAN LIVING | CREATE, UPDATE, REMAKE

Scary Pom-Pom Spider

YOU NEED:
- Card stock
- Chunky yarn (black, brown or a combination)
- 4 dark brown pipe cleaners
- 2 beads (red, black or brown)
- Scrap white paper
- Compass and pencil
- Scissors
- Craft glue

TO MAKE:

1| Using compass and pencil, on card stock draw two 7.5 cm (3-inch) diameter circles; draw 1.3 cm (½-inch) diameter circle centred inside each. Cut out each outer circle, then each inner circle; cut 1 slit through each ring. From yarn, cut 1 pom-pom tie, 38 cm (15 inches) long. With edges even and slits aligned, hold circles together. Holding in other hand, and starting and ending at slit, wind yarn evenly and thickly counterclockwise around circle through centre hole, until hole is full.

2| Holding yarn firmly in place at centre, slip scissors between circles at outside edge and cut yarn all around; still holding firmly in centre, slip tie between circles and around yarn at centre, then tightly knot. Trim tie ends.

3| Gently push pipe cleaners through centre of pom-pom and bend to shape legs. Glue beads in place for eyes (see photo, opposite). On scrap white paper, draw 2 sets of fangs and cut out. Shade lightly with pencil if desired; glue in place.

Dancing Skeleton Cookies

Makes: about 32 cookies

¾ cup (175 mL) **butter,** softened
1 cup (250 mL) **granulated sugar**
1 **egg**
1 tsp (5 mL) **vanilla**
2¼ cups (550 mL) **all-purpose flour**
⅓ cup (75 mL) **cocoa powder**
½ tsp (2 mL) **baking powder**
¼ tsp (1 mL) **salt**

ICING:
2½ cups (625 mL) **icing sugar** (approx)
3 tbsp (45 mL) **milk**

In large bowl, beat butter with sugar until fluffy; beat in egg and vanilla. In separate bowl, whisk together flour, cocoa powder, baking powder and salt; stir into butter mixture in 2 additions to make smooth dough. Divide dough in half and flatten into discs; wrap each and refrigerate until firm, about 1 hour.

On lightly floured surface, roll out each disc to ¼-inch (5 mm) thickness. Using 3-inch (8 cm) gingerbread man cutter, cut out shapes, rerolling scraps. Place, 1 inch (2.5 cm) apart, on parchment paper–lined baking sheets. Freeze until firm, about 15 minutes, or refrigerate for 30 minutes.

Bake in 350°F (180°C) oven until firm to the touch and edges begin to darken, 18 to 22 minutes. Transfer to racks and let cool.

Icing: In bowl, mix icing sugar with milk, adding up to ¼ cup (60 mL) more sugar if needed to make smooth icing that holds its shape when piped. Cover with damp towel to prevent drying out.

Using piping bag fitted with small plain tip, pipe icing onto cookies to resemble skeletons. Let dry, about 1 hour. (Store in airtight container for up to 3 days.)

PER COOKIE: about 136 cal, 1 g pro, 5 g total fat (3 g sat. fat), 23 g carb, 1 g fibre, 17 mg chol, 56 mg sodium, 38 mg potassium. % RDI: 1% calcium, 4% iron, 4% vit A, 9% folate.

Herb and Spice Bundles

These fragrant little bundles make pretty hostess gifts, and are ready to steep in your favourite dishes or beverages.

YOU NEED:

Bundles

- Cheesecloth, reusable cloth tea bag or other clean, porous undyed cloth

- Mulling Spices or Bouquet Garni (recipes, page 231) or other herb or spice blend of your choice

- Embellishments, such as Dried Citrus Slices (page 230), cinnamon sticks and/or dried herb sprigs

- Scissors

- Kitchen string

Dried Citrus Slices (page 230)

- Lemons, limes, navel oranges or blood oranges

- Bodkin or small knitting needle

- Twine, raffia or ribbon

- Sharp knife

- Parchment paper and baking sheet

- Cooling rack

Bundles

TO MAKE:

1| Fold cheesecloth to make double thickness. Cut into 10 to 15 cm (4- to 6-inch) squares. Brush edges to remove any stray threads. Cut kitchen string to desired length.

2| Mound desired herb or spice mixture in centre of double-thickness cheesecloth square.

3| Bring edges of cloth up over spices, pinching together to form fairly tight bundle. Twist bundle slightly to ensure a good seal at the top.

4| Wrap string around bundle and tie tightly. Tie decoratively around embellishments. For Mulling Spices, embellish with cinnamon sticks and/or Dried Citrus Slices. For Bouquet Garni, use lavender or bay leaves.

Dried Citrus Slices

TO MAKE:

1| Using sharp knife, slice citrus fruit into 3 mm (⅛-inch) thick rounds. Bake on parchment paper–lined baking sheet in 200°F (100°C) oven for 1 hour, opening door to let steam escape every 15 minutes.

2| Turn slices over and bake until dried but not browned, 1 to 1½ hours, letting steam escape every 15 minutes. (Watch small slices toward end of baking and transfer to rack as they become dry.)

3| Transfer slices to rack; let stand until completely dry, at least 12 hours. The slices can stand for up to 3 weeks.

4| Using bodkin, pierce fruit. Thread twine through holes and affix to packages.

Tip:
Use extra slices as Christmas tree decorations, or add to potpourri.

Mulling Spices

Makes: enough for
4 bundles

Steep this fragrant mix in apple cider, wine or cranberry juice. Each bundle is enough for about 6 cups (1.5 L) of liquid.

8 slices (⅛ inch/3 mm thick) **gingerroot**
6 strips (1 inch/2.5 cm wide) each **orange rind** and **lemon rind**
¼ cup (60 mL) **whole cloves**
2 tbsp (30 mL) **whole allspice**
12 **cinnamon sticks** (3 inches/8 cm long), smashed

Arrange ginger, orange rind and lemon rind on rack; let stand until dry and brittle, about 24 hours. Break into ¼-inch (5 mm) pieces in bowl. Add cloves, allspice and cinnamon; stir to combine.

Bouquet Garni

Makes: enough for
8 bundles

This classic French herb combination is wonderful to simmer in soups and stews. It's especially nice made with dried herbs from your garden.

¼ cup (60 mL) **dried bay leaves**
¼ cup (60 mL) **dried parsley**
¼ cup (60 mL) **dried thyme**

Combine bay leaves, parsley and thyme.

Snowball Cake Pop
Centrepiece

Flowers are great, but who doesn't love decorations you can eat?

YOU NEED:

• Styrofoam block

• Craft glue or spray adhesive

• Fake snow or iridescent glitter

• Ribbon

• Snowball Cake Pops (recipe, opposite)

TO MAKE:

1| One side at a time, brush or spray Styrofoam block with glue. Press on fake snow, making sure all surfaces are covered evenly. Let dry.

2| Tie ribbon around sticks of Snowball Cake Pops as desired.

3| Insert bottoms of candy sticks into foam block decoratively. Place block on plate or tray to catch any stray snow or glitter.

Tip:
Look for long candy sticks at bulk food or candy-making supply stores.

Snowball Cake Pops

Makes: 36 pops

Chocolate coating wafers are designed to be melted and moulded. They coat thinly and are ideal for this recipe, especially in comparison to finicky white chocolate. Look for them, in a variety of colours, at bulk food stores.

½ cup (125 mL) **salted butter,** softened

¾ cup (175 mL) **granulated sugar**

2 **eggs**

½ tsp (2 mL) **vanilla**

1½ cups (375 mL) **all-purpose flour**

1½ tsp (7 mL) **baking powder**

½ tsp (2 mL) **baking soda**

Pinch **salt**

⅔ cup (150 mL) **milk**

⅓ cup (75 mL) **amber rum** or apple juice

1¾ cups (425 mL) **white chocolate coating wafers** (such as Merckens)

1 cup (250 mL) **sweetened flaked coconut**

In large bowl, beat butter with sugar until fluffy; beat in eggs, 1 at a time. Beat in vanilla.

Whisk together flour, baking powder, baking soda and salt; stir into butter mixture alternately with milk, making 3 additions of flour mixture and 2 of milk. Scrape into greased, parchment paper–lined 9-inch (2.5 L) square metal cake pan.

Bake in 350°F (180°C) oven until cake tester inserted in centre comes out clean, about 30 minutes. Let cool in pan on rack for 10 minutes. Turn out onto rack; peel off paper. Let cool. (Wrap in plastic wrap; overwrap in foil and freeze for up to 2 weeks.)

Trim darkened edges off cake. Crumble cake into food processor; drizzle with rum. Process until in fine crumbs; transfer to bowl.

Press by heaping 1 tbsp (15 mL) into balls; insert candy stick into each. Refrigerate on parchment paper–lined baking sheet until firm, about 30 minutes.

Meanwhile, in heatproof bowl over saucepan of hot (not boiling) water, melt chocolate wafers until smooth. Remove from heat.

Dip balls in chocolate, letting excess drip back into bowl; refrigerate until set, 30 minutes. Dip again; sprinkle all over with coconut. Refrigerate until firm, about 1 hour or up to 2 days. Serve at room temperature.

PER POP: about 128 cal, 2 g pro, 7 g total fat (4 g sat. fat), 15 g carb, trace fibre, 18 mg chol, 69 mg sodium, 51 mg potassium. % RDI: 3% calcium, 3% iron, 3% vit A, 6% folate.

Autumn Cookie Pop Centrepiece

Dress up your fall table with a centrepiece that's as tasty as it is cute.

YOU NEED:

- Assorted decorative gourds

- Container that fits gourds, such as small planter, mini-urn or small window box

- Metal skewer or awl

- Jack-o'-Lantern Cookie Pops (recipe, opposite)

- Ribbon (optional)

TO MAKE:

1| Arrange gourds in container, ensuring a snug fit to prevent them from shifting.

2| Using skewer, poke hole through gourd skin, 2.5 to 5 cm (1 to 2 inches) deep.

3| Insert Jack-o'-Lantern Cookie Pop stick into hole. Repeat as desired, arranging cookie pops decoratively in gourds.

4| Tie ribbon around container if desired.

Jack-o'-Lantern Cookie Pops

Makes: 30 pops

If jack-o'-lanterns aren't your style, you can cut this dough into just about any shape you like, to fit just about any occasion. You'll need thirty 6-inch (15 cm) candy sticks.

¾ cup (175 mL) **butter,** softened
1 cup (250 mL) **granulated sugar**
1 **egg**
1 tsp (5 mL) **vanilla**
2½ cups (625 mL) **all-purpose flour**
½ tsp (2 mL) **baking powder**
¼ tsp (1 mL) **cinnamon**
Pinch **salt**

ROYAL ICING PAINT:
2 tbsp (30 mL) **meringue powder**
2⅓ cups (575 mL) **icing sugar**
Paste food colouring
Candies or other decorations

In large bowl, beat butter with sugar until fluffy; beat in egg and vanilla. Whisk together flour, baking powder, cinnamon and salt; stir into butter mixture in 2 additions. Divide in half and flatten into discs; wrap each and refrigerate until firm, about 1 hour or up to 24 hours.

Scoop dough from 1 disc by 1 tsp (5 mL) to make 30 pieces; roll into balls. Set aside.

On lightly floured surface, roll out remaining dough to scant ¼-inch (5 mm) thickness. Using 3-inch (8 cm) pumpkin or jack-o'-lantern cookie cutter, cut out shapes, rerolling scraps.

Place 6 balls, 4 inches (10 cm) apart, on parchment paper–lined rimless baking sheets. Press into ¼-inch (5 mm) thick discs. Press lollipop stick onto each disc. Top with cutout, pressing lightly to adhere and sandwich stick. Repeat with remaining balls and cutouts.

Bake in top and bottom thirds of 350°F (180°C) oven, switching and rotating pans halfway through, until light golden on bottoms and edges, about 12 minutes. Transfer to racks; let cool completely. (Store in airtight container for up to 1 week or freeze for up to 1 month.)

Royal Icing Paint: In bowl, beat meringue powder with ¼ cup (60 mL) water until foamy, about 2 minutes. Gradually beat in icing sugar until stiff, about 9 minutes. Tint with food colouring as desired.

Spread heaping 1 tsp (5 mL) icing over top of cookie; decorate with candies. Let dry.

PER POP (WITHOUT CANDIES): about 107 cal, 1 g pro, 5 g total fat (3 g sat. fat), 15 g carb, trace fibre, 18 mg chol, 40 mg sodium. % RDI: 1% calcium, 4% iron, 4% vit A, 10% folate.

Lined Gift Boxes with Dividers

Craft store gift boxes are easy to customize. These, with pretty cardboard dividers, are perfect to hold sweet or savoury food gifts.

Fruitcake Bites with Marzipan, page 238

YOU NEED:

- Medium or large cardboard candy or pastry box*

- Kraft paper, parchment paper or waxed paper

- Card stock or light cardboard

- Ruler and pencil

- Scissors or X-acto knife and specialty scrapbooking scissors or pinking shears (optional)

- Self-healing cutting mat (optional)

Available at bulk food stores or bakeries

gifts and food

CANADIAN LIVING | CREATE. UPDATE. REMAKE

TO MAKE:

1| For paper liners: Measure height and width of candy box to determine length of paper. Add height to width and multiply by 2; add 2.5 cm (1 inch) for overlap.

2| Measure length of box to determine width of paper.

3| Using ruler and pencil, mark rectangle, using determined length and width, on paper. Using desired scissors, cut just within pencil line.

4| Centre box on paper. Fold paper up and around box, creasing lightly at folds.

5| Place paper inside box, adjusting creases as necessary to fit snugly.

6| For dividers: Measure inner height, width and length of box. On card stock, draw 2 rectangles, 1 with height and length, the other with height and width. Cut out rectangles, rounding corners if desired. Fit, 1 at a time, into box; trim if necessary.

7| Using same rectangles as templates, trace required number onto wrong side of card stock and cut out. (For example, to divide into 4 compartments, you'll need 1 divider for length and 1 for width; for 6 compartments, you'll need 1 for length and 2 for width.)

8| Using ruler and pencil, make mark(s) at top edge of long piece(s) as follows: in centre for 4-compartment box; at desired intervals for a box with 6 or more compartments. Draw line(s) two-thirds of the way to bottom edge. With scissors or X-acto knife, cut along line(s).

9| Repeat with wide piece(s) of card stock, making marks at bottom edge and drawing line(s) two-thirds of the way to top. With scissors or X-acto knife, cut along line(s).

10| Matching slots, slide pieces together to join. Tap lightly on flat surface to make flush. Fit into box.

gifts and food

Fruitcake Bites with Marzipan

Makes: 36 pieces

These adorable individual fruitcakes make perfect gifts. Dust the cookie cutter with icing sugar to prevent the marzipan from sticking.

½ cup (125 mL) **golden raisins**

½ cup (125 mL) **sultana raisins**

½ cup (125 mL) **candied citrus peel**

½ cup (125 mL) **brandy**

¼ cup (60 mL) **dried currants**

½ cup (125 mL) each chopped **walnuts** and chopped **pecans**

1 cup (250 mL) **all-purpose flour**

½ tsp (2 mL) **baking powder**

¼ tsp (1 mL) each **cinnamon** and **ground allspice**

¼ tsp (1 mL) **salt**

Pinch each **nutmeg** and **ground cloves**

½ cup (125 mL) **unsalted butter,** softened

½ cup (125 mL) packed **brown sugar**

2 **eggs**

½ tsp (2 mL) **vanilla**

TOPPING:

¼ cup (60 mL) **brandy**

Icing sugar

1 pkg (200 g) **marzipan**

36 **silver dragées** or coloured dragées

In large bowl, combine golden raisins, sultana raisins, citrus peel, ¼ cup (60 mL) of the brandy and currants; toss well. Cover and let stand for 4 hours, stirring occasionally. Add walnuts and pecans.

Whisk together flour, baking powder, cinnamon, allspice, salt, nutmeg and cloves; remove ½ cup (125 mL) and toss with fruit mixture.

In large bowl, beat butter with sugar until fluffy. Beat in eggs, 1 at a time. Beat in vanilla. Stir in remaining flour mixture just until incorporated. Stir in fruit mixture until combined. Scrape into parchment paper–lined 9-inch (2.5 L) square metal cake pan, smoothing top.

Bake in 250°F (120°C) oven until cake tester inserted in centre comes out clean, about 2 hours. Let cool in pan on rack.

Remove cake from pan; peel off paper. Soak double-thickness cheesecloth in remaining brandy; wrap around cake. Wrap in plastic wrap then foil; refrigerate for 1 week or up to 1 month.

Topping: Unwrap cake; brush with brandy. On icing sugar–dusted surface, roll out half of the marzipan into 9-inch (23 cm) square; drape over fruitcake. Cut into 36 squares.

Roll out remaining marzipan; using small snowflake cookie cutter, cut out 36 snowflakes. Lightly brush tops of squares with water; place snowflake on each. Press dragée into centre of each.

PER PIECE: about 126 cal, 2 g pro, 7 g total fat (2 g sat. fat), 15 g carb, 1 g fibre, 17 mg chol, 27 mg sodium, 94 mg potassium. % RDI: 2% calcium, 4% iron, 3% vit A, 5% folate.

Walnut and Rosemary Crackers

Makes: 72 pieces

These crackers are delicious with a blue cheese spread or any fine artisanal cheese.

¾ cup (175 mL) **walnut pieces**
½ cup (125 mL) **large-flake rolled oats**
1½ cups (375 mL) **all-purpose flour**
1 tbsp (15 mL) finely chopped **fresh rosemary**
1 tsp (5 mL) **salt**
⅓ cup (75 mL) cold **salted butter,** cubed
1 **egg white,** lightly beaten

In food processor, finely chop walnuts with rolled oats. Add flour, rosemary and salt; pulse to combine. Pulse in butter until in coarse crumbs. Add ⅓ cup (75 mL) cold water; pulse until dough starts to come together into ball.

Turn out onto lightly floured surface and press together. Divide in half; knead each until smooth, about 2 minutes. Form each into square; cover and let rest for 20 minutes.

On lightly floured surface, roll out each into 10-inch (25 cm) square; trim edges. Cut each into 6 strips; cut crosswise into 6 rows. Transfer to greased baking sheets. Prick each piece 3 times with fork; brush lightly with egg white.

Bake in 400°F (200°C) oven until golden, 12 to 14 minutes. Transfer to racks and let cool. (To store, seal in airtight container for up to 1 week.)

PER PIECE: about 28 cal, 1 g pro, 2 g total fat (1 g sat. fat), 3 g carb, trace fibre, 2 mg chol, 39 mg sodium. % RDI: 1% iron, 1% vit A, 3% folate.

Dressed Up Coffee Cans

Novel packaging guarantees success at any bake sale. These cans are easy to make from household supplies.

YOU NEED:
- Clean coffee cans or other cans with lids
- Decorative paper or fabric scraps
- Twine, ribbon or other decorations
- Cellophane (optional)
- Pencil, ruler, compass and scissors
- Glue stick

Fruity Hermits, page 255

gifts and food

240

TO MAKE:

1| Wash cans well in hot soapy water. Remove any labels. Dry well.

2| Measure height and circumference of can; add 2.5 cm (1 inch) to circumference for total width. Using pencil and ruler, mark rectangle, height x total width, on paper; cut out. With glue stick, secure to can.

3| Adorn can with twine, or other decorations as desired.

4| Mark and cut out paper to cover lid of can. If you can't find cans with lids, wrap treat-filled cans in cellophane and tie with ribbon.

Mustard-Spiced Nuts

Makes: 4 cups (1 L)

This quick mix is not only irresistible but also easy to make. Use other combinations of nuts if you prefer.

1 cup (250 mL) **walnut halves**

1 cup (250 mL) **whole unblanched almonds**

1 cup (250 mL) **raw cashews**

1 cup (250 mL) shelled **pistachios**

1 tbsp (15 mL) **extra-virgin olive oil**

1 tbsp (15 mL) **Dijon mustard**

2 tbsp (30 mL) packed **brown sugar**

1 tbsp (15 mL) **dry mustard**

1½ tsp (7 mL) **ground coriander**

1 tsp (5 mL) **salt**

½ tsp (2 mL) **cayenne pepper**

¼ tsp (1 mL) **black pepper**

In bowl, combine walnuts, almonds, cashews, pistachios, oil and Dijon mustard; toss to coat. Combine sugar, dry mustard, coriander, salt, cayenne and black pepper; toss with nuts to coat.

Bake on parchment paper–lined baking sheet in 300°F (150°C) oven, stirring once, until fragrant and lightly toasted, about 20 minutes. (Seal in airtight container for up to 1 week.)

PER 2 TBSP (30 mL): about 101 cal, 3 g pro, 8 g total fat (1 g sat. fat), 5 g carb, 1 g fibre, 0 mg chol, 79 mg sodium, 120 mg potassium. % RDI: 2% calcium, 6% iron, 4% folate.

Luscious Liqueurs

Give someone the gift of homemade liqueur in a pretty bottle. Attach a recipe for a tasty cocktail and get ready to celebrate!

**From left:
Cran-Raspberry
Cordial, Limoncello
and Irish Cream
Liqueur, pages
244 to 245**

**LIMONCELLO
CREAM COCKTAIL**

2 oz   Limoncello   60 g
1 tbsp whipping cream 15 mL

*Fill cocktail shaker with ice.
Add limoncello and cream;
shake vigorously to blend and
chill. Strain into sherry gla...
Makes 1 serving.

YOU NEED:

• New or vintage
  bottles with stoppers

• Small-mouth funnel

• Cran-Raspberry
  Cordial or Limoncello
  (recipes, page 244),
  or Irish Cream
  Liqueur (recipe,
  page 245)

• Decorative or kraft
  paper, card stock
  and/or self-adhesive
  labels

• Regular or
  decorative
  scrapbooking
  scissors, or pinking
  shears

• Embellishments,
  such as Dried Citrus
  Slices (page 230) or
  small charms

• Ribbon or cord

• Hole punch

• Craft glue

gifts and food

242

TO MAKE:

1| Wash bottles well with hot soapy water. Let dry completely, upside down if necessary to prevent condensation from building up inside.

2| Using funnel, pour in liqueur. Wipe rim clean. Seal with stopper.

3| For Cran-Raspberry Cordial, print or write cocktail recipe on paper; cut to tag size. Cut piece of decorative paper or card stock slightly larger than cocktail recipe, leaving enough room to punch hole in corner. Glue recipe to card stock and punch hole in corner. Glue on charm if desired. Let dry. Thread ribbon through hole and tie around neck of bottle.

4| For Limoncello, print or write cocktail recipe on self-adhesive label. Using scrapbooking scissors or pinking shears, trim label to make decorative edge. Peel off backing and adhere to bottle. Thread ribbon or cord through Dried Citrus Slice; wrap decoratively around bottle and tie.

5| For Irish Cream Liqueur, cut kraft paper into wide rectangle. Using pinking shears, trim long sides to make decorative edges. Fold paper lengthwise so that 1 decorative edge comes almost to centre. Wrap paper around bottle; overlapping ends, glue at back of bottle. Print or write cocktail recipe on separate paper; roll into tiny scroll. Roll another smaller piece of decorative paper around scroll. Tie ribbon around bottle, securing scroll.

Cran-Raspberry Cordial

Makes: about
6 cups (1.5 L)

Tart, sweet and brimming with fruity flavour, this infused vodka looks beautiful mixed into cocktails.

2 cups (500 mL) each
    frozen **cranberries**
    and frozen **raspberries**
2 cups (500 mL)
    granulated sugar
1 bottle (750 mL) **vodka**

In food processor, coarsely chop together cranberries, raspberries and sugar; transfer to 8-cup (2 L) airtight jar.

Pour in vodka; seal and shake. Refrigerate for 2 weeks, shaking often.

Strain through double-thickness cheesecloth into large measuring cup, squeezing and twisting to extract juice. Pour into bottles and seal. (Store in cool, dark place for up to 1 year.)

PER 1 OZ (30 ML): about 70 cal, 0 g pro, 0 g total fat (0 g sat. fat), 9 g carb, 0 g fibre, 0 mg chol, 0 mg sodium. % RDI: 3% vit C.

Cran-Raspberry Sipper

Makes: 1 serving

1½ oz (45 mL)
    Cran-Raspberry Cordial (recipe, left)
1 tbsp (15 mL) **lime juice**
⅓ cup (75 mL) chilled
    soda water
Lime slice

Fill old-fashioned glass with ice. Add cordial and lime juice. Top with soda water; stir just to blend. Garnish with lime.

PER SERVING: about 108 cal, trace pro, trace total fat (0 g sat. fat), 15 g carb, 0 g fibre, 0 mg chol, 18 mg sodium, 36 mg potassium. % RDI: 1% calcium, 1% iron, 12% vit C, 2% folate.

Limoncello

Makes: about
6 cups (1.5 L)

Lemon, or *limone* in Italian, provides the refreshing, sweet kick in this simple liqueur. If possible, use organic lemons.

8 **lemons**
1 bottle (750 mL) **vodka**
2½ cups (625 mL) **water**
2 cups (500 mL)
    granulated sugar

Scrub lemons in hot soapy water; rinse well and dry. With vegetable peeler or zester, peel off rind, avoiding white pith. Place rind in 4-cup (1 L) airtight jar; pour in vodka. Seal and let steep in cool, dark place for 5 days.

In small saucepan, bring water and sugar to boil; boil gently for 15 minutes. Let cool to room temperature.

In large measuring cup, stir vodka mixture with sugar mixture; strain through coffee filter–lined or cheesecloth-lined funnel into bottles, discarding rind. Seal. (Store in cool, dark place for up to 1 year.)

PER 1 OZ (30 ML): about 33 cal, 0 g pro, 0 g total fat (0 g sat. fat), 4 g carb, 0 g fibre, 0 mg chol, 0 mg sodium.

gifts and food

CANADIAN LIVING | CREATE. UPDATE. REMAKE

Limoncello Cream Cocktail

Makes: 1 serving

2 oz (60 mL)
  Limoncello (recipe, opposite)
1 tbsp (15 mL)
  whipping cream

Fill cocktail shaker with ice. Add Limoncello and cream; shake vigorously to blend and chill. Strain into sherry glass.

PER SERVING: about 181 cal, trace pro, 5 g total fat (3 g sat. fat), 17 g carb, 0 g fibre, 19 mg chol, 7 mg sodium, 13 mg potassium. % RDI: 1% calcium, 6% vit A.

Irish Cream Liqueur

Makes: about 5½ cups (1.375 L)

This easy-to-make liqueur has a glorious, silky texture. It's delicious on its own, as a cocktail base or in coffee or Irish Mint Hot Chocolate (recipe, right).

2 cups (500 mL)
  whipping cream
2 cups (500 mL) **Irish whiskey**
1 can (300 mL)
  sweetened condensed milk
1 tbsp (15 mL) **instant coffee granules**
1 tbsp (15 mL)
  chocolate syrup
1 tsp (5 mL) **vanilla**
⅛ tsp (0.5 mL) **almond extract**

Using whisk or in blender, blend together cream, whiskey, condensed milk, coffee granules, chocolate syrup, vanilla and almond extract until coffee dissolves. Pour into bottles. Seal. (Refrigerate for up to 2 weeks.)

PER 1 OZ (30 ML): about 89 cal, 1 g pro, 5 g total fat (3 g sat. fat), 6 g carb, 0 g fibre, 17 mg chol, 17 mg sodium, 48 mg potassium. % RDI: 3% calcium, 5% vit A.

Irish Mint Hot Chocolate

Makes: 1 serving

1 oz (30 mL) **Irish Cream Liqueur** (recipe, left)
½ oz (15 mL) **white crème de menthe**
¾ cup (175 mL)
  hot chocolate
Whipped cream
  (optional)
Dark chocolate shavings

In mug, stir liqueur with crème de menthe; stir in hot chocolate. Top with whipped cream (if using). Sprinkle with chocolate.

PER SERVING: about 382 cal, 7 g pro, 16 g total fat (10 g sat. fat), 40 g carb, 2 g fibre, 29 mg chol, 75 mg sodium, 360 mg potassium. % RDI: 19% calcium, 7% iron, 11% vit A, 6% folate.

Recycled Jar Schnapps

Rustic and always useful, canning jars are a bargain at thrift stores and yard sales (who doesn't have a few lying around?). Fill them with a batch of luscious, fruity schnapps to give away to friends and family.

YOU NEED:

• New or vintage canning jars (large for steeping and smaller ones to give as gifts)

• Lids and screw bands (use new to prevent smells and flavours from transferring)

• Small-mouth funnel

• Cheesecloth

• Cranberry Almond Schnapps or Pineapple Lime Schnapps (recipes, opposite)

• Decorative tags, paper, card stock or self-adhesive labels

• Ribbon, twine or raffia

• Glue (optional)

• Hole punch

Cranberry Almond Schnapps and Pineapple Lime Schnapps

Cranberry Almond SCHNAPPS

Pineapple Lime SCHNAPPS

TO MAKE:
1| Wash jars and lids in hot soapy water and dry well.

2| Using funnel and cheesecloth, strain any remaining solids from schnapps. Pour into small jars. Screw on lids and bands.

3| Print or write name of schnapps on decorative tags. Glue or press onto jars.

4| Print or write accompanying cocktail recipe on decorative paper or tags. Punch hole in corner and thread ribbon through hole. Tie decoratively around jar.

Cranberry Almond Schnapps

Makes: 3 cups (750 mL)

Enjoy this tipple on its own or in a Festive Cosmo (recipe, right).

¼ cup (60 mL) **blanched almonds**
1 pkg (300 g) **fresh cranberries** or thawed cranberries
⅓ cup (75 mL) **granulated sugar**
¼ cup (60 mL) chopped **crystallized ginger**
4 thin strips **orange rind,** white pith removed
1 bottle (750 mL) **vodka**

Toast almonds in 350°F (180°C) oven until fragrant, 7 to 8 minutes. In saucepan over medium-low heat, bring cranberries, sugar, nuts, ginger, orange rind and ¼ cup (60 mL) water to boil. Boil, stirring, until sugar dissolves and cranberries pop, 5 minutes. Let cool to room temperature. Stir in vodka. Seal in large jar; steep in cool, dark place for 2 weeks, shaking jar occasionally.

Strain through cheesecloth-lined sieve, pressing out all liquid. Seal in jar or bottle. (Refrigerate for up to 3 months.)

PER 1 OZ (30 mL): about 83 cal, 0 g pro, 0 g total fat (0 g sat. fat), 4 g carb, 0 g fibre, 0 mg chol, 1 mg sodium. % RDI: 2% vit C.

Festive Cosmo

Makes: 1 serving

Fill cocktail shaker with ice. Add 1½ oz (45 mL) Cranberry Almond Schnapps (recipe, left) and ½ oz (15 mL) orange-flavoured liqueur; shake to blend and chill. Strain into martini glass.

Pineapple Lime Schnapps

Makes: 3 cups (750 mL)

You can keep some of this in the freezer for a chilly shot of schnapps at any time. Or use as a base for a Pineapple Mimosa (recipe, right).

1 **pineapple**
Juice of 1 **lime**
1 tbsp (15 mL) **granulated sugar**
1 bottle (750 mL) **vodka**

Peel, core and cut pineapple into 1-inch (2.5 cm) cubes. In large jar, combine pineapple, lime juice and sugar. Seal and refrigerate for 2 hours. Stir in vodka; seal and steep in cool, dark place for 2 weeks, shaking jar occasionally.

Using sieve lined with double-thickness cheesecloth, strain into pitcher, pressing out all liquid. Seal schnapps in jar or bottle. (Refrigerate for up to 3 months.)

PER 1 OZ (30 mL): about 79 cal, trace pro, 0 g total fat (0 g sat. fat), 3 g carb, 0 g fibre, 0 mg chol, 1 mg sodium. % RDI: 1% iron, 13% vit C, 1% folate.

Pineapple Mimosa

Makes: 1 serving

Pour 1½ oz (45 mL) Pineapple Lime Schnapps (recipe, left) into champagne flute; top with 5 oz (150 mL) chilled sparkling wine, cava or Prosecco. Strain into martini glass.

Sturdy Cello Gift Bags

Clear cellophane bags are a great way to give small edible gifts. Why not dress them up and make them sturdier with pretty ribbon and paper?

gifts and food

CANADIAN LIVING | CREATE, UPDATE, REMAKE

YOU NEED:

• Clear food-grade cellophane bags

• Card stock (preferably patterned on 1 side) or scrapbooking paper

• Candy or treats

• Ribbon

• Pencil and ruler

• Scissors and hole punch

Maple Fudge Walnuts and Chocolate Chili Nuts

TO MAKE:

1| Measure width and height of bag; open bag and measure depth of bottom.

2| On card stock, draw rectangle with short sides slightly smaller than width of bag and long sides equal to height plus depth of bottom. Cut out.

3| Place rectangle on work surface, patterned side up if applicable. Fold bottom up 2.5 cm (1 inch), making sharp crease. Unfold. Measure up from fold to depth of bag bottom; fold up to this mark, making sharp crease. Unfold.

4| Insert card stock into bag, pressing to make flat bottom between creases.

5| Fill with candy or treats. Fold bag top down and toward back. Punch 2 holes through all layers of bag and card stock, about 5 cm (2 inches) apart and 2.5 cm (1 inch) down from fold at top of bag.

6| Thread ribbon through holes and tie bow in front.

Maple Fudge Walnuts

Makes: 4 cups (1 L)

You'll want to make several batches of these because they disappear much too quickly.

4 cups (1 L) **walnut halves,** broken
1 cup (250 mL) packed **brown sugar**
½ cup (125 mL) **whipping cream**
¼ cup (60 mL) **maple syrup**
1 tbsp (15 mL) **butter**
½ tsp (2 mL) **salt**
½ tsp (2 mL) **maple extract**

On baking sheet, toast nuts in 350°F (180°C) oven until fragrant and light golden, 12 to 15 minutes; transfer to large bowl.

Meanwhile, in saucepan, bring sugar, cream and maple syrup to boil; boil until reduced to 1¼ cups (300 mL), about 8 minutes. Stir in butter until melted. Stir in salt and maple extract.

Pour over walnuts; toss to coat. Spread on greased foil-lined tray. Let cool. Break into pieces. (Store in airtight container for up to 5 days.)

PER 2 TBSP (30 ML): about 130 cal, 2 g pro, 10 g total fat (2 g sat. fat), 10 g carb, 1 g fibre, 6 mg chol, 43 mg sodium. % RDI: 2% calcium, 4% iron, 2% vit A, 5% folate.

Chocolate Chili Nuts

Makes: 4 cups (1 L)

Chili and chocolate are a vibrant Mexican flavour combo – and the perfect partners to rich mixed nuts.

4 cups (1 L) **unsalted mixed nuts**
⅔ cup (150 mL) **icing sugar**
¼ cup (60 mL) **cocoa powder**
2 tsp (10 mL) **chipotle chili powder**
1 tsp (5 mL) **salt**
½ tsp (2 mL) **cinnamon**
Pinch **cayenne pepper**
1 **egg white**
3 tbsp (45 mL) **vegetable oil**

On baking sheet, toast nuts in 350°F (180°C) oven until fragrant, 7 to 8 minutes.

Meanwhile, in bowl, whisk together sugar, cocoa powder, chili powder, salt, cinnamon and cayenne; stir in egg white and oil. Add hot nuts; toss to combine.

Spread on foil-lined baking sheet; roast in 350°F (180°C) oven for 5 minutes. Let cool on pan on rack. Break into pieces. (Store in airtight container for up to 2 weeks.)

PER 1 TBSP (15 ML): about 66 cal, 2 g pro, 6 g total fat (1 g sat. fat), 3 g carb, 1 g fibre, 0 mg chol, 38 mg sodium. % RDI: 1% calcium, 3% iron, 4% folate.

Vintage Cups Gift Box

Flea-market finds make delicate dividers in a gift box
filled with homemade candies.

YOU NEED:

• Vintage silver, glass or ceramic cups

• Large round cookie tin

• Linen or other fabric napkin

• Nonslip drawer liner

• Bittersweet Amaretti Bark, Two-Tone Peppermint Bark, Whisky Walnut Fudge and/or Chocolate Caramel Bites (recipes, pages 251 to 253)

• Ribbon

• Cellophane (optional)

• Scissors

Clockwise from top left: Bittersweet
Amaretti Bark, Two-Tone Peppermint Bark,
Whisky Walnut Fudge and Chocolate
Caramel Bites, pages 251 to 253

TO MAKE:

1| Wash cups in warm, soapy water and dry well. Polish silver-plated cups if desired.

2| Line cookie tin with napkin. Cut nonslip drawer liner to diameter of cookie tin; place in bottom of tin.

3| Fit cups into tin as snugly as possible. Fill with assorted candies.

4| Tie ribbon decoratively around outside of tin. Fit lid on top if possible, or wrap cellophane around and over tin, and tie with ribbon.

Chocolate Caramel Bites

Makes: 24 pieces

This chewy caramel requires a watchful eye and constant stirring.

1 cup (250 mL) **pecan halves**

Pinch **salt**

⅔ cup (150 mL) **sweetened condensed milk**

½ cup (125 mL) packed **dark brown sugar**

½ cup (125 mL) **unsalted butter**

2 tbsp (30 mL) **corn syrup**

½ tsp (2 mL) **vanilla**

2 oz (60 g) **bittersweet chocolate,** chopped

2 tbsp (30 mL) **whipping cream**

Grease 24 mini muffin or tart cups; set aside.

On rimmed baking sheet, sprinkle pecans with salt. Bake in 350°F (180°C) oven until fragrant and golden, 7 minutes. Let cool.

Remove 24 pecan halves and set aside. Chop remaining pecans; divide evenly among tart cups.

In small saucepan, melt condensed milk, sugar, butter and corn syrup over medium heat, stirring. Simmer over medium-low heat, stirring constantly, for 25 to 27 minutes or until thickened and deep caramel in colour, and candy thermometer registers 215 to 220°F (101 to 104°C). Remove from heat. Immediately stir in vanilla. Spoon 1 tbsp (15 mL) into each cup; tap pans to spread evenly. Let cool on rack.

Meanwhile, in bowl over saucepan of hot (not boiling) water, melt chocolate with cream; remove from heat and stir until smooth.

Spoon scant ½ tsp (2 mL) chocolate mixture onto centre of each candy. Top with pecan half. Refrigerate until firm, 30 minutes. (Layer between waxed paper in airtight container and refrigerate for up to 2 weeks.)

PER PIECE: about 130 cal, 1 g pro, 9 g total fat (4 g sat. fat), 12 g carb, 1 g fibre, 15 mg chol, 16 mg sodium. % RDI: 3% calcium, 2% iron, 5% vit A, 1% folate.

Quick Tempering Chocolate:

• Chop chocolate [A]. In bowl over saucepan of hot (not boiling) water, melt two-thirds of the chocolate. Remove from heat.

• Add remaining chocolate [B], stirring until melted and cooled to about 90°F (32°C).

Whisky Walnut Fudge

Makes: about 64 pieces

The most important thing to know when making fudge is that it sets very quickly. As soon as it starts to lose its gloss, immediately scrape it into the pan.

2 cups (500 mL) packed **brown sugar**
1 cup (250 mL) **granulated sugar**
¾ cup (175 mL) **whipping cream**
2 tbsp (30 mL) **corn syrup**
2 tbsp (30 mL) **unsalted butter,** cubed
¼ tsp (1 mL) **salt**
Pinch **baking soda**
3 tbsp (45 mL) **whisky**
1 tsp (5 mL) **vanilla**
½ cup (125 mL) **chopped walnuts**

Line 8-inch (2 L) square metal cake pan with parchment paper; set aside.

Completely grease inside of heavy saucepan. Add brown sugar, granulated sugar, cream, corn syrup, butter, salt and baking soda; stir over medium-low heat. Bring to boil over medium heat; boil, without stirring, for 4 to 6 minutes, or until reaches soft-ball stage, 234°F (112°C) on candy thermometer (or when 1 tsp/5 mL dropped into cold water forms soft ball). As mixture boils, brush down side of pan with pastry brush dipped in water.

Dip bottom of saucepan in cold water. Let cool on rack, undisturbed, until lukewarm (110°F/43°C), 30 to 45 minutes.

With wooden spoon, beat in whisky and vanilla until thickened, lightened and beginning to lose gloss, 4 to 5 minutes.

Meanwhile, microwave nuts on high until warm, 20 seconds; immediately stir into fudge. Quickly scrape into prepared pan, spreading evenly. Let cool until set, about 30 minutes.

Remove fudge from pan. Using knife dipped in hot water, cut into 1-inch (2.5 cm) squares. (Layer between waxed paper in airtight container and store for up to 5 days or freeze for up to 2 weeks.)

PER PIECE: about 60 cal, trace pro, 2 g total fat (1 g sat. fat), 11 g carb, 0 g fibre, 5 mg chol, 13 mg sodium. % RDI: 1% calcium, 1% iron, 1% vit A.

Bittersweet Amaretti Bark

Makes: about 1 lb (500 g)

Chunks of amaretti cookies give this bark great texture and crunch.

1 lb (500 g) **bittersweet chocolate,** melted
1 cup (250 mL) **quartered amaretti cookies**
1 tsp (5 mL) **vanilla**

Line 15- x 10-inch (40 x 25 cm) rimmed baking sheet with foil; grease foil. Set aside.

In large bowl, stir together chocolate, cookies and vanilla. Spread to about ¼-inch (5 mm) thickness over two-thirds of the prepared pan. Refrigerate until firm, about 30 minutes.

Break bark into chunks. (Layer between waxed paper in airtight container and refrigerate for up to 2 weeks.)

PER 1 OZ (30 G): about 176 cal, 2 g pro, 11 g total fat (6 g sat. fat), 18 g carb, 2 g fibre, 0 mg chol, 9 mg sodium. % RDI: 2% calcium, 9% iron.

Two-Tone Peppermint Bark

Makes: 1½ lb (750 g)

Sweet and oh-so-minty, this bark rivals any you've seen in a gourmet store.

12 oz (375 g) **bittersweet chocolate,** melted
¾ tsp (4 mL) **peppermint extract**
12 oz (375 g) **white chocolate,** melted and warm
2 tbsp (30 mL) **coarsely crushed candy canes** or peppermints

Line 15- x 10-inch (40 x 25 cm) rimmed baking sheet with foil; grease foil. Set aside.

In bowl, stir bittersweet chocolate with peppermint extract. Spread in 10-inch (25 cm) square on prepared pan. Let stand until just set but not hard, about 15 minutes or 8 minutes in refrigerator.

Spread white chocolate over top; sprinkle with candy. Refrigerate until firm, about 1 hour. Break into chunks. (Layer between waxed paper in airtight container and refrigerate for up to 2 weeks.)

PER 1 OZ (30 G): about 162 cal, 2 g pro, 10 g total fat (6 g sat. fat), 17 g carb, 1 g fibre, 1 mg chol, 13 mg sodium. % RDI: 4% calcium, 4% iron.

Baking Mix and Sugar Jars

Storage jars come in all shapes and sizes, and you can always find a new use for them. Here, make these delicious, pretty mixes to take as hostess gifts.

Left to right: Orange Sugar, Fruity Hermits and Vanilla Sugar

YOU NEED:

- Lidded jars, such as canning jars or flip-lid jars with gaskets

- Fruity Hermits, Orange Sugar or Vanilla Sugar (recipes, opposite)

- Card stock or recipe card

- Raffia, ribbon or twine, or small artificial berry garland (optional)

- Gift tags

TO MAKE:

1| Wash jars and lids in hot soapy water and dry well.

2| For Fruity Hermits, layer dry ingredients in jar as directed in recipe, using photo (see opposite) as guide. On card stock or recipe card, write out cookie recipe (see below for instructions). Seal jar.

3| For sugars, pour sugar into jar, arranging decorative strips of orange rind or vanilla bean halves against wall of jar so they are visible. Seal jar.

4| Tie raffia decoratively around jar, or twist length of garland around mouth of jar. Attach recipe card or gift tag.

Fruity Hermits

Makes: about 36 cookies

To expose more green, vigorously rub pistachios in towel before chopping.

1½ cups (375 mL)
  all-purpose flour
½ tsp (2 mL) each
  baking powder, nutmeg and **cinnamon**
¼ tsp (1 mL) each
  ground allspice and **ground cloves**
¼ tsp (1 mL) each
  baking soda and **salt**
¾ cup (175 mL)
  granulated sugar
1½ cups (375 mL) **dried cranberries**
1½ cups (375 mL)
  chopped **pistachios**

In 4-cup (1 L) jar and using funnel, layer flour, baking powder, nutmeg, cinnamon, allspice, cloves, baking soda, salt and sugar. Top with cranberries and nuts. Store, sealed, in cool spot for up to 1 month.

For gift card: Line rimless baking sheets with parchment paper, or grease; set aside.

Sift ingredients into large bowl, setting cranberries and nuts aside.

In separate bowl, beat ⅔ cup (150 mL) softened butter, 1 egg, 2 tbsp (30 mL) 10% cream and 1 tsp (5 mL) vanilla. Stir into dry ingredients until almost blended. Mix in cranberries and nuts, using hands if needed, to make soft dough.

Drop by rounded 1 tbsp (15 mL) onto pans. Bake in 350°F (180°C) oven until bottoms are slightly darkened, 12 to 15 minutes. Let cool on pans for 5 minutes. Transfer to racks; let cool completely. (Store layered between waxed paper in airtight container for up to 5 days or freeze for up to 1 month.)

PER COOKIE: about 113 cal, 2 g pro, 6 g total fat (3 g sat. fat), 14 g carb, 1 g fibre, 14 mg chol, 56 mg sodium. % RDI: 1% calcium, 4% iron, 4% vit A, 6% folate.

Orange Sugar

Makes: 2 cups (500 mL)

Stir this aromatic sugar into whipped cream, rice pudding or yogurt.

2 cups (500 mL)
  granulated sugar
¼ cup (60 mL) chopped
  orange rind
Orange rind strips

In food processor, whirl sugar with orange rind until rind is almost blended into sugar.

Spread on large rimmed baking sheet; let dry for 24 hours, stirring occasionally. Crumble, then press through sieve. Pack into jars, adding strips of orange rind along side of jar.

MIX IT UP
Vanilla Sugar:
Omit orange rind. Slit 1 vanilla bean lengthwise; scrape out seeds. Whirl seeds with sugar; do not press through sieve. Pack into jars with vanilla pod halves.

Tea Blends

Heavenly in fragrance and taste, these tea blends are a delight to the senses. Stir up your favourite blends as gifts and package them in dressed up cello bags (page 248), boxes (page 236) or cans (page 240).

Puffed Wild Rice Green Tea

Makes: about 30 servings

Heat nonstick skillet over medium-high heat until hot. Add ¼ cup (60 mL) wild rice; toast, shaking constantly, until most kernels are puffed and brown, about 30 seconds. Transfer to bowl and let cool.

Add 1 cup (250 mL) green tea leaves (such as Japanese sencha) to bowl; mix to combine.

MIX IT UP
Wild Rose Green Tea: Reduce wild rice to 2 tbsp (30 mL). Add ¼ cup (60 mL) dried rose hips.

PICTURED, OPPOSITE:
1. Puffed Wild Rice Green Tea
2. Rose Petal Tea
3. Chocolate Chai
4. Chamomile Mint Tea
5. Green Ginger Mint Tea
6. Wild Rose Green Tea

Rose Petal Tea

Makes: about 35 servings

Using vegetable peeler, peel rind, removing pith, from 2 oranges. Place on rack; dry at room temperature until brittle, about 24 hours. Break into ¼-inch (5 mm) pieces.

In bowl, mix orange rind, 1 cup (250 mL) black or green tea leaves, and ½ cup (125 mL) each dried rose petals and hibiscus, crumbled.

Chamomile Mint Tea

Makes: about 30 servings

Using vegetable peeler, peel rind, removing pith, from 2 lemons. Place on rack with 1 cup (250 mL) fresh mint leaves; dry at room temperature until brittle, about 24 hours.

Break lemon rind into ¼-inch (5 mm) pieces in bowl. Mix in mint leaves; 1 cup (250 mL) green or black tea leaves; ¼ cup (60 mL) dried chamomile flowers, crumbled; and 1 tbsp (15 mL) dried lavender.

Green Ginger Mint Tea

Makes: about 30 servings

Peel rind from 4 tangerines or 2 oranges, removing pith; cut 1 piece (4-inch/ 10 cm) gingerroot into ⅛-inch (3 mm) thick slices. Remove leaves from 2 bunches spearmint. Place rind, ginger and mint on rack; dry at room temperature until brittle, about 24 hours. Break into 1-inch (2.5 cm) pieces.

In bowl, mix together rind, ginger, mint and 1 cup (250 mL) green tea leaves, such as gunpowder.

Chocolate Chai

Makes: about 16 servings

Cut 1 piece (2-inch/ 5 cm) gingerroot crosswise into ⅛-inch (3 mm) thick slices. Place on rack and dry at room temperature until brittle, 24 hours.

In bowl, smash 3 cinnamon sticks into 1-inch (2.5 cm) shards. Mix in ginger; 1 cup (250 mL) Earl Grey tea leaves; ⅔ cup (150 mL) shaved semisweet chocolate; 2 tbsp (30 mL) fennel seeds; 24 whole cloves; 12 green cardamom pods, cracked; and 1 tsp (5 mL) peppercorns.

diagrams

Easy Apron

(page 20)

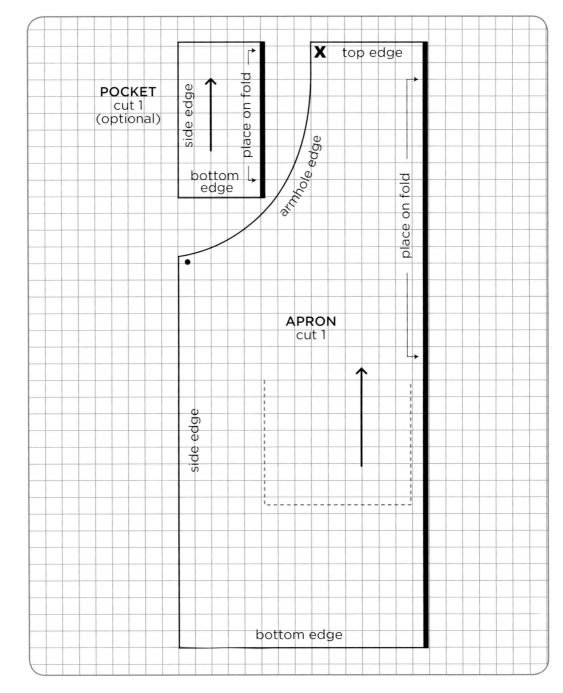

POCKET
cut 1
(optional)

side edge

place on fold

bottom edge

X top edge

armhole edge

place on fold

APRON
cut 1

side edge

bottom edge

each square on grid = 2.5 cm (1 inch)

diagrams

CANADIAN LIVING | CREATE. UPDATE. REMAKE

Upcycled Necktie Tea Cosy

(page 24)

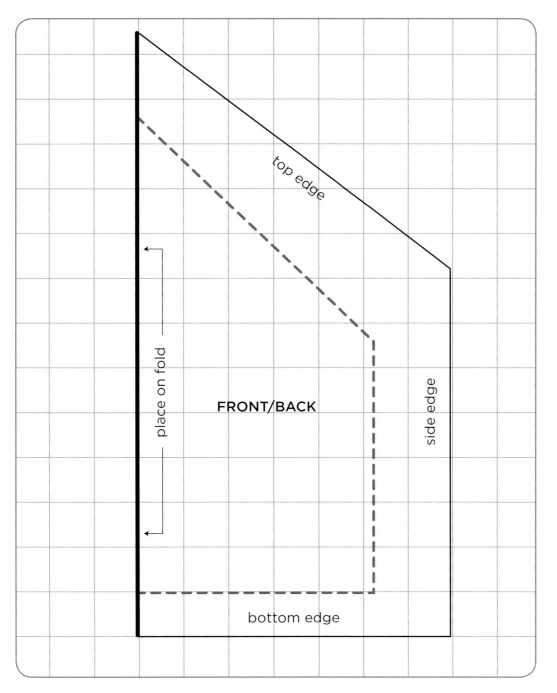

top edge

place on fold

FRONT/BACK

side edge

bottom edge

each square on grid = 2.5 cm (1 inch)

Lynx Sock Toys

(page 34)

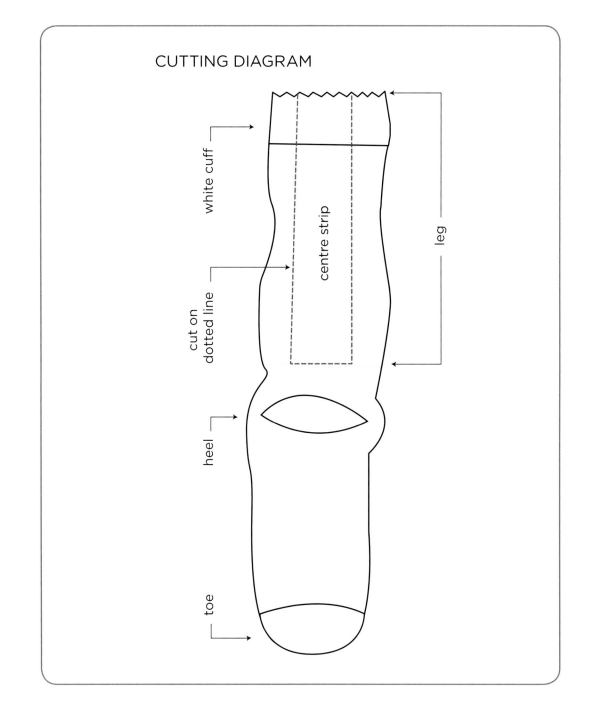

CUTTING DIAGRAM

white cuff

centre strip

leg

cut on
dotted line

heel

toe

Lynx Sock Toys

(page 34)

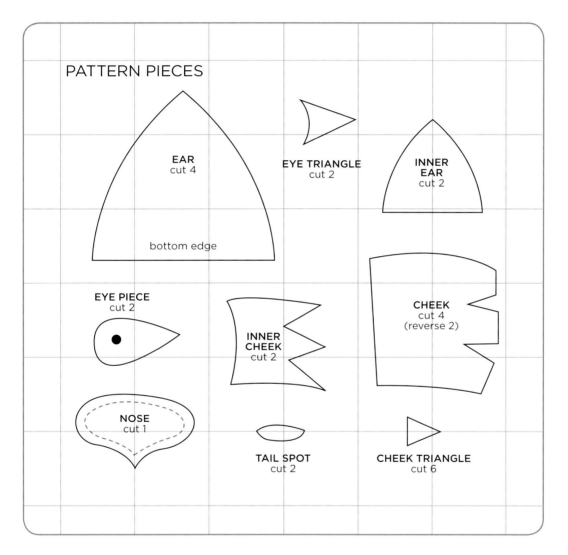

PATTERN PIECES

EAR
cut 4

bottom edge

EYE TRIANGLE
cut 2

INNER
EAR
cut 2

EYE PIECE
cut 2

INNER
CHEEK
cut 2

CHEEK
cut 4
(reverse 2)

NOSE
cut 1

TAIL SPOT
cut 2

CHEEK TRIANGLE
cut 6

each square on grid = 2.5 cm (1 inch)

diagrams

CANADIAN LIVING | CREATE. UPDATE. REMAKE

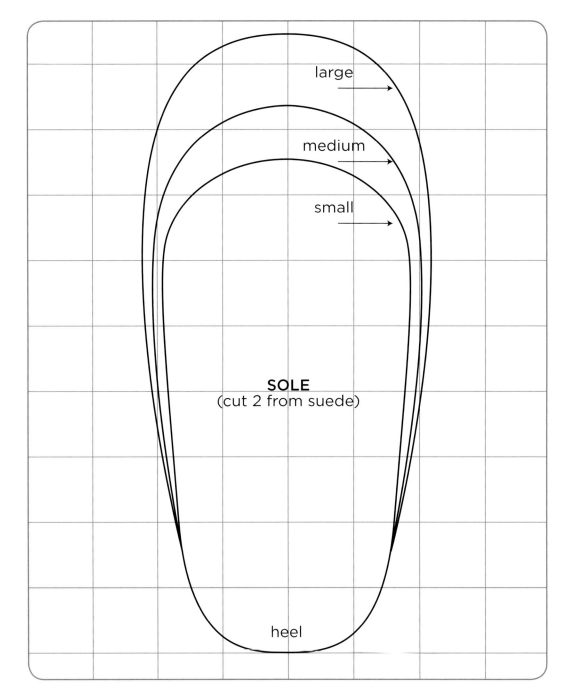

large

medium

small

SOLE
(cut 2 from suede)

heel

each square on grid = 2.5 cm (1 inch)

Wire Family Photo Tree

(page 70)

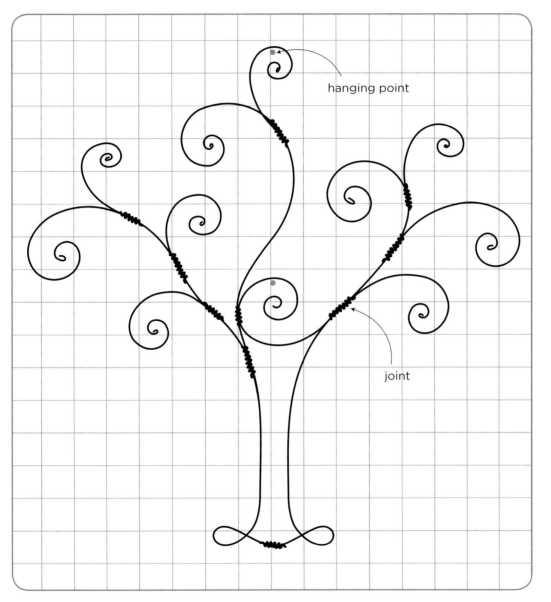

hanging point

joint

each square on grid = 2.5 cm (1 inch)

Plate Shelf

(page 76)

PATTERN PIECES

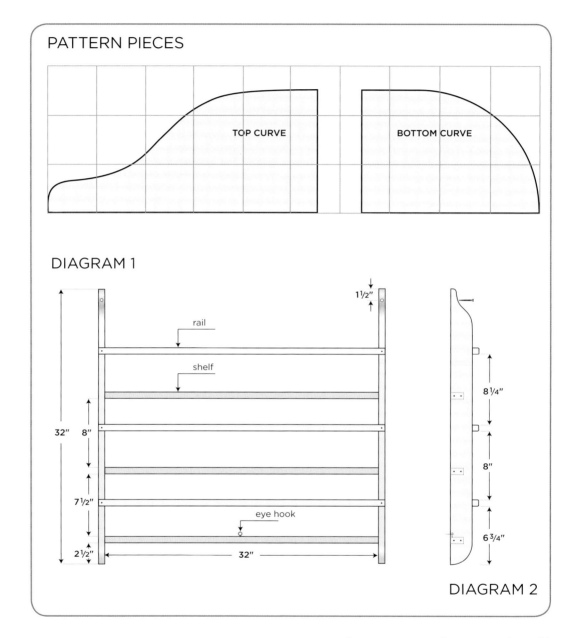

TOP CURVE

BOTTOM CURVE

DIAGRAM 1

rail

shelf

eye hook

1½"

32" | 8"

7½"

2½"

32"

DIAGRAM 2

8¼"

8"

6¾"

each square on grid = 2.5 cm (1 inch)

diagrams

CANADIAN LIVING | CREATE. UPDATE. REMAKE

Tin Tile Hanging Pot

(page 80)

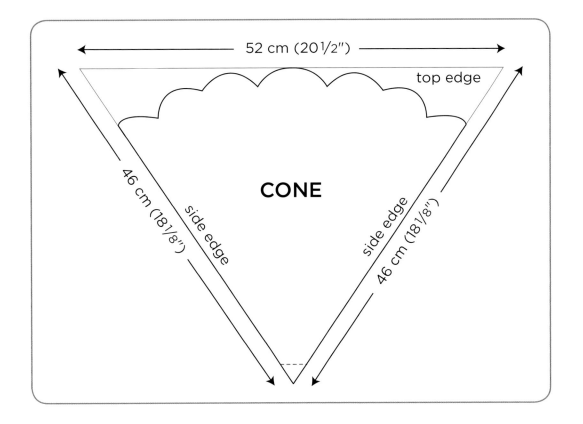

52 cm (20½")

top edge

46 cm (18⅛")

side edge

CONE

side edge

46 cm (18⅛")

Versailles Latticework Planter

(page 116)

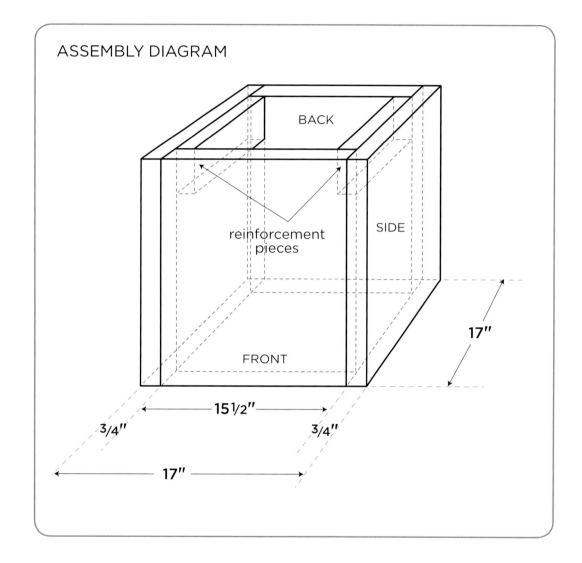

ASSEMBLY DIAGRAM

BACK

SIDE

reinforcement
pieces

FRONT

17"

15½"

3/4"   3/4"

17"

Leftover Lattice Window Box

(page 118)

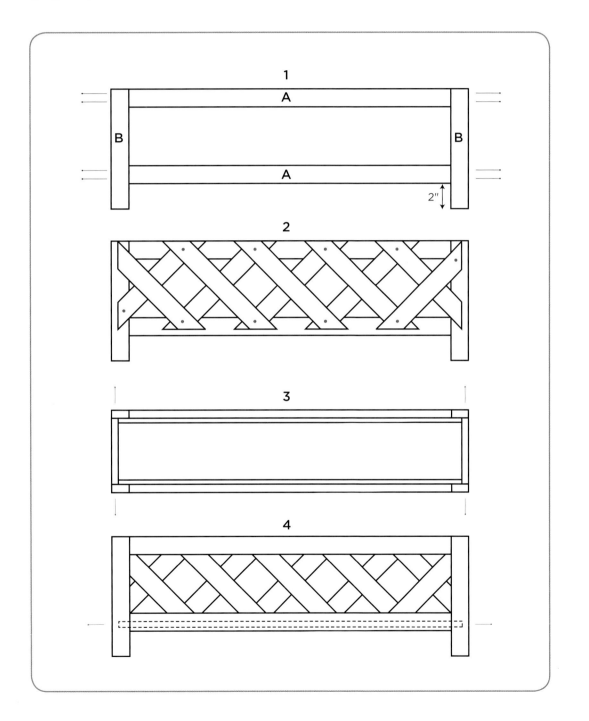

269

diagrams

CANADIAN LIVING | CREATE, UPDATE, REMAKE

Boxy Birdhouses

(page 126)

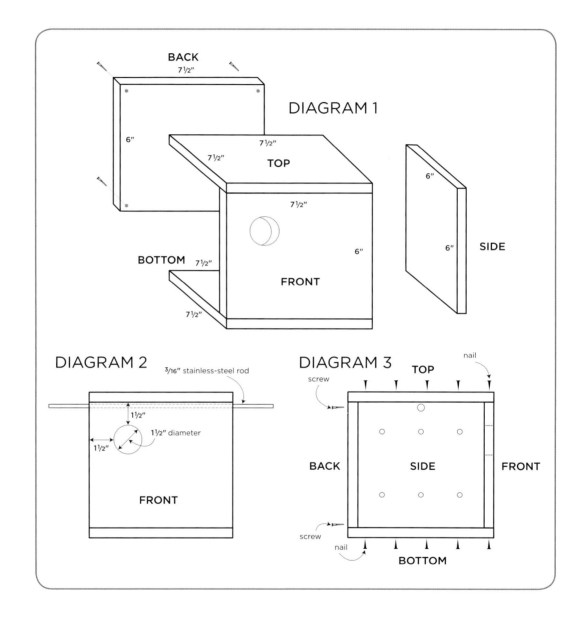

CANADIAN LIVING | CREATE, UPDATE, REMAKE

Nest Shelf

(page 138)

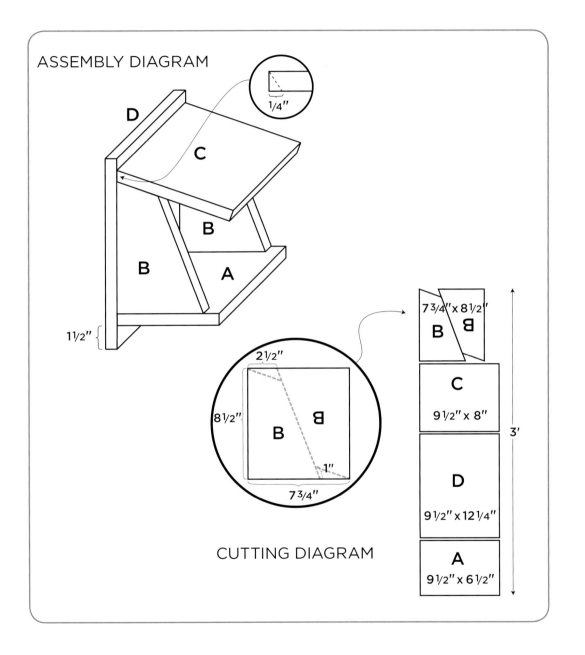

ASSEMBLY DIAGRAM

1/4"

D

C

B

B

A

1 1/2"

CUTTING DIAGRAM

2 1/2"

8 1/2"

B

B

1"

7 3/4"

7 3/4" x 8 1/2"

B B

C

9 1/2" x 8"

D

9 1/2" x 12 1/4"

A

9 1/2" x 6 1/2"

3'

Woven Finger Puppets

(page 146)

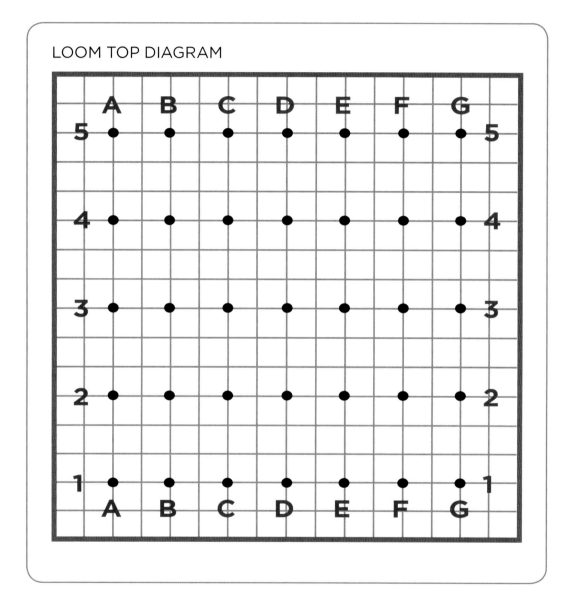

LOOM TOP DIAGRAM

The Five-Minute Kite

(page 150)

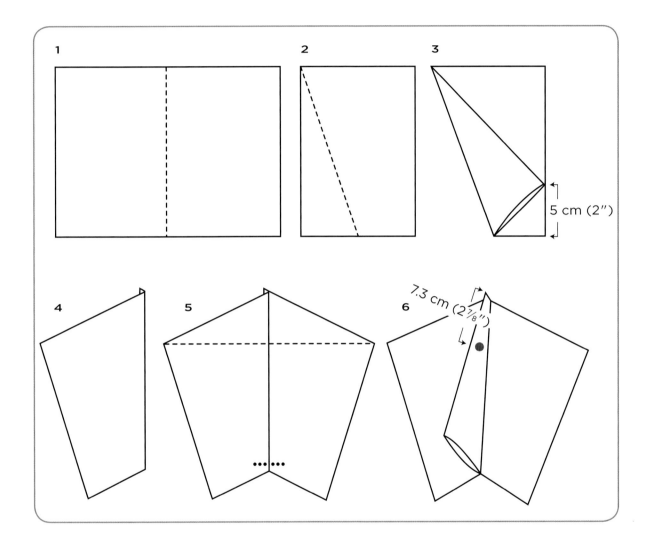

Dragon and Princess Puppets

(pages 158 and 160)

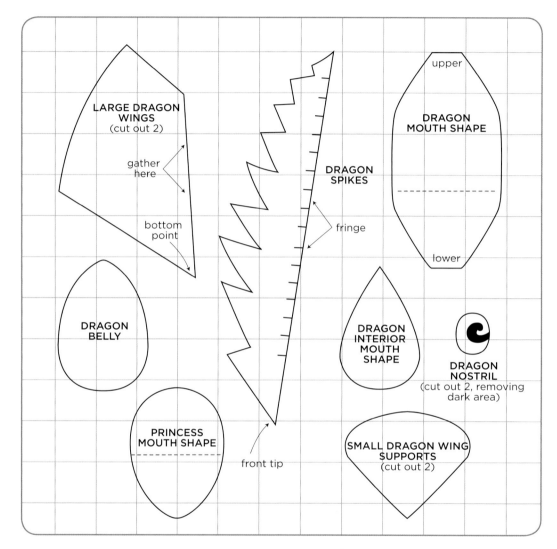

LARGE DRAGON WINGS
(cut out 2)

gather here

bottom point

DRAGON SPIKES

fringe

DRAGON MOUTH SHAPE

upper

lower

DRAGON BELLY

DRAGON INTERIOR MOUTH SHAPE

DRAGON NOSTRIL
(cut out 2, removing dark area)

PRINCESS MOUTH SHAPE

front tip

SMALL DRAGON WING SUPPORTS
(cut out 2)

each square on grid = 2.5 cm (1 inch)

In Like a Lion Tote

(page 164)

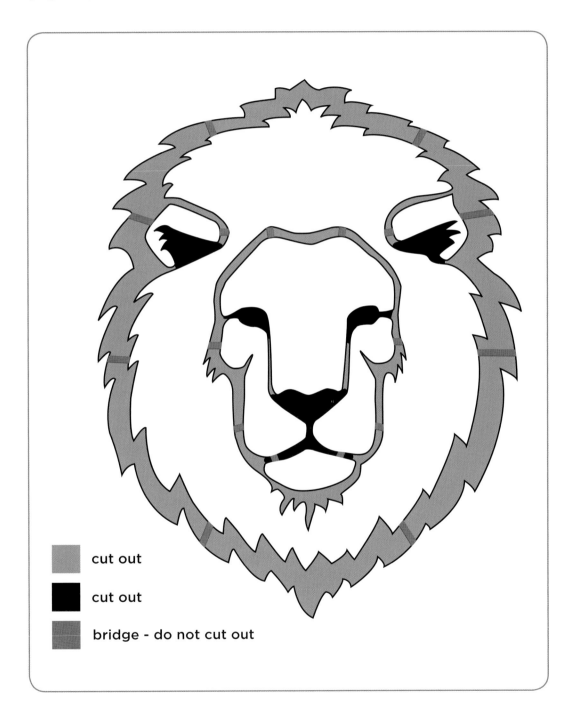

cut out

cut out

bridge - do not cut out

Sweet Valentine Packages

(page 176)

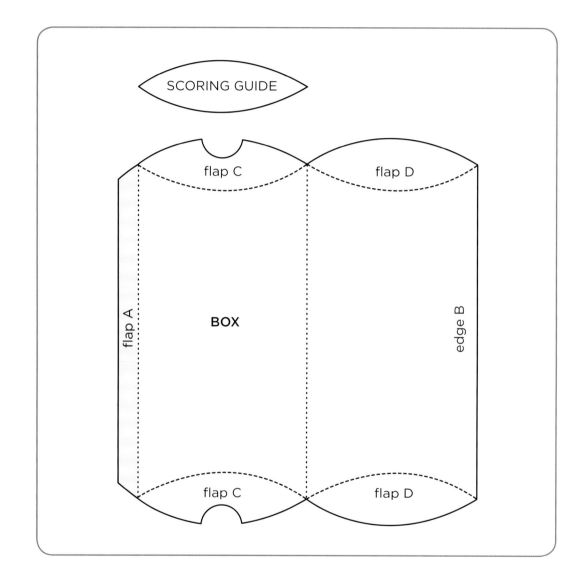

SCORING GUIDE

flap C

flap D

flap A

BOX

edge B

flap C

flap D

"Be Mine" Bunting

(page 178)

Easter Gift Bag

(page 180)

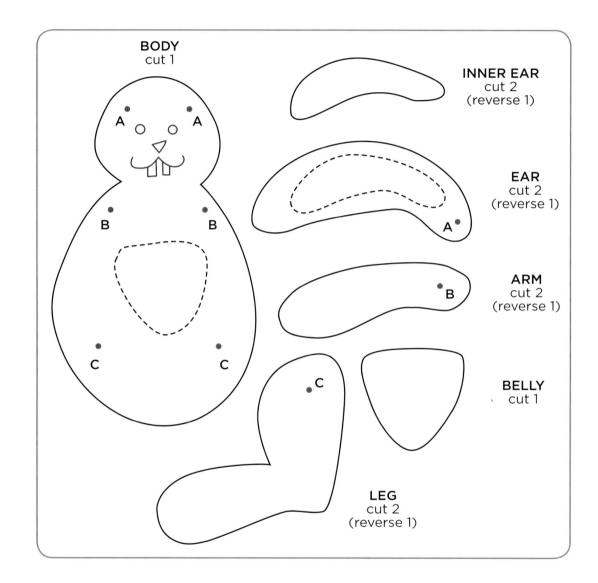

BODY
cut 1

A   A

B   B

C   C

INNER EAR
cut 2
(reverse 1)

EAR
cut 2
(reverse 1)

A

ARM
cut 2
(reverse 1)

B

BELLY
cut 1

C

LEG
cut 2
(reverse 1)

Canada Day Maple Leaf Birds

(page 184)

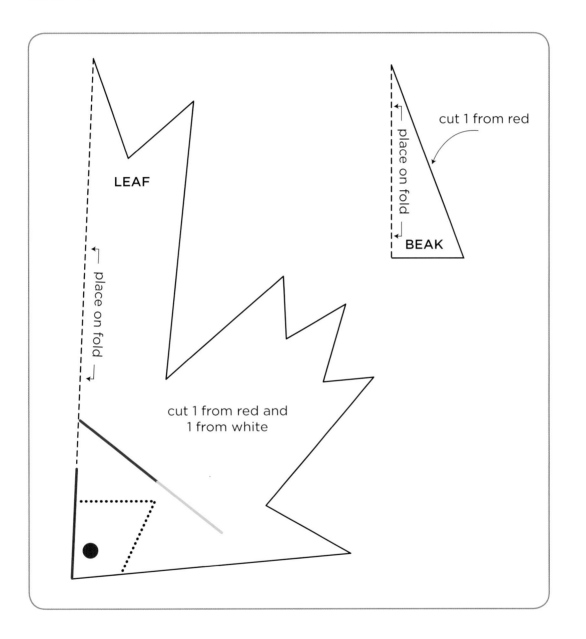

LEAF

place on fold

cut 1 from red and
1 from white

cut 1 from red

place on fold

BEAK

Autumn Table Runner and Quick Place Card Holders

(pages 186 to 188)

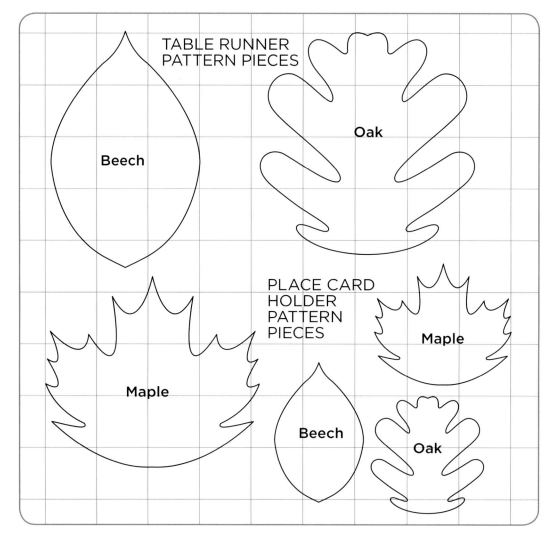

TABLE RUNNER
PATTERN PIECES

Oak

Beech

PLACE CARD
HOLDER
PATTERN
PIECES

Maple

Maple

Beech

Oak

each square on grid = 2.5 cm (1 inch)

Five-Minute Napkin Rings

(page 188)

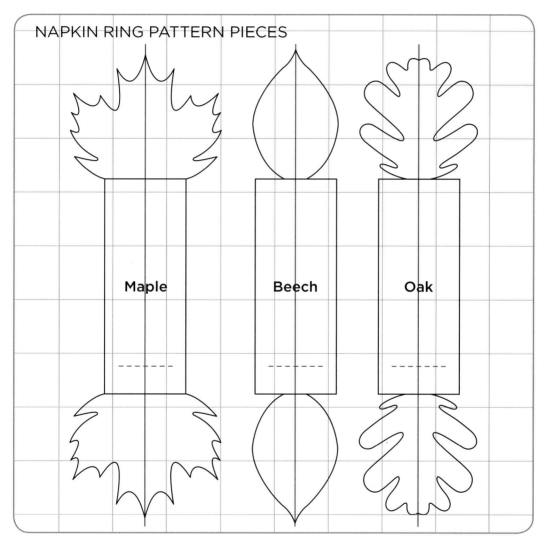

NAPKIN RING PATTERN PIECES

Maple

Beech

Oak

each square on grid = 2.5 cm (1 inch)

Spooky Pencil Toppers

(page 194)

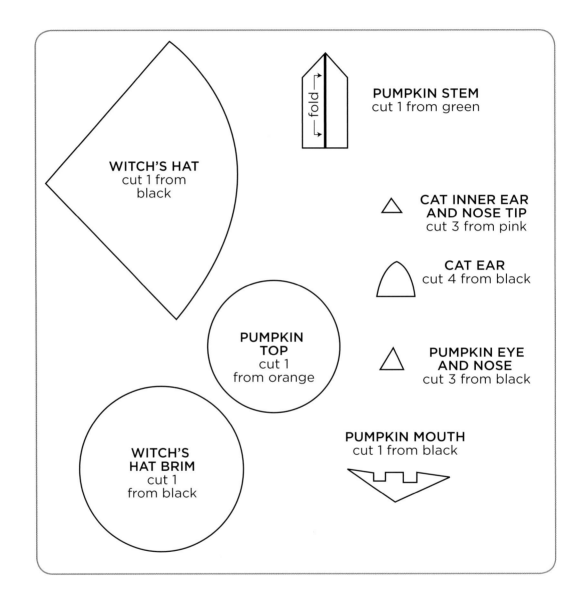

PUMPKIN STEM
cut 1 from green

fold

WITCH'S HAT
cut 1 from
black

**CAT INNER EAR
AND NOSE TIP**
cut 3 from pink

CAT EAR
cut 4 from black

**PUMPKIN
TOP**
cut 1
from orange

**PUMPKIN EYE
AND NOSE**
cut 3 from black

PUMPKIN MOUTH
cut 1 from black

**WITCH'S
HAT BRIM**
cut 1
from black

diagrams

CANADIAN LIVING | CREATE, UPDATE, REMAKE

Bookmarks

(page 196)

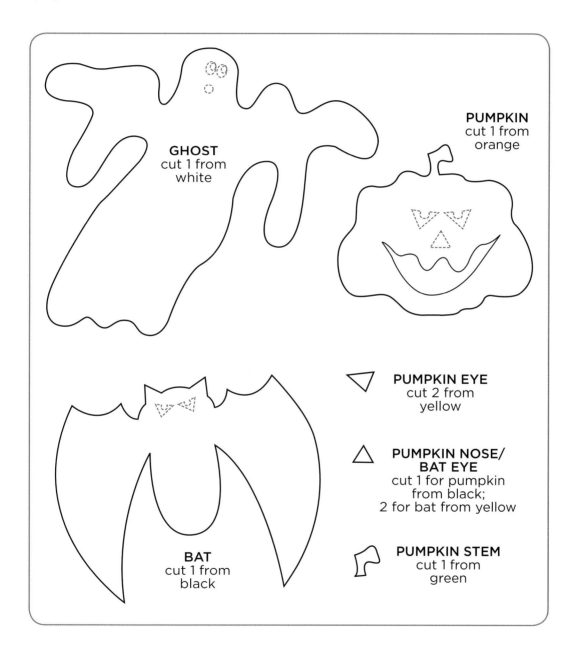

GHOST
cut 1 from
white

PUMPKIN
cut 1 from
orange

PUMPKIN EYE
cut 2 from
yellow

**PUMPKIN NOSE/
BAT EYE**
cut 1 for pumpkin
from black;
2 for bat from yellow

PUMPKIN STEM
cut 1 from
green

BAT
cut 1 from
black

Resources

General Guidelines:

We want you to enjoy the projects we have collected here, and to end up with a finished product that you are proud of – whether you're making something for your home, yourself or to give as a gift. To ensure a successful DIY experience, we recommend doing the following.

1| Read the project instructions all the way through, and review assembly diagrams and step-by-step photographs before you begin.

2| Gather all tools and materials, and keep them close at hand as you work.

3| Plan ahead. Make sure you have enough time to complete each step.

4| Be safe. Keep your work area tidy. Keep sharp, hot or otherwise dangerous tools out of the reach of children. Read instruction manuals before using power tools.

A Note About Measurements:

You will notice that our craft and food instructions usually provide measurements in both metric and imperial, in the order they are most commonly used. For example, as fabric is sold by the metre in Canada, our sewing projects list metric measurements first. On the other hand, because Canadians still use teaspoons, tablespoons and cups when cooking, our recipes list imperial measurements first. If you only see one measurement listed (for example, we call for a 5 mm bead or a length of 1x2 lumber), that is how the material is sold. If you are working on a project for which both metric and imperial measurements are provided, you'll get the best results if you choose one set of measurements and stick to it, rather than switching back and forth between the two.

Knitting and Crochet Standard Abbreviations:

beg = beginning

ch = chain

cn = cable needle

CO = cast off

dc = double crochet

dec = decrease(s)(d)(ing)

hdc = half double crochet

inc = increase(s)(d)(ing)

k = knit

kbf = increase one stitch by knitting into front and back of stitch

k1tbl = knit one through back loop

lp(s) = loop(s)

m1 = make 1 stitch by picking up horizontal loop in front of next stitch and knitting into back of it

p = purl

pat = pattern

psso = pass slipped stitch(es) over

rem = remain(ing)

rnd(s) = round(s)

RS = right side

sc = single crochet

sk = skip

sl = slip

sl st = slip stitch

sp = space

ssk = decrease one stitch by slipping two stitches knitwise, one by one; insert tip of left-hand needle into fronts of these two stitches and knit them together

st(s) = stitch(es)

st st = stocking stitch

tog = together

wyib = with yarn in back

wyif = with yarn in front

WS = wrong side

yfwd = yarn forward

yo = yarn over

yoh = yarn over hook

yon = yarn over needle

yrn = yarn round needle

Reference Books:

A comprehensive reference book is an invaluable companion to the avid crafter – it's always there to help you, even at midnight on Christmas Eve! Here are a few of our favourites.

• *Canadian Encyclopedia of Gardening,* Christopher Brickell (Dorling Kindersley, 2004)

• *The Comfortable Home,* Mitchell Gold and Bob Williams (Crown, 2009)

• *The Complete Canadian Living Baking Book,* Elizabeth Baird and The Canadian Living Test Kitchen (Transcontinental, 2008)

• *The Complete Encyclopedia of Needlework,* Thérèse de Dillmont (Running Press, 2002)

• *Decorating Is Fun! How to Be Your Own Decorator,* Dorothy Draper (Pointed Leaf Press, 2007)

• *Embroidery Stitches,* Mary Webb (Firefly, 2006)

• *How to Make a Garden: The 7 Essential Steps for the Canadian Gardener,* Marjorie Harris (Random House, 2007)

• *The Knitter's Companion,* Vicki Square (Interweave, 2010)

• *The New Complete Guide to Sewing,* Reader's Digest (2010)

• *The Ultimate Sourcebook of Knitting and Crochet Stitches,* Reader's Digest (2003)

Sources

We recommend getting to know the proprietors of your local art or craft supply and fabric or yarn stores. In addition to supplying your material needs, shop owners and employees are often great sources of technical know-how. Sadly, it would take more room than we have to list all the small stores across Canada, so this list includes major retailers that are represented across the country or online. Before you shop, check your local listings.

Miscellaneous Supplies:

Art and craft supplies: DeSerres, deserres.ca; Mary Maxim, marymaxim.ca, Michaels, michaels.com

Candy-making supplies: Bulk Barn, bulkbarn.ca; Golda's Kitchen, goldaskitchen.ca

Cookie cutters: Golda's Kitchen, goldaskitchen.ca

Flowers and floral supplies: Michaels, michaels.com

Freezer paper: Reynolds, reynoldspkg.com; available at major grocery stores

Hardware: Home Hardware, homehardware.ca

Microwave flower press: elizabeths-flowers.com

Sewing supplies: (embroidery floss and supplies, fabric, notions, sewing essentials, and quilting supplies), Fabricland, fabricland.ca

Yarn:

Although the yarns we feature in this book were available at the time of printing, product and colour names and availability can change without notice. Check with your local yarn store or with the yarn company's website to ensure the product is available, or to find out more about appropriate substitutions.

Briggs and Little: (yarn and carded fleece), briggsandlittle.com

Louet: louet.com

Malabrigo: malabrigoyarn.com

Mirasol: mirasolperu.com, diamondyarn.com

Mission Falls: missionfalls.com

Patons: patonsyarns.com

Sirdar: sirdar.co.uk, diamondyarn.com

acknowledgments

Like most DIY projects, this book got more fun the more people got involved. Each offered a small piece of the puzzle, and helped lighten our load with their contributions.

Foremost, we'd like to thank the artists, artisans and crafters who designed the projects in these pages (for a complete list, see page 288). Without their creativity, this book would not have come to life. Their inspirations are an inspiration to us all.

Crafts just don't work if you don't have pictures to follow. Heartfelt thanks go to the many talented photographers who documented the steps, tricks and techniques it takes to create these projects. At the top of the list is our friend Paul Chmielowiec, who shot (among many other things) the gorgeous closeups you see on our chapter openers. Thanks also to our food and prop stylists, who ensure that our food images look positively mouthwatering. (For a list of all of these contributors, see page 288.)

Close to our hearts (and always hovering nearby with page proofs) was our brilliant art director, Chris Bond. He's never afraid to take on an artistic challenge, and his own DIY decorating experience gave him helpful insights into creating a book that fellow creative people will enjoy and find easy to navigate. Thanks, too, to Miguel Cea, who cheerfully created all of our diagrams with incredible precision.

Nowhere is accuracy more important than in a book like this. Special thanks go to our copy editor, Jill Buchner, whose skill (and cookies) are legendary. Kate Atherley, our knitting and crochet technical editor, took the burden of stitch math off our plates and ensured that everything you knit or crochet will come out perfectly.

Merci beaucoup to our Transcontinental Books publisher, Jean Paré; our group publisher, Lynn Chambers; and our fearless editor-in-chief, Susan Antonacci. Without their support, we'd never have been able to produce this dream project.

Thanks also to our distribution team at Random House Canada, including (but not limited to) Duncan Shields and Janet Joy Wilson.

Stay crafty,
Christina Anson Mine and
Austen Gilliland

Credits

Recipes
The Canadian Living
Test Kitchen

Diagrams
Miguel Cea

Illustration
Kate Fox-Whyte:
page 127

Project designers
Leslie Ashton: page 184
Margot Austin: page 90
Conrad Biernacki:
page 123
Glenna C: pages 44, 52
and 64
Jo Calvert: pages 10, 18,
26, 32, 38, 40, 46, 124,
130 and 132
Circle Home and
Design: page 136
Janet Clark: page 56
Noreen Crone-Findlay:
page 146
Gail Davis: page 24
Trudy Duivenvoorden
Mitic: page 114
Stephanie Earp: page 58
Susan Filshie: page 210
Kate Fox-Whyte:
page 126
Jon Gillette: pages 70,
76, 138 and 150
Austen Gilliland: pages
22, 28, 108, 110, 164, 168,
178, 182, 186, 216, 236
and 240
Heather Gilmour
Herbert: page 198
Amanda Herman:
page 72
Roxie Hood and Clara
McFayden: page 61
Kelly Kainz: page 118

Dorotea Kemenczy:
pages 116, 176 and 180
Karen Kirk: pages 74, 82,
94, 134, 140, 197, 202,
209 and 212
Carol Knowlton-Dority:
pages 155, 156, 158
and 160
Mary Lou Kuipers: pages
20, 162, 166, 189, 190, 224
and 226
Montana Labelle: pages
104 and 204
Sabrina Linn: pages 12
and 14
Bill Loney: page 120
Colin McMurray:
page 102
David Overholt: page 30
Patons Design Studio:
pages 48, 50, 54 and 206
Renée Schwarz: pages
34, 144, 152, 170, 174, 194,
196 and 200
Kate Seaver: page 78
Michael Simardone:
pages 84, 86, 88, 96, 98,
100 and 106
John Sorensen: page 80
Ralph Swan: page 92
Patricia Unger: page 16
Joanne Wittig: page 57

Photography
Luis Albuquerque:
pages 10, 11, 20, 38, 39,
197, 202 and 203
Brandon Barré: pages
92, 93, 102 and 103
Stacey Brandford:
pages 98 and 100
Ryan Brook,
Transcontinental
Premedia: page 53
Mark Burstyn: pages 22,
23, 46, 47, 70, 71, 78, 79,

84, 85, 96, 97, 152, 154
and 210
Paul Chmielowiec:
pages 1, 8, 28, 29, 42, 48,
49, 54, 68, 82, 83, 94,
95, 104, 105, 112, 123, 126,
128, 142, 155, 162, 172, 178,
182, 183, 186, 188, 198,
199, 209, 212, 214, 228,
229, 240 and 254
Christopher Dew:
page 61
Yvonne Duivenvoorden:
pages 86, 88, 89, 124,
138, 184, 185, 204, 205,
220, 222, 232, 234, 238,
239, 242, 246, 248, 250,
252, 253 and 256
Nancy Falconi: pages
170, 171, 189, 190, 224
and 226
Angus Fergusson: pages
57, 110, 111, 156, 158, 160,
216, 218 and 219
Geoff George: pages 5
(bottom), 52, 108, 109,
166 and 251
Jon Gillette: page 150
Alvaro Goveia: page 56
Michael Graydon: pages
40, 41, 44, 74, 75, 76,
106, 107, 130, 131, 151
and 164
Daniel Harrison: page 18
Kevin Hewitt: pages 116,
117, 133, 144, 145, 174, 175
and 176
Bert Klassen: pages 114
and 115
Virginia MacDonald:
pages 58, 90, 146, 147
and 148
Monica McKenna:
page 16
Margaret Mulligan: pages
24, 25, 26, 27 and 50

James Noble: pages 12,
13, 14, 15, 30 and 31
Edward Pond: pages 64,
72, 73, 168, 169 and 227
Jodi Pudge: pages 230,
231 and 236
Seed9 Photography:
page 5 (top)
Nina Teixeira: pages 32,
33, 34, 35, 37, 136, 137,
180, 181, 194, 195, 196,
200 and 206
Curtis Trent: page 132
Ted Yarwood: pages 80,
118 and 119
Roger Yip: pages 120,
121, 122, 134, 135, 140
and 141

Food styling
Donna Bartolini:
page 256
Joanne Lusted: pages
228, 229 and 254
Lucie Richard: pages
232 and 238
Claire Stancer: page 234
Claire Stubbs: pages
220, 222, 227, 246, 248,
250, 252 and 253
Rosemarie Superville:
pages 242 and 251

Prop styling
Catherine Doherty:
pages 28, 29, 232, 238
and 242
Extra Touches: pages
189, 190, 224 and 226
Oksana Slavutych:
pages 220, 222, 234,
246, 248, 250, 251, 252,
253 and 256
Genevieve Wiseman:
page 227